Bodhisattva 4.0

Bodhisattva 4.0

A PRIMER FOR ENGAGED BUDDHISTS

John Harvey Negru

Bodhisattva 4.0
A Primer for Engaged Buddhists
John Harvey Negru

Published by
The Sumeru Press Inc.
Ottawa, ON
Canada

Library and Archives Canada Cataloguing in Publication

Title: Bodhisattva 4.0 : a primer for engaged buddhists / John Harvey Negru.
Names: Negru, John, author.
Description: Includes bibliographical references.
Identifiers: Canadiana 20190163380 | ISBN 9781896559537 (softcover)
Subjects: LCSH: Buddhism—Social aspects. | LCSH: Religious life—Buddhism.
Classification: LCC BQ4570.S6 N44 2019 | DDC 294.3/37—dc23

For more information about The Sumeru Press
visit us at *sumeru-books.com*

CONTENTS

>

Bodhisattva 4.0

INTRODUCTION

May all beings be happy. That's where it all begins. But what does it mean, here and now?

This book is a collection of simple conversation-starters about very difficult questions. It is not meant to provide answers, but rather to encourage mindful reflection and action. We all have a stake in our future, and the consequences of our decisions have enormous import. We have only to look to the past for proof. Whatever your station or passion, there are ways to make a positive difference in the world. Just start where you are, work with what you have, and do what you can.

The ideas presented here come from a Buddhist perspective, but not in an exclusive way. Good ecology embraces biodiversity and adaptation. In that spirit, Buddhist ecology draws upon ideas that will benefit all of us, irrespective of their origins. And as the Buddha said, don't believe me just because I say so; try it on for size and see if it works for you in your life. Then decide how to proceed.

Technology is the key characteristic of our world today. We swim in it like fish in water; it surrounds us, sustains us, delights us, drives us, and defines us. We think we know what technology is. We don't.

And what of the future? We will each die; of that we can be sure. But what of future generations, the future human and non-human inhabitants of our blue planet? What will their world look like? Does it matter?

I am one of those who will not be here. I am an elder. This book is my gift to the future.

THE BOOK

We are poised on the inflection point of the fourth industrial revolution. Hence the title of this book, *Bodhisattva 4.0*. To some, it appears as the dawning of a brave new world. To others, it appears as the precipice above the inferno. In each generation, Buddhist practitioners have had to re-imagine what it means to be a Bodhisattva. For those of us alive today, it remains the essential path.

You have before you 108 meditations. They are organized into twelve subject areas, and each area comprises nine topics. Each topic is presented as a two-page spread that includes resources for further study. The journey is non-linear, so partake as you will. This is not a book intended to be read in one sitting.

Engaged Buddhism is a relatively new field, which sprang from the environmental movement. Few books exist on the topic, but the web is alive with sites of interest to Eco-Buddhists. For example, **His Holiness the Karmapa** has been very active in the sphere of environmental action. This book is a humble contribution to the aspirations of all who cherish life and accept a responsibility to enhance it.

Laudate Si, the recently published encyclical from **Pope Francis**, illumines our common ground. While there is far to go, the fact that people are beginning to understand the issues and debate them, and that the concepts of ecology have permeated global culture, are very encouraging.

Our planet has been around for more than four billion years. Our human presence on it has been about two hundred thousand years, a mere blink of the eye. For most of that time, we were a relatively insignificant branch on the Tree of Life. In the short time we have been here, we have become the dominant species, and the effects of our presence are visible to all, particularly since the Industrial Revolution some 150 years ago. We have burned through 30,000,000 years of photosynthesis in less than 200 years. The amount of fresh water behind dams is five times greater than the amount flowing free. At the rate we are going, we will need six planets to sustain ourselves, and this is clearly impossible. Technology has amplified both the best and worst of our human nature. It has become the lens through which we conceive life's challenges and solutions, often to the exclusion of other options.

The way forward is not easy. Few politicians or media celebrities have any stomach for presenting the unvarnished truth. Entrenched elites will fight tooth and nail to preserve their privilege. The chaos brought about by our increasingly degraded environment pits groups against each other for scant resources. And for most people, the prospects are simply overwhelming. As individuals, we all too often feel insignificant. And the environment is just one of multiple flash points....

To solve the problems we face, we need not just "better" technology, but a renewal of spirit; we need a different set of priorities. Happiness comes from inner contentment, not more stuff. Peace comes from communal respect, not chauvinist ideologies. Sustainability is a fundamental necessity, not an option. **His Holiness the Dalai Lama** has eloquently charted that course in *Ethics for a New Millenium*.

THE AUTHOR

I have been a Buddhist for all of my adult life. I've met many teachers, immersed myself in practice, including five years in a residental monastic setting, and been involved in Sangha activities for more than 40 years. As coordinator for the Toronto Buddhist Federation, and later as the Toronto coordinator for the Buddhist Council of Canada in the 1980's, I had the privilege of assisting many communities with intrafaith and interfaith initiatives. As the founder of Canada's leading independent Buddhist book publishing company, news agency and directory of Buddhist organizations, I've had the opportunity to participate in many community development projects.

On a parallel track, I have been a technology pioneer and teacher for almost as long – as graphic designer, typographer, print production specialist, writer (three books and 100+ feature articles on technology subjects), contributing editor for multiple technology periodicals, university instructor (print and web production for publishers) and high school teacher (notably in graphic, product and architectural design, urban planning, geomatics, project management, and computer engineering).

When I was in the design business between 1975 and 2000, many of my clients were environmental activists, such as Pollution Probe, Energy Probe, the Canadian Environmental Law Association, Ecology House, etc. Others included activist groups, such as the Nonsmokers Rights Association, the Multicultural History Society of Ontario, The Skills Exchange, The Network for Learning, LGBTQ organizations, and the Urban Alliance on Race Relations. Then there were the arts organizations, multinational corporations, banks, government agencies, entrepreneurs, and just about every major publisher in Canada. It was quite an education!

As a teacher, much of my focus is on design process, project management, systems thinking and sustainability. Together with my left-of-centre Jewish humanist upbringing (my mother a social worker, my father a newspaper editor), these life experiences have hopefully equipped me well to tackle the thorny issues explored in this book.

Thank you for joining me in this journey.

THE ROAD AHEAD

History is a narrative we tell ourselves to make sense of our experience. Sense-making is all the buzz these days. Some might say we walk backwards into the future while gazing fixedly on the artifacts of our past. Others might say we walk forwards toward a future we dream into being. Some say time is circular; others, a collaborative construct. Somehow, we've gone from the Age of Aquarius in the 1960's to our current *zeitgeist* of End of Days, in the span of one generation.

In any scenario, one thing upon which we can all agree is that our situation is critical, the challenges are complex, and this is no time for inaction.

The bad news: No super-hero or saviour is going to rescue us; we have to do this ourselves. The good news: No one of us has to accept responsibility for saving the entire planet; we each just have to do at bit more from day to day. In other words: The Pure Land must be crowdsourced.

It's time for Buddhists to hear the concerns of the larger community, to study the evidence, get up off our meditation cushions, and add our voices more confidently to the global conversation with direct solutions to the challenges ahead.

A NOTE ABOUT THE RESOURCES

I have tried to include each resource only once, and to reference the homepage whenever possible. This makes the websites easier for you to find. However, it also means some websites which are full of great information and apply to a variety of topics but are not included as resources there. Generally speaking, each website is worthy of more than a passing glance.

It was not always easy to winnow down resources for some topics, but in the interest of brevity, many were omitted. My choices were rather subjective. For any topic of interest to you, a bit of diligent online research will yield more results (usually).

Unfortunately, in some cases (particularly with the search string, "Buddhism and...") very little of value can be found on the web. This is a problem I address repeatedly throughout the book.

TECHNOLOGY

TOOLS

1

What is technology? Tools. Extensions of our senses and powers. Whether they are physical, like a hammer, or intangible and cognitive, like smartphone apps, they are all of a kind. They are means, rather than ends.

> Each technology is an extension of human lives: someone makes it, someone owns it, some oppose it, many use it, and all interpret it.
>
> *David Nye*
> Technology Matters

When we talk about technology, particularly in the Buddhist literature of the West, we tend to focus on digital technology. But this is only one small subset of the technology that sustains and defines us.

Focusing on one technology, or one type of impact, to the exclusion of others, misses the point. Hi-Tech is sexy, but Lo-Tech is a much more powerful quality-of-life determinant. Similarly, to discuss technology outside the context of civil society is dealing in half-truths.

Technology is not a monolith. It is not one thing, but many things depending on how we look at it. We have to wrestle with technology like a zen koan. It's slippery, and we're only able to see it from outside our habitual mindset with great difficulty.

The unifying principle in technology is that, unlike nature, it is designed. Our capacity to design our world is a core aspect of our humanity, and it speaks to the plasticity of our reality. Indeed, we're rather proud of that ability, and design frequently becomes the end rather than the means in our search for happiness.

Animals have, at best, very limited abilities to shape their world; we take it for granted. Were it not for this openness, we could not conceive of change, progress, growth, transformation. The corollary of this openness is that, turning inward, we see ourselves as evolving, able to change and grow, to master our destiny. We are essentially unfinished.

As in any gestalt, technology exists not as a thing, *per se*, but as a relationship between things, existing in the undefined interaction of disparate elements. Just as Buddhists say there is no self, but only dependent arising, so too could we say technology has no defining self-existence.

To truly understand the impact of our technologies, we need to see the big picture; we need to take a systems approach. We need to look through different lenses: political, social, cultural, economic, environmental and ethical. We need to question the unspoken assumptions we have of our relationship with technology, without taking anything for granted. We need to look for synergistic outcomes not implicit in any one technology.

TECHNOLOGY

There is no question that, on balance, technology has been a wonderful boon to humanity. Who would give up shelter, food, clothing, healthcare, transportation, and the like? But, these have not come without a cost and we have turned away all too often from the truth of that cost, preferring to externalize it rather than own it. It's human nature. Technology is seductive, exhilarating, intoxicating. Just watch an automobile commercial and you'll understand instantly what I'm talking about.

For millennia, humans employed their best technology to survive in a wild world. With the industrial revolution, all that changed. The collective global consciousness took a leap into new powers of invention and execution. Since that point, our tool use has become so sophisticated as to appear magic.

Under the enchantment of technology, it's easy to forget that we are still subject to the laws of nature. We still get sick, we still die, we live on a planet with finite resources; no amount of technology can change that.

The fruits of technology have blinded us to our larger reality, our larger potential. We perceive happiness as a bounty of products and services. We seek our entertainment in technologically mediated activities (often of a very passive nature). So much of our life has fallen under the control of technology that we have lost sight of our essential mode of being.

Once invested in this image of reality, we then convince ourselves it is the way things actually are. When we realize that, we can begin to address the problems we face. Our answers will require forward thinking, using technologies only now emerging. Like **Alvin Toffler**, we need to be futurists. Like **Ray Kurzweil**, we need to design with the tools of the future, so when they are developed we will be able to use them wisely. And, like **David Nye**, we need to deconstruct our relationship with technology to help us make sound choices.

TOOLS RESOURCES
- www.historyoftechnology.org
- www.alvintoffler.net
- www.kurzweilai.net
- portal.findresearcher.sdu.dk/en/persons/david-nye
- moralmachine.mit.edu
- ec.europa.eu/futurium/en/ai-alliance-consultation/guidelines#Top

DESIGN

2

When we shape our environment, we have some goal in mind. This is the premise behind all design; it is the true mother of invention.

We all know good design when we see it, although we may not understand the process of what went into its creation. It's a bit of a black box for most people. Professional designers use a rigorous process to get from the initial challenge to the final product. The process involves left- and right-brain thinking, not wishful thinking.

> There's the whole Buddhist thing about the essence of a bowl being its emptiness – that's why it's useful. Its emptiness allows it to hold something. I guess that means that design must talk about something else. If you make design about design, you're just stacking bowls, and that's not what bowls are for.
>
> Frank Chimero

The public only see the creative, right-brain side and that's where TV and magazine articles often gravitate. They think like consumers. However, the real world of designers involves a lot more than some spark of genius. It is born at the nexus of technology, business and art, all in equal measure. It is a team effort.

Thinking like a designer begins with clearly understanding the goal, the stakeholders, the constraints, and the path.

Our design education starts with thirteen fundamental concepts: aesthetics, control, energy, ergonomics, environmental sustainability, fabrication, function, innovation, material, mechanism, safety, structure, and system. In the design of digital products, we add three more key concepts: information, intelligence and interaction. On the business side, project management, supply chain management, and marketing skills are all essential, as well as basic business operations.

Humans are now the dominant evolutionary force on planet Earth. Our individual decisions and actions now overlap on a global scale. This is the Anthropocene. Our goal is a healthy planet and we are the designers. We need a holistic approach and a plan, in order for us to to achieve success.

To go a step further, some say it is already too late for our planet. They say it's all over but the crying. But suppose you have a Bodhisattva vow. Like Ksitigarbha (Jizo), you are prepared to spend eternity in Hell to ease the suffering of beings there. Your work is never-ending. So here you are on Planet Earth today. What will you do?

For starters, you'll need to train for the job. You need to master the dominant paradigm – technology.

TECHNOLOGY

"Technology" as we know it today didn't exist until around 1800, even though the word has its origins in ancient Greece. The first decade of the 19th century was when the Jacquard loom (arguably the first computer) was invented, and also when Eli Whitney (inventor of the mechanical cotton ginny) conclusively demonstrated the value of interchangeable parts. Together they transformed design and production from craft into manufacturing, launching the Industrial Revolution.

In the 150 or so years that followed, until the advent of digital computers and the Information Age, design and invention became the twin evangels of the mechanical bride. Luminaries like **Edison**, **Fessenden**, **Ford**, **Hollerith**, **Marconi**, **Massey**, and **Niépce** were stars in the firmament, championing the way forward. In architecture, traditionalists like **Frank Lloyd Wright** gave way to modernists like **Philip Johnson**. **Frederick Law Olmstead** transformed urban planning with his ideas of public space.

Out of this evolving culture of technology and urbanization, two radical thinkers would turn the entire proposition on its head, in spite of the fact that they met fierce resistance from vested interests at the time. Their legacy is huge, even though rarely acknowledged.

The first was **Buckminster Fuller**, whose revolutionary geodesic architectural designs and Dymaxion philosophy brought synergy and sustainability into the public consciousness. The second was **Rachel Carson**, whose 1962 book, *Silent Spring*, launched the environmental movement. They are the intellectual parents of human ecology.

With the advent of computers, then personal computers, then the world wide web, and then the leap to making physical things from digital data with 3D printing, it all keeps changing. The transformations are accelerating, the implications compounding exponentially. Information, intelligence and interactivity are the keys to our iFuture. Or are they?

DESIGN RESOURCES

- bfi.org (Buckminster Fuller's website)
- rachelcarson.org
- www.ideou.com/blogs/inspiration/what-is-design-thinking
- www.interaction-design.org/literature/topics/design-thinking
- www.khanacademy.org/science/biology/ecology/intro-to-ecology/v/ecology-introduction

DESIGNED

■
3

When we look at how we consume design in the larger context of the mass production infrastructure required to deliver that design to us, we see that our individual, qualitative choices (this design versus that design) take on cumulative, quantitative consequences on a global scale. In short, to understand design, we need to take a systems approach to how design became a commodity.

Everything is designed. Few things are designed well.
Brian Reed

Way back in 1948, mathematician **Norbert Weiner** coined the term "cybernetics," and wrote a book about it called, *Cybernetics: Or Control and Communication in the Animal and the Machine*. We conventionally use the catch-phrase "cyber" as shorthand for activities in the computer realm, but that really isn't a complete metaphor. His book was the first modern instance of applying a systems approach to human activity, with embedded concepts like interdisciplinary methodology, symbiosis, gestalts and universals, feedback loops, and so on.

Weiner's book was influential outside the arena of computing, as seen in **Maxwell Maltz**'s 1960 book, *Psycho-Cybernetics: A New Way to Get More Living out of Life*, which has become a classic of the self-help genre. I would go further, to say it is also one of the foundation stones for modern Western Buddhist practice (rightly and wrongly).

Since so much of our modern experience involves our relationship with technology (the manifest child of design), we can learn much about ourselves from studying design. In the cybernetic context, both our design for living and our designed environment are goal-driven.

For a deeper look into design and its larger impact, I recommend two wonderful documentaries by independent filmmaker **Gary Huswit**, *Objectified* and *Urbanized*. The former movie explores product design, whereas the latter explores architectural design and urban planning.

Whether we are talking of product design or the built environment, it's important to recognize that both rest on the foundation of industrial design, which is to say the design of the machines and processes that make the components that are fabricated into products. In this sense, we can think of architecture and civil engineering as the fabrication of a particular subset of products (windows, doors, shingles, light standards, sewers, and so on).

In the world of industrial design, industrial ecology is the systems approach which weighs all the material and energy inputs flowing through industrial systems. According to *Wikipedia*, the global industrial economy can be modeled as a network of industrial processes that extract resources from the Earth and transform those resources into commodities which can be bought and sold to meet the needs of humanity. A more holistic, Buddhist ecology would not be so anthropocentric. It's still goal-driven, but the goals are different.

To get a deeper sense of the failure of industrial ecology, watch *Detropia*, directed and produced by **Heidi Ewing** and **Rachel Grady**. It's a documentary about the death and resurrection of Detroit after the crash of the US auto industry in 2008.

From a cultural perspective, aesthetics has become synonymous with design and a dominant criterion for purchase. That's the sales proposition for Apple computer products. In the digital realm, aesthetics becomes the elegance of the user experience (UX) and the interface.

Design gives us the illusion of choice without radically up-ending the supply chain. I follow **Naomi Klein** on this topic. For example, all those 25+ competing brands of designer eyewear at the mall actually come from the same Luxottica company.

That illusion of choice feeds consolidation by corporations. For example, a handful of agribusiness companies now control the vast majority of the world's seed stock, and their GMO intellectual property patents are the cornerstone of the "nature by design" mindset.

Even in realms where the technology is stagnant, design can substitute a cult of the new for real benefits. Just look at your mobile phone.

To get beyond the shiny, happy surface of modern design, we need to stop thinking like narcotized consumers and follow the money. We need to dig into the dark corners of what everything really costs, as crusader **Annie Leonard** has done with the "Story of Stuff" movement. If design is the cause, what is the effect?

DESIGNED RESOURCES

- www.psycho-cybernetics.com
- hustwit.com
- detropiathefilm.com
- naomiklein.org
- storyofstuff.org

SOCIETY

■■■
4

We are all dependent upon one another, and on our planet, for our life and well-being. This is the truth of our interbeing.

Since we are living in this created environment and mesh of relationships, this thing we call society, what are the implications? What does it mean to be beholden to design and technology?

> The personal ego already has a strong element of dysfunction, but the collective ego is, frequently, even more dysfunctional, to the point of absolute insanity.
>
> *Eckhart Tolle*

For starters, most of us live in cities. Urbanization has been our growth medium for centuries. With urbanization comes a great deal of infrastructure, forming the basis for our communal enterprise. Now most of us live in a global village. That trend is predicted to accelerate.

Growth has been the prime directive in our evolution. It has been synonymous with progress, but in the 1970's we reached a tipping point: the growth paradigm was shown to have limits. We need a sustainable model, not just for individuals, but for society as a whole, over a longer timeframe.

Many of us in the developed world live in post-productive societies. We benefit from the resources and labour of others, but contribute little of substance. We "manage" things. But we still cling to the conjoined myths of growth and progress. The conflict is not new. **Fritz Lang**'s 1927 silent sci-fi movie classic, *Metropolis*, revealed the uneasy nature of capitalism and the rapacious demands of technology in modern industrial society, more than a decade before **Charlie Chaplin**'s better-known film, *Modern Times*. State-run economies appear to have even less respect for their citizens. Either way, oligarchy is the default mode.

Technology itself (the "Technium" – a neologism coined by **Kevin Kelly**, founding editor of *Wired* magazine) requires us to play by a certain set of rules if we want to enjoy its benefits. Problems arise, however, when we approach all aspects of life and culture from the perspective of what technology wants.

Another issue with communal living is colloquially known as the tragedy of the commons. The age-old problem, stated in modern terms by **Garrett Hardin** in 1968, denotes a situation where individuals acting independently and rationally according to each's self-interest behave contrary to the best interests of the whole group by depleting some common resource, because everyone thinks it is somebody else's responsibility to care for it.

The new paradigm of sustainability will require transformation. We need at least to recognize we are a post-growth society, and from there to actively create a degrowth society.

In the slums outside the nurture of state-supported society, self-organizing groups of citizens form bootstrap communities to get things done. Much can be learned from this type of open-source democracy, where it does not seek merely to replicate the errors of society at large.

Scanning the news, you will be hard-pressed to hear the concept "degrowth." The powers that be would prefer to maintain the status quo, would prefer you to shop, and would prefer to make soothing noises while rearranging the deck chairs on our sinking ship.

It takes a long time to turn big systems around! Long before **Al Gore**'s *An Inconvenient Truth*, the **Club of Rome** was looking to the future with their groundbreaking book, *Limits to Growth*, published in 1972.

For the engaged Buddhist, liberation has to be about more than ourselves. The elimination of suffering is not unique and personal; our liberation cannot be at the expense of another. It extends to animals, plants and the planet itself.

The choice to live simply within our means was always there. Renunciation is not new, but Samsara is vicious and it's not going to change.

To play devil's advocate: the world is going to end, we are all going to die, we're taking a lot of plants and animals with us when we go, and the world will endure spasm after spasm in the Kali Yuga. There's really no point in calling for others to please make a change before it's too late. Act as if it's already too late.

We must each, personally, make the change in our own lives right now. We must each stand up and be the pocket of enlightenment through the darker age to come.

SOCIETY RESOURCES

- kk.org (Kevin Kelly's website)
- clubofrome.org
- occupytogether.org
- bodhimonastery.org
- plumvillage.org/letters-from-thay/thich-nhat-hanhs-statement-on-climate-change-for-unfccc/

ECOLOGY

■ 5 Ecology is the the branch of biology that deals with the relations of organisms to one another and to their physical surroundings.

Industrial ecology applies the same systems approach to material and energy flows in the ecosphere of design, manufacturing and infrastructure. It is a tool used in supply chain management and business planning. But the tail must not wag the dog.

> Fully rooted in the complexities of the historical moment, Eco-Dharma contributes to the ongoing revitalisation of the Dharma, staying responsive and relevant, challenging institutionalised greed, hatred and ignorance, nurturing a dharma that stands in courageous and compassionate defence of the earth, a Dharma that stands in solidarity with life.
>
> *ecodharma.com*

Much of what we know about the impact of our technology-driven lifestyle comes from application of industrial ecology tools. For example, we can find our carbon footprint, or that it takes the equivalent of five bottles of water to manufacture each bottle of water we drink, or that it takes 1500 liters of water to grow a kilogram of wheat. However, there is no ethical component to biological or industrial ecology. For that, we need something more.

Deep ecology (a term first coined by **Arnold Næss** in 1973) is an environmental movement and philosophy that regards human life as just one of many equal components of a global ecosystem. Its goal is a sustainable future for all beings.

Buddhist ecology is a form of engaged Buddhist practice focusing on environmental issues. Buddhist ecology and deep ecology are spiritual twins, drawing inspiration from a shared perspective.

Don't think of ecology as preserving national parks or saving the oceans (as important as those goals are). Think of it as the very fabric of your life, right where you are. In our cybernetic global village, the mobile phone in your hand has a critical impact on the life of a family in central Africa. A backyard chicken farm in southern China could be the source of your next attack of influenza.

Reduce, re-use, recycle. That has been the environmentalist mantra for most of my adult life. Are you old enough to remember **Stewart Brand** and the first *Whole Earth Catalogue* in 1968? If not, look him up. I've seen widespread acceptance of these ideas, innovative education, and social programs to get people on board. But now I'm hearing an increasing number of expert voices telling us we aren't doing nearly enough. The momentum of our "progress" is taking us past another tipping point, and this time the tragedy of the commons is going to affect the entire world. Simultaneously, I'm hearing a torrent of fake news and anti-science cant designed to maintain the status quo for the benefit of the oligarchs. Not good. Not good at all.

So, you can sit on your meditation cushion and imagine you are becoming one with the universe, or you can get mad as hell and get busy fixing things.

We all know the powerful energy that anger can unleash. We applaud the anti-heroes who buck the system and tell us the unvarnished truth. That anger is seductive, and social media is full of the world's justifiable outrage at bigotry, corruption, injustice, and stupidity.

The problem, as I see it, is that for most people, expressing that anger is as far as they go. They know they've been marginalized by the one per-centers, the powers-that-be, but have no solution beyond making sure they get whatever crumbs they can off the big man's table. It's a corrosive mix of frustration and meaninglessness. The seeming catharsis of express-ing our "righteous outrage and scorn" on social media is a self-sustaining feedback loop. It may be the first step of our awakening, but it certainly shouldn't be the last. We need more than memes. What if we could design a better world? How would it look?

For an outstanding place to begin, download **Dr. David Henning**'s 2002 e-book, *A Manual for Buddhism and Deep Ecology*, freely available on the Buddhanet website. It's a workbook, and each page of text is faced with a page for comments, questions and discussion points.

Taking it a step further, Buddhist ecology is not just about being an environmentalist. It's about being engaged in improving all dimensions of human activity.

ECOLOGY RESOURCES

- ecology.com
- deepecology.org
- footprintnetwork.org
- is4ie.org
- industrial-ecology.com
- www.buddhanet.net/pdf_file/deep_ecology.pdf

PRAJNA

6

Many articles have been published about the relationship between Buddhism and science. Some focus on cosmology and quantum physics. Others, notably projects involving **Ven. Matthieu Ricard**, have looked at neuroscience and meditation. The findings can be quite esoteric, but there appear to be significant congruencies between Buddhist and Western scientific thought on these subjects.

Don't go by reports, by legends, by traditions, by scripture, by logical conjecture, by inference, by analogies, by agreement through pondering views, by probability, or by the thought.
Shakyamuni Buddha
Kalama Sutra

Buddhist practice is primarily experiential and evidence-based, like the scientific method; rejecting science has never been an article of faith for Buddhists. Shakyamuni Buddha himself famously said: "If you were to follow the Dharma purely out of love for me or because you respect me, I would not accept you as disciple. But if you follow the Dharma because you have yourself experienced its truth, because you understand and act accordingly – only under these conditions have you the right to call yourself a disciple of the Exalted One."

This is a great foundation. Ironically, however, Buddhist monks receive little science education. The **Bobby Sager** Family Foundation's *Beyond the Robe* project hopes to change that but, for the most part, the initiative is coming from the Western scientific community and donor class, not the reverse. To overlook that problem is to create a bigger one!

Most of us experience science through the technology we use on a daily basis – the effects of science – rather than through pure scientific inquiry. The upshot is that Buddhist teachers traditionally don't have much to say about the nuts and bolts of how to negotiate between practice and daily living in a tech-saturated society.

It is also important to note that our Western scientific paradigm is not without problems of its own, as explored in **Thomas Kuhn**'s landmark 1962 book, *The Structure of Scientific Revolutions*. Scientific research is often muzzled by political agendas or spun by corporate interests. Objective truth is obscured. Inferences based on limited or faulty data are equally flawed.

Long ago, people thought of the universe as a living organism and/or the work of a Creator God. With the advent of higher mathematics, the universe was thought of as the music of the spheres. With the advent of the Industrial Revolution, the universe was thought of as a giant machine. With the advent of Darwinism, the universe was thought of as a giant, continually transforming set of forces. With the advent of cybernetics, the universe was thought of as a self-regulating system. With the advent of computers, information has been thought of as the key to understanding the workings of this system. While all these metaphors have merit, none of them is the truth. They merely illustrate that believing is seeing. As in the Zen koan, neither the flag nor the wind is moving.

The extreme of relying exclusively on the scientific paradigm leads us to the materialistic nihilism of scientism, while the results of rejecting rational science can be seen in the hostility of theistic ideologies that seek to deny, confront or mystify our sense of reality. The *deus ex machina* pretzel logic of so-called Intelligent Design is an example of the latter.

History is full of examples of technological "solutions" that turned out to create entirely new sets of problems that require even more technological solutions to fix. Sometimes, we can see the problems coming, often of an ethical nature, but we don't seem to be able to slow down the momentum of technological progress. Sometimes we get so frustrated at the difficulty of working with humans that we put all our faith in technology.

By the same token, calling Buddhist practice an "inner technology" is another example of how a dominant cultural paradigm becomes the lens through which everything is viewed. It's an example of spiritual materialism, co-opting and commodifying Buddhism so it can exist denatured within the status quo. Much of the course of modern Buddhism is about breaking free from those assumptions.

We need a new Middle Way paradigm: Engaged Buddhism. Prajna cannot exist without Upaya. Modern Buddhism cannot nourish us if it does not present anything of relevance to the modern world.

PRAJNA RESOURCES
- blogs.scientificamerican.com/guest-blog/is-buddhism-the-most-science-friendly-religion/
- matthieuricard.org
- beyondtherobe.org
- en.wikipedia.org/wiki/The_Structure_of_Scientific_Revolutions

HAPPINESS

█ 7

There is no doubt that technology has brought great happiness to humans. Agri-tech has fed us all. Medi-tech has improved our health. Transpo-tech has enabled us to travel, to trade, and so on. The infrastructure of our cities sustains us. Scientific technology enables us to learn about the natural world and not be powerless. Communications technology connects us.

There is no way to happiness – happiness is the way.

Thich Nhat Hanh

Our conundrum is that technology is also implicated in terrible injustices and tragedies: obscene riches for the one-percenters, weapons of war, pollution, industrial accidents, climate change, mass extinctions.... The list is long.

The information revolution has globalized, equalized, and harmonized us (except where governments prevent it), educating us in ways never before possible. We are history's most knowledgeable generation. Yet the information revolution has also brought about new crimes, and new problems. Again, the list is long.

So let's be clear: nobody is willingly going to give up the benefits of technology. But we have to make a distinction here between using technology and rampant consumerism, which is the belief that our sole path to happiness is through procurement and consumption of things and experiences (however "green"). Unbridled growth in our late-stage civilization is malignant. It's fantasy to think that technology itself will provide us the magic ability to pull ourselves up by our bootstraps. Each step forward on that path comes with too much baggage.

We must look for happiness elsewhere, within ourselves and within intentional communities dedicated to sustainability and equality. This is the essence of renunciation. It is not a flight from life, but a credo for a higher calling.

Buddhism is well acquainted with simple living, renunciation of materialism, and turning toward cultivation of the mind. The challenge, then, is to transform those from something individual into something societal: an idea that Bodhisattvahood is congruent with good citizenship. Good citizenship, in this context, means supporting the best, taking an activist stance against the status quo and for better ways of being.

Perhaps, in traditional Buddhist societies, monastic institutions provided such a progressive model and extended it into their communities. It may have been so, but that societal structure is dead and buried. The world doesn't work like that now. The Zen masters are out in the marketplace, perforce, hawking their wares along with all the rest of us. To make matters worse, since the monastic institutions of yore are no more, most Buddhist teachers are functioning in a precarious gig economy.

Can we be happy if our happiness comes at the expense of our children and our global community? Can we separate technology that helps us achieve that goal of sustainability from technology that leads to mutual assured destruction? During the Zen Boom of the 60's and 70's, it was all about awakening to now. In 1996, **Stewart Brand** (the *Whole Earth Catalogue* guy) started the Long Now Foundation, to promote foresight and strategic planning with a 10,000 year span. Can we focus on the Long Now rather than the short-term moment?

Mindfulness is an aspect of Buddhist practice now in vogue. Sadly, as **Jeff Wilson** recounts, it is often neutered, commodified and subverted – no threat to the dominant cultural paradigm. In Zen, that type of practice is known as Bompu Zen. It's concerned with health and individual well-being. That's well and good, but we need something far more radical.

Many people say that fulfilment comes not from accumulating material things, or self-actualization, or even from attaining rarified mental states, but from a meaningful life helping others. World literature is full of stories of people who exemplify that truth. So let's make it the starting point of our Great Vow, as Bhutan has done with their Gross National Happiness pledge. We love to make those people celebrities, and the bigger the number of people they helped, the better they must be (or so the logic goes). It's as if you're only a hero if you get a million "Likes."

Of course, we can't, as individuals, solve all of the world's problems, but we can each do something. To quote **Arthur Ashe**: Start where you are, use what you have, do what you can.

HAPPINESS RESOURCES

- longnow.org
- professorjeffwilson.wordpress.com
- grossnationalhappiness.com
- arthurashe.org
- www.glennwallis.com
- www.pwc.com/gx/en/issues/economy/the-world-in-2050.html

RESPONSIBILITY

8

We people of the world are clamoring for democracy and self-control. We are calling for a more equitable and nonviolent world. We want an end to the domination of oligarchs and their transnational corporations. We want an end to the rule of the gun.

Today, more than ever before, life must be characterized by a sense of universal responsibility, not only nation to nation and human to human, but also human to other forms of life.

HH the Dalai Lama

We want a world built on rational foresight and strategic planning, not religious fanaticism that flies in the face of all the progress that civilization has achieved. We want a culture of caring, not conflict.

We've seen that a better way is possible. We need to consume less, consume more wisely, develop appropriate technologies to enhance the lives of those with limited means, speak truth to power, take back control from those who seek to exploit us, and put our efforts into caring for each other and our planet.

There as many ways to help as there are beings. The list of possibilities is endless. To begin, we need simply to think globally and act locally.

The above memes now permeate our discourse, thanks to our virtually instant communications infrastructure. Information technology has transformed our modern age, just as electricity did a century ago.

Personal computers, smartphones, the Internet, artificial intelligence, and the computerization of an ever-expanding array of devices from vacuum cleaners to surgical robots – the dizzying impact of computers – can seduce us into believing that our future is endlessly bright or sedate us with entertainment. We're willing to accept the problems since the overall impact has been so overwhelmingly positive. There's no going back.

One of the most promising developments in information technology has been open-source computing, which has turned the proprietary paradigm on its head (in spite of push-back). Open-source media has empowered each of us: from citizen scientists, intentional communities, and activists to the general public. From Wikipedia to Innocentive, Kickstarter to Etsy, Facebook to blogs the world over, we are stepping up. We are re-wiring global consciousness.

His Holiness the Dalai Lama has long been a champion for the concept of Universal Responsibility. Although the phrase may invoke images of dreary moral duty for many of us, he counters that it is, in fact, the true gateway to personal happiness. He is not alone in that position. The idea has deep roots in Buddhism and many other world religions. Hence organizations like Sarvodaya Shramadana in Sri Lanka.

When Shakyamuni Buddha sought to systematize his teaching more than 2500 years ago, he relied on what he called the Four Noble Truths: of suffering, its cause, its end, and the path. That path, eightfold in structure, included Right Livelihood as its fifth component. Right livelihood is a way of life based on the ethical principle of non-exploitation.

In today's world, the nature of work has changed, the web of causes and consequences has become more complex, but the ethical opportunity remains. Life outside the "developed world" bubble is much worse than inside, and they are inextricably linked. Neither turning a blind eye nor empty sloganeering nor #slacktivism will suffice.

If design is about beginning with the goal in mind, we must consider what the world will look like 25 years from now, 250 years from now. Our choices must go beyond self-interest or local enrichment at the expense of others.

Recently, more than one thousand AI and robotics scientists signed an open letter to the the United Nations calling for a ban on weaponized artificial intelligence with the capability to target and kill without meaningful human intervention. Are governments listening?

The Pandora's Box of problems that technology can unleash is not limited to a war of the artilects (to use **Dr. Hugo de Garis**' term). The future of carbon-based energy production may drown us. The future of robotic production may leave most of us without meaningful jobs. The future of money may put control of our capital in the "hands" of algorithms. The future of bio-technology may simply wipe us all out.

Suddenly, Right Livelihood is Mission Critical.

RESPONSIBILITY RESOURCES

- furhhdl.org
- futureoflife.org
- innocentive.com
- profhugodegaris.wordpress.com
- www.sarvodaya.org

DEGROWTH

9

The key to OUR sustainable future is not just switching to "green" products. Nor is it just a matter of switching to clean energy sources. We can't "just say no." It will require a complete re-think of how we live. According to **Buckminster Fuller**, we need to think of our planet like a spaceship, millions of miles from the mothership (the sun), needing to sustain itself in a closed-loop system.

> The idea of unlimited growth... needs to be seriously questioned on at least two counts: the availability of basic resources and... the capacity of the environment to cope with the degree of interference implied.
>
> *E.F. Schumacher*

As **Stephen Jenkinson** points out in his 2015 book, *Die Wise*, "Nothing naturally occurring in this world depends upon human beings for its life. Humans are not a mandatory part of the natural order's health or ways. On the other hand, *our* capacity to live at all requires the interdependence of all those other things, and so *our obligation to what gives us life is greater than that borne by any other living being.* Human life means what it means because of how life is, of which humans are a small and deeply obligated, dependent part. *We are heirs to the meaning of life and not its creators...*"

What will it look like to step back from the trajectory upon which we find ourselves? That is a conversation most pundits are reluctant to entertain. But it is a logical corollary of a Buddhist perspective. The vector of progress without limits has been an illusion. The parameters that sustain human life are narrow and inflexible. If we don't respect those boundaries (our modern understanding of karma), no amount of magical thinking will change the course of things.

When we talk about Buddhist economics, it must necessarily include the idea of embracing voluntary simplicity, not just welcoming more of the world's population into the tent through social justice.

Here's a definition of degrowth from one of it's leading proponents, degrowth.org: "Sustainable degrowth is a downscaling of production and consumption that increases human well-being and enhances ecological conditions and equity on the planet. It calls for a future where societies live within their ecological means, with open, localized economies and resources more equally distributed through new forms of democratic institutions. Such societies will no longer have to 'grow or die'. Material accumulation will no longer hold a prime position in the population's cultural imaginary. The primacy of efficiency will be substituted by a focus on sufficiency, and innovation will no longer focus on technology for technology's sake but will concentrate on new social and technical arrangements that will enable us to live convivially and frugally. Degrowth does not only challenge the centrality of GDP as an overarching policy objective but proposes a framework for transformation to a lower and sustainable level of production and consumption, a shrinking of the economic system to leave more space for human cooperation and ecosystems."

This new world order sounds a lot like the interbeing advocated by Vietnamese Zen Master **Thich Nhat Hanh**. Bhutan has also taken this approach with their vow to become the world's first carbon-negative country, and to focus on Gross National Happiness instead of Gross National Product.

This is not just an idle philosophical debate about how many angels can dance on the head of a pin. Nature abhors a vacuum. It's going to continue, with or without us. We can wake up and live consciously, or like some monumental species-wide Darwin Award winner we can take ourselves out of the gene pool through our own stupidity.

Sure, you say, but I'M only going to live another 60 years or so, tops. And I want the Good Life now. Screw the future. Well, if you're not one of the one-percenters right now, and have kids, how's that workin' out for ya? Not so good, I'll bet.

In a recent article in *Nature*, the weekly science journal, researchers noted that climate change is not nearly as big a threat to biodiversity as is human activity: over-exploitation, agricultural activity, urban development being the big three. That means there are real things we can do right now to get it right.

So, it's time to roll up our sleeves and get to work...

DEGROWTH RESOURCES

- orphanwisdom.com
- www.degrowth.info
- degrowth.org
- www.degrowus.org
- degrowthcanada.wordpress.com
- www.postgrowth.org

FUTURE

EMERGING

10

The world is transforming right before our eyes. The changes are diverse, complex and radical. Those changes will be seen in how we work, play, live, and share this planet.

If you are old enough, you will remember the whimsical futures of Buck Rogers, Captain Future, or Tom Swift. More recently, you may have grown up on the Star Trek or Star Wars franchises. In any event, for a more realistic (if less emotionally engaging) vision of the near future, it's best to turn to the professional futurists.

> Most long-range forecasts of what is technically feasible in future time periods dramatically underestimate the power of future developments because they are based on what I call the 'intuitive linear' view of history rather than the 'historical exponential' view.
>
> *Ray Kurzweil*

While thinking about the future is an age-old human activity, the field of professional futurists is relatively recent. Few universities offer programs in the area. There is a World Future Society and an Association of Professional Futurists. The members of these organizations can be found offering strategic foresight to governments, assisting corporations to exploit new technologies, prognosticating in the media, and so on. But there is no widely-accepted credential required to be a futurist. I only know of one university in Canada that offers a post-graduate program in foresight and strategic planning.

The tech industry has its superstars (such as **Steve Jobs**, **Elon Musk**, **Ray Kurzweil**, **Sergey Brin**, or the next guy to ring the NYSE bell for his IPO) but that is not the whole picture. We still have daily reminders of "Whoa, didn't see that coming!" Our vision of the future is not without its weaknesses; for example, less than 25 percent of the World Future Society's members are women, according to its CEO, **Amy Zalman**. Strategic foresight consultants (for example: SciFutures, whose clients include General Mills, Pepsico, and VISA), are fully invested in the prevailing economic paradigm because they are beholden to the companies that hire them. Futurists often find themselves analyzing trends in technology evolution and use, rather than leading transformative values shifts.

Amidst all this chaos, it is possible to tease out three key themes:

While we need to take a long view (planning for the next 10,000 years), our actions in the next 50 years will be critical in determining the future. Given that human nature is not about to morph radically any time soon, technology is the fulcrum for meaningful sustainability. To evaluate new technologies, an interdisciplinary approach is required.

Futurists predict that the most transformative new technologies will emerge in artificial intelligence (AI), the Internet, interfaces, sensors, ubiquitous computing (ubicomp), robotics, biotechnology, materials, energy, space and geoengineering. These changes will be profound and they are already happening.

Utopians and dystopians present alternative futures, but who is right? The emotional toll of unresolved anticipatory grief over our potential impending doom is crippling. The promise of a bright future seems limited only to a fortunate few. Somehow, we must draft an operating manual for Spaceship Earth based on these realities, but the old "growth, progress, jobs" mantra will not suffice. The new technologies seem to be more of a Trojan horse or a Pandora's box than we can control. Tomorrow is here and there is no Plan(et) B. Procrastination is not an option.

As ecologists, we will want to look at outputs as well as inputs, consequences as well as drivers. Our manual must be more than a "how-to" fan club for new technology.

The impacts of tech are more difficult to predict than the technologies themselves, but it's easier if we look at where those new technologies have already begun to transform our lives: governance, jobs, finance, healthcare, education, conflict, food, entertainment, and so on. And we need to hear from spiritual leaders – not just **The Pope** and **The Karmapa**, but from broad global coalitions such as GreenFaith or the Alliance for Religion and Conservation, and grassroots groups like Rebellion Earth.

If we put the impacts into types, it's even easier. We'll look at impacts that are social, political, economic, cultural, environmental, and ethical.

This way we can begin to comprehend the bigger picture to chart our way forward.

EMERGING RESOURCES

- wfs.org
- associationofprofessionalfuturists.org
- iftf.org
- horizons.gc.ca/eng
- singularityhub.com
- www.humansandnature.org

ANTHROPOCENE

There is no such thing as a "natural" disaster. A volcano may explode, and nature adapts. People typically don't consider it a disaster unless it threatens human activity. Conversely, looking at the major disasters of the modern world (climate change, the Pacific Ocean garbage patch, extinctions, Fukushima, or the BP Gulf oil spill, to name just a few), there's no place to look for the causes other than humans. As famous cartoonist **Walt Kelly** had his character Pogo confess in a 1970 Earth Day poster, "We have met the enemy and he is us."

It's no longer us against "Nature." It's we who decide what nature is and what it will be.

*Paul J. Crutzen +
Christian Schwägerl*

Environmentalist **Bill McKibben**, one of the first scientists to bring global warming to popular awareness, picked up the theme in his 1989 book, *The End of Nature*. He is now a leading advocate for global social action on climate change. The end of nature is now a keystone of postmodern environmental philosophy.

We call this era the Anthropocene (Age of Humans). It's not a well-known term. Google it and get 617,000 hits, compared to "twerking," which will give you more than 20 million; that statistic alone could well capture the world's entire problem in a nutshell – but I digress.

In the sphere of climate change, fossil fuels are the carbon bomb. However, the Anthropocene is not simply a way of looking at climate change. From the perspective of deep ecology, it is a framework for evaluating all human activity: the modern avatar of karma. Our impact has transgressed nine planetary boundaries for life. Pulling back is up to us. How we pulled back from the ozone hole boundary shows us we can do this.

There's an old Korean Zen saying, often hung on a plaque in the monastery kitchen: "What right have you to waste even a single grain of rice?"

How could we not look at the world situation today and realize it is condition critical? Each one of us can step up and become an ecosattva; all that is required is the intention to do so. From that intention, opportunities will present themselves.

For example, in Cambodia, monks have ordained trees to prevent illegal logging. In Nepal, Shechen Monastery has an active eco-group. In Myanmar, monks play a role in educating laypeople about conservation. In Japan, since 1995, a Green Plan has been part of the official Soto Zen strategy to engage pressing contemporary issues.

In the West, Dharma teachers have taken an even more activist role, such as **Jun Yasuda** and the Grafton Peace Pagoda's antinuclear peace walks, or **Shodo Spring** and the Compassionate Earth Walks. Many Dharma centres have environmental policies and groups in place too.

At issue here is bridging our well-established Buddhist conservation efforts, with their relatively strong sutra foundation, from a strictly environmental focus into broader areas of technological change. Renunciation of consumerism, divestiture of investments in retrograde energy companies, support for more equitable supply chains, or advocacy for farmers are all great for the planet. But they don't address the challenges of artificial intelligence, robotics, ubicomp, biotechnology, and so on.

Buddhist practice has to be about more than *kensho* or preserving age-old traditions and social conventions. Buddhists represent less than one percent of the North American population. So either we are irrelevant or elitist. The Buddha said finding that human life is rare, and finding the Dharma even more rare. He didn't suggest we should turn our backs on all other living beings (who greatly outnumber us, by the way). It is in our enlightened self-interest to ensure the planet stays within the parameters necessary for life. I believe that Buddhists can have an outsized voice in this work, if we just enter the conversation and speak up. Hence this book.

Are Right Livelihood and technology fundamentally at odds? What does it mean to be human in a world run by computers? Is Mindfulness merely a neurological process? Can a robot attain enlightenment? Does your True Nature include gene splicing? These are no longer just hypothetical questions.

We are hanging from a cliff, suspended from a network RS232 pinout cable by our teeth, while hackers are chewing through it. Quick, why did Bodhidharma e-mail from the West?

ANTHROPOCENE RESOURCES

- billmckibben.com
- 350.org
- e360.yale.edu
- graftonpeacepagoda.org
- compassionateearth.wordpress.com

TECHNOCRACY

■ 12

Eighty years ago, **Edward Sapir** and **Benjamin Lee Whorf** put forward the idea of linguistic relativity: the notion that the structure of a language affects the ways in which its respective speakers conceptualize their world. In a similar fashion, we could say that our relationship with technology, the language and process of design and manufacture, similarly shapes the way we conceptualize our world.

I point out to you, Marcus Claire Luyseyal, a lesson from past over-machined societies which you appear not to have learned. The devices themselves condition the users to employ each other the way they employ machines.

Frank Herbert
God Emperor of Dune

Consider the Western historical record. In ancient times the world was conceived of by animists as a living thing comprising gods and spirits as well as physical beings. With the advent of mechanical clocks abour 700 years ago, we began to speak of the universe as a giant machine, moving in teleological time. In the Age of The Enlightenment, we began to look for the principles by which this universal machine functioned. With the advent of digital technology, we "decided" information was the key to the universe. The search for universal principles has led us to applying the principles of information technology to all spheres of exploration in our search for the master code. Ironically, our search has taken us back to our biological basis, but with the revolutionary notion that our information tools now enable us to control biology like never before.

At each stage of this evolution, old paradigms fell out of favour as they became increasingly incongruent with experience. As explained by **Thomas Kuhn** in his 1962 book, *The Structure of Scientific Revolutions*, paradigms are constantly clashing like tectonic plates. The prevailing world-view suppresses the others.

Taking it a step further, **Marshall McLuhan** said, "We create our tools; thereafter, they create us." In his numerous books, papers, and lectures on media theory, he enumerated the many ways this happened with the advent of print, radio, television and other forms of communications technology.

As the saying goes: to a hammer, everything looks like a nail. These days we could say: to a computer, everything looks like an algorithm.

So here we are, in the Anthropocene. It's the end of nature; everything is design, technology and human intention. How do we deal?

What Technology Wants, a 2011 book by **Kevin Kelly**, publisher of *Wired* magazine, explored the question. *You Are Not A Gadget*, a 2011 book by virtual-reality pioneer **Jared Lanier**, provided the counterpoint. From our vantage point almost ten years later, it appears Kelly's vision has proven to be the dominant paradigm. Just the other day, I heard a discussion on the radio of how the promise of open source, net neutrality, and the democratizing influence of the Internet has been a failure; digital communications technology has simply proven to be the most successful advertising medium we've yet developed, and for the most part, that controls the conversation. We see our digital future as all about buying and selling. After all, isn't **Jeff Bezos** the richest man in the history of the planet?

From the perspective of Buddhist ecology, technology should follow, not lead. Our engagement must be intentional, selective. In this Middle Way, we're acknowledging the technological roots of our current suffering, accepting that the solutions too may be technological, but advocating for a different goal. We're looking in from outside the paradigm.

This is a huge challenge. It's important to remember technology is not a monolith and it does not control us. So far. Ceding control to the nascent artificial intelligence we have created may result in a different story 50 years from now.

Deposing the gods of technocracy will not be easy. We have a long history of being in love with our tools, as **David Nye** points out in his book, *The American Technological Sublime*.

Well, as the saying goes: Speak truth to power. I interpret that to mean we have to get up off our meditation cushions, turn off our mindfulness apps, join like-minded secular organizations, and put our sweat equity into the larger arena. As I said before, the Zen Masters are out in the marketplace. Let's get out there and sell "nothing."

TECHNOCRACY RESOURCES
- marshallmcluhan.com
- jaronlanier.com
- doubleoperative.files.wordpress.com/2009/12/nye-david-e-american-technological-sublime.pdf
- quillette.com/2018/06/04/the-trouble-with-technocracy/

DYSTOPIA

■■■
13

There is no shortage of books, movies and television shows premised on a dystopian future. The difference now is that many of them seem either already to have come true (*Candide, 1984, Brave New World*) or about to come true (*The Road, Wall-E, Mad Max, The Matrix*).

The tropes of human frailty and history as a litany of unintended consequences play well in art, especially when coupled with a solitary hero like Superman or James Bond, but really our problems today require us to discard that notion in favour of a concerted, global effort by every individual, working on a variety of fronts.

I am of the opinion that most mass media plays upon our fears in order to disempower us. Just listen to the nightly news, with its clamorous teasers of:

- Shocking, breaking news...
- Disturbing new details...
- Chilling video...
- Another mass shooting...
- Bus crash on the other side of the planet kills 25...
- Trump (anything)

You're screwed, people are savages, the world is insane, the system's too big to fight, you knew all along that's how it goes so you're complicit, now cut to commercial. Here, buy this to improve the one tiny, miserable bit of the world that you CAN control: your underarm sweat (or fill in the blank). Then back to that one feel-good, human interest story to let you know the reporting was balanced. Up next: funny videos, dancing celebrities, pet antics, singing wanna-bes, or a variety of misfits more screwed up than you. When **Jon Stewart** was doing *The Daily Show*, he used to end the episode with a crystallized clip of WTF insanity, he dubbed "Our moment of Zen." (Note to self: is that really what Zen is all about?) Now other newscasters use the same technique to cap off their shows, although they call it "Our moment of the day."

Unplug. Be here now. Wake up. OK, now what? Isn't this *kensho* where Siddhartha's journey began, with realizing the fallacy of conventional wisdom? He then spent six years learning from others and moving deeper into his journey. He didn't rest on those laurels. He didn't simply stop at his first breakthrough.

Yes, samsara is vicious and beings are numberless. If we vow to save them all, it's not going to happen on the cushion. After coming to Enlightenment, Siddhartha spent the next 40 years walking all over India devoting every minute of every day to making things better for people, animals and the environment. Zen Masters don't preach "form is emptiness," bliss out, and then do nothing; they work for the betterment of all every day. Practice and action go hand in hand. If peace is every step, you have to keep walking the walk.

We all know the list of what's wrong. We suffer from crisis fatigue and all we want to do is cocoon. We desperately want it to be somebody else's problem. Sorry, but that just isn't going to happen.

Some of us are angry. We're mad as hell and we're not going to take it any more (to quote **Peter Finch**, in that 1976 movie, *Network*). That isn't a solution, but it does provide a starting place; it shows us that things don't have to be the way they are. If we can see the potential harm in our system, we can correct course.

Appropriate technology and social entrepreneurship have been eye-openers for my students, trying to see outside their First World bubble where the biggest challenge is Apple iPhone x versus Samsung Galaxy s10.

Even if everything goes to hell in a handbasket, perhaps we can have a dystopia where people help each other. Indeed, that seems like the most likely near-future scenario. What could that look like? **Illac Diaz** and the Liter of Light Foundation are a fantastic example of how disadvantaged people in the slums of Manila found an appropriate technology to enhance their lives, go beyond the limits of their overwhelmed electrical grid, and make use of discarded pop bottles, to do it. It has been a triple win.

Dr. Govindappa Venkataswamy, provider of free cataract surgery to millions of people around the world, is another role model.

DYSTOPIA RESOURCES

- dark-mountain.net
- www.michaelmann.net
- literoflight.org
- en.wikipedia.org/wiki/Govindappa_Venkataswamy

UTOPIA

14

Some would argue that technology is in fact the *only* thing that has advanced civilizations and, therefore, it is likely to be our saving grace in future. Progress in building structures, energy production and distribution, food production and storage, transportation, health, communications, and security, are some examples. It is true that every advance has come with a cost, but in hindsight it would appear that the changes have been incrementally positive, when considered cumulatively.

> Most human beings have an almost infinite capacity for taking things for granted.
> *Aldous Huxley*
> Brave New World

So what is our fear of technology? Perhaps at the heart of the matter is fear of how technology is used or withheld, and that is an issue of human nature. Developing countries have a very different perspective than those countries who are at the top of the technology pyramid. Should Buddhists be anti-technology?

As **Stewart Brand** points out in his 2009 book, *Whole Earth Discipline: An Ecopragmatist Manifesto*, our misunderstandings about the nature of technology often make our vision cloudy, our resolve shaky. A devotion to new technology is not the solution either. For all the good that technology has done, it is a fallacy to think that technology alone is the thaumaturge for all our problems.

Venerable Prayudh Payutto (Phra Bhramagunabhorn), one of Thailand's most well-known Buddhist scholars, and recipient of the 1994 UNESCO Prize for Peace Education, has written extensively on the problems of society, the environment, economy, law, and science and technology from a Buddhist perspective. His 1991 book, *Toward Sustainable Science*, and his 1994 book, *Buddhist Solutions for the 21st Century*, both compiled and translated by **Bruce Evans**, are particularly relevant. Phra Payutto's work is a bit hard to find in English now, but you can find selections on the Internet Wayback Machine. In his work, you can find many orthodox scriptural bases for a progressive perspective.

For example:

> On the level of everyday life, or satisfying the everyday needs of humanity, science plays the vital role of paving the way for technological development and encouraging the production, development and consumption of lopsided technology.

On the other hand, social preferences for a particular kind of technology encourage scientific research aimed at producing, developing and consuming that technology.

From what we have seen, science, supported by the beliefs in the efficacy of conquering nature and producing an abundance of material goods, has spurred the production and development of technology along a path resulting in serious problems. Science and technology may have actually done more harm than good.

The kind of production, development and consumption of technology which has caused these problems is one geared to feeding greed (selfishly and wastefully catering to desires on the sensual plane), hatred (causing exploitation, destruction, power mongering), and delusion (encouraging heedlessness, time-wasting activities, and the blind consumption and use of technology).

In the development of science on the technological level, it will be necessary to change some of the basic assumptions it is based on, by encouraging the development of constructive technology, which is free of harmful effects, within the constraints of these three principles:

1. Technology which is moderate.
2. Technology which is used for creating benefit.
3. Technology which serves to develop understanding and improve the human being.

What I particularly like about Phra Payutto's critique is that he takes a holistic approach to science, technology, and human society.

UTOPIA RESOURCES

- sb.longnow.org
- www.abuddhistlibrary.com/Buddhism/B%20-%20Theravada/Teachers/Ven%20Payutto/Buddhist%20Solutions%20for%20the%20%20Twenty-First%20Century/Buddhist%20Solutions%20for%20the%20Twenty-First%20Century.htm
- www.urbandharma.org/pdf/Buddhist_Economics.pdf

HISTORY

A little more than 1200 years ago, we humans had perfected the art of architecture to a degree that major monuments were being built all over the planet. Buddhists built some in India at Ajanta, Ellora and other sites, but their largest effort by far was the construction of Borobudur in Java, Indonesia, where Atisha had settled. It is not only the largest Buddhist monument on the planet, but also one of the wonders of the ancient world by any measure: a psycho-cosmological legacy writ in stone.

In the district of *Bóro*, in the province of *Kedú*, and near to the confluence of the rivers *Elo* and *Prága*, crowning a small hill, stands the temple of *Bóro Bódo*, supposed by some to have been built in the sixth, and by others in the tenth century of the Javan era.

Sir Stamford Raffles
The History of Java, 1817

After more than 100 years to complete, it was buried by ash in a volcanic eruption, lost to human knowledge for a millennium, and then "re-discovered" by **Sir Stamford Raffles**, who was the British ruler in Java in the early 1800's.

The structure (known as a *candi* or *stupa*) was constructed with no modern architectural tools – an engineering triumph and testament to the dedication of its many artistic contributors. It is allegorical in nature, a Vajrayana mandala dedicated to Akshobya, with layers of progressive abstraction until the topmost level. What would a contemporaneous visitor have thought of that technological marvel?

The architect who built it miscalculated the load-bearing capacity of the soil foundation, and even before the structure was completed, it began to sink precipitously. To rectify the problem, the bottom layer of the allegory was buried in buttressed ramparts.

Painstakingly restored in the late 1970's and declared a UNESCO World Heritage site in 1991, it's now revealed again in all its glory, save for the Buddha statues and heads that were looted over the years since Sir Stamford's revelation.

Meanwhile in China, in a Silk Road oasis called Dunhuang on the edge of the Taklamakan Desert, Buddhists spent more than 1000 years, starting around 366 CE, building a complex of more than 400 cave temples known as the Caves of the Thousand Buddhas, or Mogao (now also a UNESCO World Heritage site). Five hundred years after they started, their library acquired the first book ever printed with moveable type (traceable to 868 CE), a copy of the *Diamond Sutra* – predating the *Gutenberg Bible* by some 600 years. The library, which grew to be very extensive, was sealed and hidden in the 12th century CE to protect it from invaders, and subsequently lost to human knowledge for almost a millenium.

What, we wonder, was the impact of that printed sutra when it first appeared in the lineage of direct transmission? How did the technology of printing transform our understanding of ourselves in that milieu?

In 1907, **Sir Aurel Stein**, fresh from his adventures exploring the Silk Road, stumbled upon the ancient Mogao Buddhist cave temples at Dunhuang, where a humble Taoist monk who lived amongst the forgotten ruins told him of a treasure cave filled with ancient manuscripts. Over the course of the next little while, Stein induced the hermit with various blandishments to give him access to the trove, which Stein then plundered and shipped off to the Victoria & Albert Museum in London. The many manuscripts, paintings and books he acquired still reside there.

Meanwhile, in Cambodia in the early 12th century, a Hindu dynasty began to build the enormous city of Angkor. Converting to Buddhism over the next hundred years, the original Hindu focus of the city's many Wats (temples) took on a Buddhist character they maintain to this day. Ongoing archeological study and recent surveys with LiDAR technology have revealed the vast scale of the city's design, its complex urban planning, and its astounding hydrological infrastructure supporting a large agricultural population.

Simply to say that Angkor is a UNESCO World Heritage site scarcely does it justice; it is a wonder and a profoundly inspiring manifestation of all that it is to be human. The work took hundreds of years. It was a collective effort. What would possess a people to build hundreds of temples, sited with the best geomantic principles, encompassing vast water parks?

These three examples show how past Buddhists have engaged with technology for centuries, dedicated to a higher purpose.

HISTORY RESOURCES
* whc.unesco.org/en/list/592 (Borobudur)
* whc.unesco.org/en/list/440 (Mogao)
* whc.unesco.org/en/list/668 (Angkor)

ETHICS

■ 16   Don't kill. Don't steal. Don't lie. Don't be sexually irresponsible. Don't use intoxicants. Buddha's five basic precepts are pretty clear. The modern moral landscape is, alas, not so clear.

How about texting while driving? Drone strikes? Employers scoping your social media posts? Genetically-modified food patents? Stem cell research? Offshore oil drilling in Alaska? Fracking? Refugee policy? Cosmetic surgery? TV evangelists? Spying on environmental groups? Gangsta rap? Torrents? Wikileaks? LGBTQ rights? Tasers? Video games? Caffeine-enriched energy drinks? Facebook using your data to overthrow governments? Poaching?

> He is not noble who injures living beings. He is called noble because he is harmless towards all living beings.
>
> Dhammapada, 270

From pre-birth to end-of-life and disposal of the dead, advances in technology have taken us from simplicity to complex choices about right and wrong. Technology has enabled us to see the effects of our choices ripple out across the world, and forced us to weigh the implications of our actions multiplied by billions.

We can't separate the personal from the social. We can't rigidly adhere to a fundamentalist refuge that flouts the spirit of religion while flaunting the letter of the "law." We can't rest on a minimalist *via negativa* of "do no harm" instead of actively pursuing a path of engagement. And we most definitely cannot simply condemn technology or other people as "the problem."

So, what do we do? What would Buddha do? What would Buddha do with historical literalism, fundamentalism, revisionism, or relativism?

Since he's not around for us to ask him, we are left with the task of embracing the challenge like a koan. In fact, that was one of Shakyamuni's final messages to us: don't rely on my words simply out of faith in me; test my teachings in the context of your experience and see what works. Granted, our experience is radically different from pre-modern India, but some things haven't changed.

In other words, as complex as our modern world can be, we still have a set of principles against which to evaluate good and evil. And as the *Dhammapada* verse above illustrates, those principles are very clear.

Buddhists place a lot of emphasis on intention. That's important, but as the saying goes, "The road to hell is paved with good intentions." Complex problems require serious investigation and oversight by many stakeholders. New situations call for new solutions, innovations based on previous learning. Buddhist awakening should not stand in mutual obstruction to our innate cognitive abilities. They are part of the vitality of Tathagatagarba.

One of the first thinkers to take this on was **E.F. Schumacher**, whose 1973 book, *Small Is Beautiful: A Study of Economics As If People Mattered*, popularized a term he had first coined in Burma in 1955: Buddhist economics. His later book, *A Guide for the Perplexed*, published in 1977 after his death, presents the deeper philosophical basis for his earlier work. Buddhist economics is now a "thing" and each year new books come out based on that approach.

Thinkers in many spheres beyond economics, whether professing to Buddhism or not, are tackling thorny questions with the same critical eye.

For example, **David Suzuki** is a tireless champion for the environment. **Cory Doctorow** blogs, writes and speaks extensively about intellectual property and information policy. **Michael Pollan** does the same for food issues. When experience speaks, we Buddhists need to listen. Good ideas are good regardless of where they come from.

Harm reduction is an important concept to bear in mind here. Recognizing that perfection is the enemy of the good, absolutist roadblocks give way to sensible solutions, such as needle exchange programs for addicts, the decriminalization of prostitution, or Light Rapid Transit instead of more expensive subway lines. Now, if only we could extend the same care and consideration to the planet!

Small personal commitments matter too. Give up plastic, single-use grocery bags, or at least use them a couple of times before discarding them. Don't use plastic straws. Ease up on the meat. Take the bus. Plant a garden that is bee- and butterfly-friendly.

ETHICS RESOURCES
* blogs.dickinson.edu/buddhistethics (*Journal of Buddhist Ethics*)
* @buddhistethics
* centerforneweconomics.org
* davidsuzuki.org
* craphound.com (Cory Doctorow's website)
* michaelpollan.com

MAGIC

When we talk about technology these days, we tend to think of hi-tech: smartphones, bioengineering, cyborgs, space travel, and so on. As seductive as these technologies are, they are merely a sideshow. The main event is still low-tech: fire, light, shelter, food, safety. It's all well and good to talk about whether we can build a space elevator to assist us with interplanetary travel, but what good is it if we can't feed and clothe the people on earth, or keep them safe? Hi-tech is not always high value.

Any sufficiently advanced technology is indistinguishable from magic.
Arthur C. Clarke

Magical thinking is defined by psychologists as believing that one event happens as a result of another without a plausible link of causation. It's the exact opposite of Buddha's dependent origination. In order to wake up from that state, one must face the realities of cause and effect, and follow the ripples outward.

The seduction of digital technology takes us from being truly present into magical thinking. It is the opposite of authentic living. Think of it as hold music, playing a Beatles song on the Pan pipes with somebody coming on occasionally to say, "We're experiencing a higher than usual call volume; please continue to hold. Your call is important to us."

Life is not a selfie. Your Twitter analytics mean nothing. You have more passwords than you can possibly remember. Self-driving cars will not result in hours of leisure. When you die in real life, you really die.

If the power went out, you wouldn't know what to do with yourself. Most of the world knows that, because they are still living it. But the Gods and Titans of the developed world appear to have forgotten.

On the other hand, rejection of technology is just as magical. It's just nostalgia for a golden age that never was. Returning to a medieval worldview is no solution. Antibiotics, vaccination, and family planning really work. Living off the grid is impractical for almost everyone.

To diagnose our technology addiction, we can start with some of the symptoms: dissociation from nature, loss of social cohesion, glorification of violence, a variety of physical ailments from obesity to myopia, and so on. The list is long.

Good public health policy always looks for social causes to personal problems. In this case, we find (on one hand) a barrage of advertising messages promoting the cult of the new, heavy investment in the illusion of choice in consumer goods, and an endless assortment of diversions and entertainments. On the other hand, we've got over-leveraged economies, inability to deal with disruptive technologies in the workplace, a jobs-trump-all mantra, Kafka-esque bureaucracy, scapegoating, and a sense of lurching from one crisis to the next. No wonder we're all experiencing cognitive dissonance!

Right about here, you are probably expecting me to reveal the answer to our dilemma, the hopeful uplift that will characterize the rest of this book. Sorry. I am completely dis-illusioned but have no answers. All I know is: our current way of life is based on unsustainable delusion.

As Abraham Lincoln once said:

> We are not enemies, but friends. We must not be enemies.
> Though passion may have strained, it must not break our
> bonds of affection. The mystic chords of memory will
> swell when again touched, as surely they will be, by the
> better angels of our nature.

In Lincoln's time, he was talking about the northern and southern States being friends. In our time, we are talking about humans and Planet Earth, and the stakes are infinitely higher. In these dark days, it is rare and precious to find those angels.

Social discounting, the cost-benefit notion that we would give up something now for a greater good for others later, on a sliding scale representing our social distance from them, is a key concept in modern project management. It's frequently considered where environmental initiatives have an impact on property, jobs, and so on. Such sanguine acceptance of human nature makes for more realistic outcomes. Consider, if you will, the work of **Richard Louv**.

MAGIC RESOURCES

- www.pc.gov.au/research/completed/cost-benefit-discount/cost-bene-fit-discount.pdf
- richardlouv.com
- naturesacred.org
- www.dalailama.com/messages/environment/buddhist-concept-of-nature

IMAGINE

18 There's a famous Zen koan: you've swallowed a blazing hot iron ball and it's halfway down your throat. What do you do?

Like it or not, that is the situation in which we find ourselves, with nothing to assist us but our own ingenuity. Necessity is the mother of invention.

Never doubt that a small group of thoughtful, committed citizens can change the world; indeed, it's the only thing that ever has.

Margaret Mead

In any good design brief, once one has clearly defined the real problem, the next step is brainstorming possible solutions. At this point, the goal is not to come up with a finished plan, but merely to explore the possible alternative futures. It's a right-brain, imaginative activity. Analyzing, editing and evaluation come later.

So let's get started...

Here are some basic assumptions: you are a spiritual person, trying to improve yourself; you see yourself as part of the web of life; you have grasped the jist of the science, demographics and economics of what's happening to the planet; you recognize the world of tomorrow will be very different from today's; you are willing to change your way of life for the good of all; and you're looking for resources to help guide your choices. You're not alone.

What is your passion? Since you can't do it all, what do you think you CAN do, in a way you can make a difference? For me, it was writing this book. Write down your ideas here:

IMAGINE RESOURCES

- Where do you find inspiration?

PRACTICE

LIFE HACK

By calling Dharma a life hack, we mean it's a clever solution to a tricky little personal problem that many people have experienced. That is the most optimistic of definitions for the term "hack." It implies that life is good, but it could be better.

The pages of Buddhist magazines are full of it. The blogosphere reeks of it. Often, it's presented as mindfulness or consciousness hacking. We've got mindful work, sex, eating, parenting, doctoring, soldiering, and so on. This is merely self-help in a new package – like Bompu Zen, it is the narrow psychologization of transcendental wisdom. Not that there's anything wrong with that.

Improve your life one hack at a time. 1000 Life Hacks, DIYs, tips, tricks and More. Start living life to the fullest!
Clickbait from the Internet

We need to get beyond our own navels. Here's where the Sangha Jewel becomes important. As our awareness of the many dimensions of practice expands, engagement becomes a natural part of it.

What about those other definitions of "hack?" A hack is someone who botches their work, or an appointed flunky. Not very encouraging. As a verb, "to hack" is to swing away wildly at something with a blade. In the computer world, it means to infiltrate, destroy, reconfigure, or violate any sort of computer program, website, etc. through use of coding. Again, not very encouraging. Still, the idea of subversion is intriguing.

What if we propose Dharma practice as subverting Samsara, destroying conventional thinking and aspirations, replacing them with a truer (but still anthropocentric) picture of reality? That's the premise behind movies like *The Matrix* or TV shows like *Kung Fu*, and part of the reason for their quasi-mystical, popular appeal.

We can go further. What if we propose that our individual life is like that of a cell in a larger body, and that body is Life on Earth, the biosphere? We need to function as best we can to do our job as a healthy cell, whatever that specific function is. However, the goal here is to work cooperatively with all the other cells, each with their own specialized function, to maintain the health and development of the entire being. Without that, the individual cells die.

Buddhist teaching says we are all complete and perfect as we are. Our Buddha Nature is pure, but covered up by adventitious stains. The goal of practice is to clear away those stains. Could we say that finding your True Nature is finding your Truth in Nature?

In the story of the transmission of Chan from the Fifth Patriarch, **Hongren**, to the Sixth, **Huineng**, the Fifth Patriarch proposed a poetry contest to his students, saying the student whose short poem best expressed an understanding of the Essence of Mind would receive the staff and bowl of the Transmission.

Hongren's most prominent student, **Shenxui**, wrote the verse:

The body is a Bodhi tree
The mind a standing mirror bright
Polish it with diligence
And let no dust alight

However, the Transmission went to Huineng, a lowly kitchen helper and novice, who wrote the verse:

Fundamentally no tree exists
Nor stand for a mirror bright
Since all is empty from the start
Where can the dust alight?

I always feel Shenxui got short-shrift for his poem. He went on to become a wonderful teacher, but his legacy has been lost in the mists of time. Could Huineng have written his riposte, had Shenxui not given him the mirror stand?

There is no short-cut to Enlightenment. Practice is a lifelong commitment, regardless of whether or not one believes in rebirth. The goal is not individual but universal. Unlike hacks, neither life nor practice embody the phrase, "one and done."

LIFE HACK RESOURCES
- medium.com/personal-growth/the-problem-with-hack-culture-b0ddf43784e9
- tricycle.org/trikedaily/dharma-hacks/
- www.cohack.org
- thebuddhistcentre.com/westernbuddhistreview/brain-hacking-and-mind-upgrades-buddhism-future

MR. NATURAL

■ 20

Back in 1967, artist **R. Crumb** created a character called Mr. Natural. He was portrayed in Crumb's comics as an old man, bald, with a long white beard, wearing a shapeless yellow gown. Part guru and part con artist, he became an icon of the 1970's counterculture, with his aphorisms like, "Keep on truckin'," "Twas ever thus," and "Don't mean sheeit."

> All philosophies are mental fabrications. There has never been a single doctrine by which one could enter the true essence of things.
>
> *Nagarjuna*

Mr. Natural is a funny spoof on spiritual leaders, and the joke extends to Zen Masters too, even though there weren't many in North America at the time he was created.

If you want to unpack the joke, however, consider how spontaneous and irrational behaviour has become synonymous with authenticity. Now that Roshis are out in the marketplace hawking their wares with the rest of us, they've had to adapt. The results have been mixed.

Looking at practice from that perspective, where does authenticity fit in the hierarchy of cool Dharma? Does it include tie-dye shirts, hemp bags, or the vast array of Buddhist trinkets? Do Buddhists need to wear special clothing? You could be updating your blog with entries like: "I just completed 20 minutes of zazen with meditation timer! Here's a Dharma quote you just HAVE TO READ; I've put it on a picture of a flower so its emotional too. It's a quote about compassion from an important teacher!" Can you package authenticity in a meme? In your practice of authenticity, if you strive to be as natural as possible in your daily chopping of wood and hauling of water, is it okay to use a Buddhist dating app?

Part of the confusion comes from how the term "natural awakening" has been translated from the original term in Nyingma Buddhism. It's not what you might think it is at first.

What is happening in the intersection of authenticity and artificiality? How do we even define those things? Is technology inherently artificial, or can the way we use it be authentic in the service of Dharma? The question reveals a nostalgia for authenticity we impute into the past. Consider **Robert's Pirsig's** *Zen and the Art of Motorcycle Maintenance*, or **Matthew Crawford's** *Shop Class as Soulcraft*. In both books, mindfulness of our embodiedness is held up as something the world has lost: the value of craft.

Extending this into the realm of ecology, where's our path? We've all read many stories of spiritual seekers communing with nature. Will our reverence for the natural world include saving it? For example, what are we doing to divest from fossil fuels? Do we support local, organic farming over factory farming with genetically modified organisms? Where do we stand with regard to meat? How about drug residues in our water?

Many of us are so enamored with technology and the promise of a near-future, technologically-empowered utopia that we forget the basics of life on earth. Sci-Fi author **Bruce Sterling** captures this in his pithy portrayal of our current plea to our devices: "Don't make me think." While we ponder the Singularity, artificial intelligence, augmented reality, cyborgs and the like, we're killing all the bees, turning the oceans into deadzones, and burning every crumb or drop of carbon we can get our hands on. In that regard, Buddhist ecology definitely has to have an anti-technology stance. But it doesn't mean we have to go forest bathing.

We may forego the smartphone meditation timer app, or the Buddha-box, in our quest to return to our True Nature. However, sticking our heads in the sand is no solution. The Lama or Roshi blogging about the Buddha Nature of a pet dog is simply not going to cut it.

The future depends on our choices now. Can technology help us see reality without overwhelming us? My humble suggestion is that when we engage with technology in the global context rather than as a personal Dharma hack, we're on the right track. Be it through social action, art, or right livelihood, we have the wonderful opportunity to fulfil our vows through engagement.

As **Dogen** said, life is one continuous mistke. Humanity lurches from one crisis to the next. That is natural, as natural as our Buddha Nature. As **Gampopa** said, our samsaric activities are based on conflicting emotions and primitive beliefs about reality. But don't panic. Just aim for the light and keep walking, step after step.

MR. NATURAL RESOURCES

- www.rcrumb.com
- robertpirsig.org
- matthewbcrawford.com
- wired.com/category/beyond_the_beyond (*Bruce Sterling's blog*)
- www.scandinave.com/blue-mountain/en/forest-bathing/
- gofossilfree.org/divestment/

MEDITATION

■
21

Meditation is a Dharma practice fundamental. There is no shortage of material on what meditation is, how to do it, and so on. A quick gloss of the Buddhist meditation terrain includes zazen, joriki and tariki, shikan taza, chanting, dzogchen, mahamudra, nondual, yidam visualization, satipatanna, vipassana, shamatha, mindfulness, chakra work, sitting, standing, walking, dancing, lying down, lucid dreaming, neuroplasticity, MBSR, modulation of alpha waves, being "in the zone," astral travel, yogic powers, past life regression, and other techniques that are devotional or secular. There are probably 84,000 different techniques.

> To be still means to empty yourself from the incessant flow of thoughts and create a state of consciousness that is open and receptive.
>
> *John Daido Loori*

Is technique technology? No, that's a malapropism. Technique refers to a design process, whereas technology refers to a tool.

Consider, if you will, the nature of bells, gongs, blocks, incense, clocks, atomic clocks, clock radios, world clocks, factory punch-clocks, or our inherent awareness of time. All mark the passage of our minutes and hours. Yes, you may say that mechanical time is an artificial construct, but even if you aspire to "Be Here Now" (thank you **Ram Dass**), you cannot deny that time flies.

We live in an age of overly-abundant information. You could say we swim in information like fish in a bowl. The answer to everything is at our fingertips (or voice request), if we know the right question. Our every move is tracked, often with our willing participation. Big Data aggregates our statistical vectors. We suffer from Information Anxiety (the description of, and antidote to which, has been brilliantly described in several books by award-winning graphic designer **Richard Saul Wurman**).

In the world of meditation, this plays out with meditation timers and a plethora of digital assistants. The essential question is whether these are are being used as aids or substitutes. I saw a cartoon recently, in which two people are coming up to the summit of a mountain peak. As the first reaches the pinnacle, the companion following, looking at a smartphone, says, "Want to know how many steps we took?"

If tracking and sharing your meditation stats is important to you, please consider the motive. Meditation is not something to accumulate.

Back in the early days of Dharma in the West, a similar discussion arose around the use of hallucinogenic drugs either as an aid to, or a substitute for, spiritual quests. **Timothy Leary**'s encomium for psychedelics was summed up as "Turn on, tune in, drop out." As Western practice evolved, it became evident that there is no place for chemical enhancement (beyond tea) in meditation. More on that later.

Consider cars as an analogy. When you meditate, you're driving your car. When you park, that's the rest of your daily life. Now it turns out that cars are parked 90 percent of the time, and we have a huge infrastructure designed to deal with that. It's a very inefficient system; no matter how good a driver you are, most of what matters happens outside your car.

Of course, if you are a distracted driver, playing with your technology when your eyes should be on the road and your attention on what's happening, you are dramatically more likely to crash. You're a risk to yourself and to everybody else around you.

In the parlance of the Middle Way, we cannot expect to find the solution to suffering in either extreme. No amount of meditation is going to free us, if it is focused on "bettering ourselves." Nor can we engage in activism without constantly checking our intentions, reflecting on the assumptions upon which we act.

By the same token, we cannot realistically say that our way of meditating is the one true way. What we can say is that meditation provides a window of stillness, through which to disengage from worldly affairs and re-orient our aspiration, a steering wheel guiding future engagement. It is a way of maintaining that stillness while navigating life's journey. But attempts to pacify that which is unpacifiable is a fool's errand. Our stream of consciousness (or rather, the universe's stream of consciousness as manifested in each of us) flows constantly. If we see meditation as a way to stop thinking, we are merely reifying what we see as a separation of samsara and nirvana. But they are not-two.

MEDITATION RESOURCES

- ramdass.org
- wurman.com
- en.wikipedia.org/wiki/Timothy_Leary

FAITH

22

Buddhism is often portrayed as a rational way of life rather than a religion. That fits nicely with our secular perspective. But at the shallow end of the pool, it's a psychological self-help technique.

On the other hand, Buddhism is sometimes (less frequently, now) portrayed as a mystical and esoteric treasure from the East. As such, it fulfills our spiritual yearning. At the shallow end of that pool, it becomes a cultish jumble of misguided rituals.

We are what we think.
All that we are arises with
our thoughts. With our
thoughts, we make our world.
Shakyamuni Buddha

In both cases, the goal is to get to the deep end of the pool, where real practice begins.

Most of this book deals with the "rational" perspective, but I'd like to spend a bit of time looking at some faith-based practices that don't square well with our Western secular worldview. Consider, if you will...

In Theravada countries such as Thailand, Burma and Cambodia, protection tattoos are common. Scorpions are a particularly potent talisman against spirit attack. Yet representations of Buddha are very inappropriate.

In all three great Buddhist traditions, sacred relics are held in great veneration. *Sarira* (gems found in cremations of holy teachers) are placed on the heads of the faithful for blessing.

In Vajrayana foundation practices, one is encouraged to say mantras and make prostrations and mandala offerings 100,000 times in a specific time frame, while engaging in complex visualizations.

Buddhist cosmology is overflowing with unseen, parallel realities, and unexplainable phenomena, including ghosts, tulkus, omens, curses, spirits, oracles, vows, karma across the ages, flying yogis, transfer of consciousness, astral travel, Dhyani Buddhas, yidams, guardian deities, and more.

Is it cultural imperialism for us to banish these as mere quaint vestiges of a pre-technological era? When the Chinese Communist Party secretly funds movements supporting divisive spirits, or demands that reincarnating lamas have their future rebirths pre-approved by the Chinese government, what are we to make of it? Hedging their bets?

It is said that Buddhas appear and teach in whatever form can reach sentient beings. Practice takes many forms, and training many paths. The education of an oracle is no less valid than the *samu* work of a Zen monk.

Sometimes we can find bridges. For example, lucid dreaming, popularized by **Stephen LaBerge**, can offer us a window into the world of dream yoga. **Peter Fenner**'s nondual "Radiant Mind" psychology presents Madhyamaka paradoxes in terms that make sense to Western ears. But sometimes, there is no bridge and we must simply make the leap of faith. What then?

Don't be so quick to defend our scientific, technological superiority. Haven't we learned yet that science is often the handmaiden of corporate interests who skew results to suit their greedy purposes? Technology without ethics has created the greatest horrors of our time, from the atom bomb to Agent Orange, from climate change to a garbage planet, and from mindful corporate minions to all of us alone together while we jiggle our smartphones.

On the other hand, ideological assaults on science are the scourge of the 21st century. Stand strong in your faith in the validity of science; it's the only rock upon which we can build a rational future. A faith that sets itself up in opposition to facts does not deserve adherence.

So what does the deep end of the pool look like? The heroes of our time are people who have faith in the future, and whose inclusive intent is to make the world a better place. They need not be spiritual celebrities. In fact, they need not even be individuals. The melding of faith, science and technology has brought us the realization that we can join powerfully with like-minded collaborators the world over in pursuing a common, sustainable goal. In the Buddhist world, the **Global Buddhist Climate Change Collective** was one such group. In the interfaith world, **Fossil Free Faith** is a great example.

Whether one chooses devotional or esoteric path in one's personal practice is just that: a personal matter. In the sphere of our action in the world, faith has a different connotation.

FAITH RESOURCES

- lucidity.com
- radiantmind.net
- gbccc.org
- fossilfreefaith.ca

VOWS

23

For most of us, wedding vows are the only ones with which we are really familiar, but of course there are other types. There are commandments. There are precepts. There are pledges, commitments and aspirations. Each of these words hides an entire cosmology of intention, ethical context, and import. In Buddhist practice, they are all crystallized in the first of the Four Great Vows: I resolve to become Enlightened for the sake of all living beings.

> Provided I become a Buddha, if my light should be limited in measurement so that it could not illuminate a hundred thousand nayuta of kotis of Buddha-countries, then may I not attain the enlightenment.
> *Amitabha*
> Vow 12

Implicit in this vow is the understanding that we have not yet achieved the goal, that the effort of trying to achieve our aspiration is the path, even though failure is a constant companion, and that in one sense there is no goal to be achieved. Such is the way of the Bodhisattva.

It is time to set aside our notions of sin, original sin, chosen people, fathers, masters, punitive righteousness, damnation, shunning, expulsion, and ritual sacrifice. They are but cracked mirrors reflecting our conflicting emotions and primitive beliefs about reality. They are distractions. They are attempts to control others instead of liberating ourselves.

The first step in our liberation must be to cast off obedience to the strictures of deluded society. It's time to opt out of who society tells you you are supposed to be. The next step is to embrace a life of compassion: for ourselves, our fellow humans, our animal brothers and sisters, our mother Earth. Once we make this turning about in the mind, everything becomes possible. Everything we do is taken into the path.

It is important to remember that few of us will choose, or are suited, to be life-long monks, nuns, priests, spiritual teachers or anchorites. Each day, we engage with the world of family, jobs, social networks, politics, health, volunteering, entertainment, and so on. Each day, we negotiate between our aspirations and our society. This does not mean we have abandoned the path.

So where does this lead us, with regard to technology? Where is the Middle Way?

Where scientific evidence exists to support the beneficial use of a technology, we often see obstruction and obfuscation by vested interests who oppose it. This results in an ideological disconnect.

Birth control is a good example. The vast majority of sexually active Catholic women admit to using birth control, in spite of the fact that the church bans it.

In the secular arena, vaccination encounters similar hysteria from those who fear it, in spite of the fact that it has probably saved more lives than any other medical treatment, except perhaps for antibiotics.

On the other hand, we often see technologies coopted by the powerful for the purpose of control (as in surveillance) or monetary gain (as in the oil industry). We also see technologies out of control simply because our society is so complex we are unable to grasp the synergistic impact of it all (as in the adoption of 5G mobile networks).

It's so easy to get caught up in the seduction of technology. We want that new mobile phone, that car, that freshly-arrived tropical fruit in a plastic clamshell, that faster web, that tropical vacation, that social media reassurance of connection.

We're going to assume for a moment that you are a very average person. We're going to assume you may eat meat, but you're not about to kill anybody. We're going to assume you are sexually active, but not a rapist. Perhaps you are a social drinker, smoke or occasionally take other drugs recreationally. Somehow, you've come to terms with the five Buddhist precepts: not to kill, steal, lie, be sexually manipulative, or take intoxicants. You can work on those.

And what happens if you break your vows? There are repentence and purification ceremonies, if that works for you. Or, you might simply recognize that there is no stigma in failure and try again. On the societal level we have Truth and Reconciliation Commissions, and public figures who stumble have perfected the art of the broadcast apology, but that is an entirely different situation, rarely successful because it is rarely sincere.

VOWS RESOURCES

- www.lionsroar.com/my-vows-2/
- studybuddhism.com/en/advanced-studies/prayers-rituals/vows/common-root-tantric-vows
- buddhaweekly.com/broken-commitments-breaking-buddhist-vows-promises-carries-heavy-karma
- www.fgsitc.org/repentance/

SECULAR

24

Much has been made, of late in the West, of a new type of Dharma practice: secular Buddhism. The premise here is that Buddhism is a philosophy rather than a religion, and that once we strip away the cultural accretions from Shakyamuni's pith instructions, we're left with a rational plan for living that is essentially secular.

Our contributions to the world are demonstrated by what we do, not in the beliefs we cling to.

The Secular Buddhist Association

There has been plenty of push-back from various sectors of the larger Buddhist community who feel that secularizing the Dharma is a gross oversimplification, cherry-picking, an insult to Asian Buddhists, or a misguided attempt to fit a transcendent path into a worldly bottle. Be that as it may, there is still much to be valued in the secular approach.

Consider the interfaith message of Buddhist leaders. **His Holiness the Dalai Lama** says: "Kindness is my religion." The **Venerable Thich Nhat Hanh** says: "Peace is every step." These are not messages requiring adherence to any dogma at all. And if you are looking for a Buddhist teacher who has expanded what that might look like, **Stephen Batchelor** is an excellent example.

In the sutras, Shakyamuni Buddha was agnostic on the question of God. His focus, whether there is or is not such a being, was on perfecting ourselves. However, he went further, to explain that there cannot be an uncaused cause or a prime mover outside reality. Change is the only constant; no-soul is the reality which gives us the freedom to grow and evolve; our interbeing is the ground in which the work takes place.

So I would say that it does not matter what your personal practice involves, be it mindfulness, mantras or devotion. Whatever works for you is fine on your personal evolution to Enlightenment. What matters to the rest of us is how you manifest that wisdom and compassion in the world: the realm of the secular. It's not secular Buddhism, it's Buddhism engaged in the secular. And there is a difference.

Just as the vitality of Tathagatagarbha comprises a Nirvana which does not negate consciousness, it comprises an understanding of human nature which does not negate transcendental consciousness. This realization is clearly manifest in the birth and flowering of the Mahayana, with its myriad Dhyana Buddhas and Bodhisattvas. Secular Buddhism cannot be the fruition of Dharma by cutting off that vital transcendental element.

For example, in contemporary attempts to secularize Buddhism, the six realms (gods, warrior gods, humans, animals, hungry ghosts, hellions) are often anthropomorphized into psychological states. The human condition is re-cast as pathological psychology and the DSM-V becomes the paradigm for practice. I fear the mindfulness movement falls into this extreme. There is no transcendence of samsaric consciousness in it.

Another example: technological materialism is rampant, inasmuch as meditation apps, lucid dreaming headsets, biofeedback machines, and so on, are seen as the enabling vehicles that will take us to our destination. This neuro-hack approach, a purported Techno-yana, is a *deus-ex-machina* mentality in which technology will miraculously solve all our problems.

Given that we are on the brink of another fundamental change brought about by a new technology, artificial intelligence, a paradigm of technology that enhances us is outmoded. In the new paradigm, technology enhances itself and in the process replaces us. We need to re-think what it means when machines can learn and make decisions autonomously, not just in a silo application, but in a systematic way with other artilects.

The question of what it means to be human in a technology-driven world, with the inherent tension between the two vectors of sacred and profane, is well illustrated in movies such as *Metropolis* (Fritz Lang, 1927), *The Terminator* (**James Cameron**, 1984), *The Matrix* (**Wachowski brothers**, 1999), and *Artificial Intelligence* (**Stephen Spielberg**, 2001). It appears technology has run amok.

On closer inspection, human nature seems to be the source of the problem. We can't just externalize a portion of our being (the "good" part) into a machine. We still haven't figured out how to usher in *The Age of Spiritual Machines* (as the 1999 book by **Ray Kurzweil** foretells).

SECULAR RESOURCES

- secularbuddhism.org
- dhamma.org
- orderofinterbeing.org
- nondualtraining.com
- thenakedmonk.com
- stephenbatchelor.org

PRAYER

■
25

Some say prayer is a spiritual technology. Perhaps they mean "technique." Prayer is no more a technology than are speaking or reading. It is a cognitive method for expression, which may rely on a variety of technologies for its outward manifestation. It is a vehicle of meaning-making.

You carry Mother Earth within you. She is not outside of you. Mother Earth is not just your environment. In that insight of inter-being, it is possible to have real communication with the Earth, which is the highest form of prayer.

Thich Nhat Hanh

My focus here is on technology as the mediator of prayer. It may be mechanical (as in the Tibetan prayer wheel), performance-based (as in ritual implements, ceremonies, and/or garb), or virtual (as in digital applications). In any event, the challenge is for the tool to enable accomplishment rather than replace it.

For example, the benefits of saying mantras reside in the mental transformation arising from the repetition, not the accumulation of rosary counter beads slid from one end of a string to the other. It's human nature to mistake the finger pointing at the moon for the moon itself.

Looking at the plethora of meditation aids, timers, Buddha boxes, mantra counters, visualization animations, lucid dreaming visors, and so on, one may say: "Oh, that's not Dharma," and bemoan our spiritual decline. However, this merely mirrors our ambivalence about technology in general, and our reliance on digital technology specifically.

We are nostalgic for a presumably purer state of being, pre-dating digital technology, but there's just something so darn addictive about our smartphones that there is no going back. We've all become proto-cyborgs.

Along this uneasy fault line, researchers are exploring the nature of spirituality with the tools of modern science. Lots of articles for both popular and scientific audiences abound. "What Happens to the Brain During Spiritual Experiences" (*The Atlantic Monthly*, June 8, 2014) is good example of the former.

Ven. Matthieu Ricard has participated in, and written about, a variety of experiments designed to show how meditation and prayer demonstrate our neuroplasticity. Many other Buddhist teachers and practitioners have also added their experiences to this corpus of study.

Prayer in Buddhism is quite different from its theistic counterpart, regardless of some seeming similarities on the surface. In Buddhist practice, prayer is on a continuum with meditation and seeks the same goal:

transformation from within. It is not supplication to an Other, omnipotent being, from a place of essential brokenness or incompleteness.

Pure Land prayer, as intended, is an inner opening to allow the Enlightenment of Amida Buddha to manifest in us. Practitioners seek to emulate Amida, rather than obtain some boon from him. Similarly, in the Nichiren tradition, prayer is opening to the wisdom of the *Lotus Sutra*. Vajrayana deity yoga and guru pujas are about manifesting their qualities in ourselves. Adherents who pray for material benefits, or critics from other faiths and ideologies who highlight that practice, miss the point.

Turning outward, Buddhist memes have been turning up across contemporary Western culture for more than 50 years. Now the Buddhist notion of serenity has rippled out into product design, and (increasingly) interaction design. Consider the discipline of "Calm Technology."

As we move deeper into the deployment and maturity of the Internet of Things, society is struggling to maintain control over the fruits of our creations. We want to minimize the cognitive cost of our increasingly complex virtual interactions ("Don't make me think," as sci-fi writer **Bruce Stirling** sums it up) but we want to keep design human-centred.

Alas, our new virtual world is susceptible to the same flaws found in Samsara since forever. Nobody has figured out how to use technology to perfect human nature, and the risks inherent in new technologies always outstrip our ability to comprehend or manage them.

In short, technology is no substitute for practice, and practice is not a flight from technology. From where I sit, secular Buddhism is not a replacement for traditional Buddhism, but rather a mode of acting in the world that fits with our modern realities. They are like two wings of a bird: you need both to fly.

In the same way, prayer has an important place in Buddhist practice.

PRAYER RESOURCES

- buddhistgeeks.com
- calmtech.com
- designkit.org
- blog.wired.com/sterling
- wolfliving.tumblr.com

MIND ONLY

26

In the early development of Buddhism, Vijnaptimatrata (the Consciousness Only tradition) proposed that all our experiences are merely expressions of consciousness and that sunyata (emptiness) is the essential nature of this consciousness. The Madhyamaka (the Middle Way tradition), proposed that all our experiences and consciousness are part of the web of dependent origination along with the "outside world," and *sunyata* is the essential nature of this interbeing.

We have within us already the most important resources we need for living interdependence well. We have tremendous mental flexibility that allows us to adopt new positions in relation to changing circumstances.

The 17th Karmapa

In the end, it was the Madhyamaka that won the day and evolved into modern Buddhism. However, in either system, intention is only the critical first step. One must practice.

From that persepctive, the term "engaged Buddhism" is really a misnomer; all practice is engaged, and should be seen that way. Even in a monastic setting, with its institutional aspect and societal context, practitioners are engaged with the world, but the character of their involvement changes. In Yogacara training, inner and outer work are complements.

While there are many western accounts of how traditional Chinese Buddhist monasteries worked, the most comprehensive and least biased (*The Practice of Chinese Buddhism: 1900-1950*) was written by **Holmes Welch** in 1967. Analogies to other traditions are quite easy to imagine.

Practice is, of necessity, responsive to its context while true to its roots. So what is the context here and now, and what does practice look like? That exploration is the goal of this book.

Human nature hasn't changed. Political and economic structures have not changed (insofar as commerce, domination, war, and barely-contained chaos are our macro steady-state). What has changed?

Four of the biggest changes to Buddhist practice since its arrival in the modern world are: laification, democratization, feminization and secularization. These are all commendable advancements. Wonderful examples of these can be seen in the Humanistic Buddhism of **Master Hsing Yun**, the Vipassana movement of **Satya Narayan Goenka**, and the political Buddhism of **Dr. Bhimrao Ambedkar**. Mapping Dharma to modern psychology, as seen in the writings of many western Buddhist teachers regarding how to deal with feelings, is another notable transformation.

While respecting their value, it is important to distinguish that they all operate within the domain of human relationships. Engaged Buddhist practice is categorically different. It is rooted in the first of the Four Vows: I resolve to become Enlightened for the sake of all living beings.

Engaged Buddhism is inseparable from the Bodhisattva Vow! Withdrawal from the world is not even part of the paradigm of interbeing, let alone an option for us. We exist within nature, not as stewards above it. Action and inaction differ in design, not degree of consequence.

Sutra, liturgy and practice foundations for Engaged Buddhism are easy to find in traditional sources. Several that spring to mind are the Theravada forest monk lineage, the vow to practice on behalf of the many earth spirits (in *The Dharma of Repentence of the Great Compassion with a Thousand Hands and a Thousand Eyes*), the *samu* work practice of Zen students, and practices in Vajrayana such as *Tonglen*, *Chöd* or *Tsok*. The challenge is giving them life in our modern world.

The modern environmental movement, which began in 1962 with **Rachel Carson**'s book, *Silent Spring*, and which gave us Eco-Buddhism, was transformational. The concurrent peace movement, civil rights movement at home and human rights movement globally, recognition of our shared global future, and evolving understanding of the nature of transnational corporations, have similarly brought that modern world into sharp focus.

However, our uneasy relationship with ubiquitous, advanced, digital technology is much less clear. On one hand, we are enchanted by the possibilities offered by our own intelligence – objectified, externalized and enhanced. On the other, we see a world in which technology renders many of us obsolete and worthless.

We have only this present moment to act. The cursor is blinking. *Mu!*

MIND ONLY RESOURCES

- archive.org/details/practiceofchines00welc
- english.fgs2.ca
- www.dhamma.org/en-US/about/goenka
- ambedkarmission.org
- abhidharma.ru/A/Tantra/Content/Cadhana/0001.pdf

UPAYA

■
27

Wisdom, by itself, is not enough. Compassion, by itself, is not enough. The catalyst, *Upaya* (Skilful Means), igniting and uniting their powers, is represented iconographically as the many arms of the Bodhisattvas.

One of the first western attempts to articulate that union explicitly came from **E.F. Schumacher** in 1973, with his book, *Small is Beautiful: Economics As If People Mattered.*

Even though you tie a thousand knots, the string remains one.

Rumi

Since then, many different Dharma-in-action initiatives have sprung forth. Notable examples include **Joan Halifax Roshi**'s hospice and chaplaincy work through the Upaya Zen Center, Zen Peacemakers and Greyston Bakery, from the indomitable **Bernie Glassman Roshi**, the many initiatives from Plum Village, inspired by **Thich Nhat Hanh**, or the Ecological Buddhism web portal, from **John and Diane Stanley** and **David Loy**.

Pilgrimages such as **Shodo Spring**'s Compassionate Earth Walk, **Daeung Sunim**'s Journey of Spirit bicycle trek across North and South America, and ongoing peace walks by Nipponzan-Myohoji Sangha (founded by **Nichidatsu Fujii** in 1917) are other notable inspirations.

At the other end of the spectrum, various monasteries host small robo-monks to welcome visitors, answer questions, and assist with chanting. Digital prayer wheels spin eternally in cyberspace. Dharma quotes (and mis-quotes) are a staple of social media. Meditation apps will ding, count your mantras, coach your breathing, and send you inspirational text messages from the tradition of your choice. Quasi-mystical Buddhist concepts are appropriated to fuel violent popular entertainment, from *Star Wars,* to *The Matrix,* to innumerable kung-fu movies and television shows.

How do we embrace technology in our practice, without becoming entangled by our engagement? Do we use or eschew technology?

Nobody seems to have a problem with "traditional" technologies such as using construction equipment to build or repair Dharma buildings, or metallurgy to make Buddha statues, or making Sangha officiants' garments from polyester instead of silk. But digital Dharma arouses strong opinions. Why? What is qualitatively different about the digital domain?

Is it okay for a Buddhist monastery to fight a nearby wind-farm (as in the case of one in Ontario, Canada, who allege the low level hum from it will disturb the tranquility of meditators on one of its four 500+ acre properties)? Is it okay for the gold for a Buddha statue to come from a mining company destroying a South American ecosystem (as in the case of Barrick Gold's Pascua-Lama project in Chile)? Is it okay to embrace the fossil fuel industry instead of the silk industry? Is incense bad for your lungs? Are tofu and seitan bad for you? If monks make their robes out of recycled plastic bottles, what happens to the microbeads that come off in the laundry and get into the rivers and lakes? Is organic food better than locally-grown? None of these issues are clear-cut as examples of upaya.

Digital Dharma is an equally murky ethical quagmire. For example: should Buddhist e-books cost money, or be freely available without any copyright restrictions (as is the case with peer-to-peer torrents sharing Buddhist book files without publisher permission)? How should we respond to online attacks from purported fellow-Buddhists (as in the case of the NKT), or hostile states (as in the case of China's GhostNet hack on the Tibetan government-in-exile)? How do we, as Buddhists, respond to #BlackLivesMatter? Can you livestream a tantric initiation? Should you out a bad teacher online? "The world is too much with us; late and soon," as William Wordsworth wrote more than 200 years ago.

How to be, in that larger world, is the subject of the next chapters of this book. My focus here is practice as it is usually imagined: study, prayer, meditation, and ritual. Four themes emerge:

- Are devices assisting or replacing our efforts in cultivation? (*Prajna*)
- What are the ethical implications of our technology choices? (*Sila*)
- How is digital technology affecting our minds? (*Dhyana*)
- When we get up off the mat, what comes next? (*Karuna*)

What happens in the intersection of spirituality and technology? What does upaya look like in our complex society, so full of ethical ambiguities?

UPAYA RESOURCES

- upaya.org
- zenpeacemakers.org
- plumvillage.org
- ecobuddhism.org
- graftonpeacepagoda.org
- digitaldharma.com

CULTURE

CHILD

28

Having a child is considered to be the pinnacle of our existence, in common thinking. The love we feel for our children is supposed to surpass all other loves, and the love they feel for us is assumed to be a given, albeit complicated, love. Our intergenerational bond is guaranteed, without the vagaries of romantic love or fairweather friendships. At least, that's how the story goes. So much of our identity is tied up with our relationship to children that we are often willing to tie ourselves in knots trying to be congruent with the plotline. It's part of our evolutionary imperative.

Times are bad; children no longer obey their parents; and everyone is writing a book.
Cicero

When we hear of couples biologically unable to have children (or trying with IVF to overcome that), or Millennials deciding not to have children, or adults estranged from their children, or parents of a child who died or has health challenges (physical or mental, take your pick), or parents whose child struggles at life (drugs, crime, poverty, take your pick), we naturally feel a sense of tragedy in the cards dealt them.

What then are we to make of the Buddhists who renounce the householder life? It is a notion alien to most people. Conversely, for those monastics who leave home, how deep is their ability to empathize with those who don't? Then there's the question of how to make sense of perhaps giving up one's vows and returning to lay life. In my case, I gave up the monastic life because of my strong desire to have children. Was it just cultural conditioning? Lay Buddhist teachers were not the norm in traditional Buddhist cultures, so role models are hard to find. Hereditary priests in Japan performed rituals, but were not particularly regarded as highly evolved Bodhisattvas. The children who took over from their parents were often less than thrilled at the obligation.

Here in the west, we're making it up as we go along.

Furthermore, we look back at childhood from the administrivia of our lives and long for the carefree innocence, the spontaneity and wonder. We take that fetishized freedom as a new goal, as in the *Zen Mind, Beginner's Mind* of **Shunryu Suzuki**. On closer inspection, it turns out to be impulsive behaviour and lack of responsibility masquerading as wisdom, a fantasy fueled by nostalgia (and goodness knows, we've seen quite enough of that from Buddhist teachers, thank you very much).

When I conducted my national sociological survey of Canadian Buddhist organizations in association with **Dr. Frances Garrett**, at the

Centre for the Study of Religion at the University of Toronto (findings published in *The Journal of Global Buddhism* in 2013), youth programming was the focus for several questions. As it turned out, there wasn't much! We North American Buddhists are doing a terrible job of passing along Buddhism to our kids. Yes the so-called ethnic temples are doing a better job than the so-called convert temples, but even there, young people are mostly disengaged. Why? I think it is because we tend to see Buddhist practice as something volitional that we embrace as adults with free will after some rational internal exploration. However, if Buddhist practice is unable to meet the challenges of our society (as opposed to societies where Buddhism is/was the ubiquitous norm), there's not much incentive to take it up. Given the small relative numbers of Buddhists here, it's not as if children see it in the society all around them.

If you spend any time watching children's television, or see kids in their strollers staring at tablets at the mall, you know childhood has been kidnapped from the real world by franchises, brand extensions, and lack of follow-through on "viewer discretion is advised." As I write this, I'm watching a room of teen-agers flipping rapidly through Instagram pictures on their phones, desperate for that dopamine rush. The zombie apocalypse has arrived and it is thoroughly demoralizing.

When young leaders like **the Kielburgers**, **Malala Yousafzai**, or **Greta Thunberg** arrive on the scene, we are as astounded as if we saw a unicorn, or horns on a hare. We glom onto them and turn them into celebrity role models. How do we flip the paradigm so these folks become the norm rather than outliers? After all, young people under 25 are already the majority in many developing countries. Young thought leaders should be a dime a dozen. And are any of them Buddhist? Will we, and Buddhism, simply be shining artifacts of the past? (Thanks **Leonard Cohen**.)

CHILD RESOURCES

- www.unicef.org/sowc05/english/childhooddefined.html
- www.diva-portal.org/smash/get/diva2:511663/FULLTEXT02.pdf
- archive.org/details/DeschoolingSociety
- www.theatlantic.com/international/archive/2012/05/trash-bin-babies-indias-female-infanticide-crisis/257672/
- www.globalbuddhism.org/jgb/index.php/jgb/article/view/138/153

ADDICT

29

Addiction/recovery has become one of the most widely practiced constructs of contemporary therapy. It's appeal is twofold: it offers a practical path for those who are addicts, but more generally, it offers an attractive metaphor for dealing with many of life's problems. Buddhist eightfold recovery programs are, in fact, only the most recent iteration of this approach, which began with the 12-Step program of Alcoholics Anonymous.

Everyone's recovery is unique.
Vimalasara
Eight Step Recovery

Another development in addiction treatment is the switch from seeing it as a moral problem to recognizing it as a medical problem, with the attendant shift in goal: from punishment to harm reduction. This has been possible because we see more clearly the social and family dynamics that lead to (and flow from) addiction, removing it from the sphere of the personal. You could say we've recognized it as a public health issue. A positive corollary to this is a rethink of the War on Drugs, which was really a surrogate for race-based incarceration and disenfranchizement of large segments of US citizenry. Decriminalization has been successfully modelled in other countries (notably Portugal), but political battles still rage here.

Still, how comprehensive is the addiction/recovery model as a path? Is it expedient means, or something with broader application? How different is Buddhist 8-Step Recovery from Theistic 12-Step Programs?

To answer these questions, I would say for those who self-identify as addicts, any recovery model that resonates for them is going to be expedient. However, I don't think the recovery model has the breadth to replace the full range of Buddhist psychology modalities. That would be problematizing something that is bigger than a medical wellness issue. There are, of course, many dissimilarities between Buddhism and Theistic religions, but I wouldn't say Buddhist recovery programs are any more (or less) efficacious than other approaches; it really depends on what makes the most sense for an individual.

Ancient Buddhist texts speak of clinging afflictions and how they obscure our clear vision of the nature of things. Two of the five basic Buddhist precepts deal with highly addictive facets of our lives: sex and intoxicants. Advanced Buddhist texts explore ways to rid ourselves of addictive reification (even at high levels of practice where we might mistake Nirvana for something real and fall into the trap of nihilism). We call this Zen sickness.

Looking at Samsara as addiction (a good synonym for clinging?), we see the dynamic everywhere – rampant consumerism, commitment to material and technological "progress," self-medicating with ideologies or entertainment or things, denial, objectification of others who are subordinated to filling our insatiable need, and so on. What, then, does wellness look like, and what lies beyond it?

With a wellness model, we get the equivalent of Bompu Zen: great as far as it goes; but it doesn't go very far. This same criticism could be, and has been, levelled against the Mindfulness movement. Once you rise above being totally incapacitated by your addiction, are you just a "functional drunk" managing to get through each day of "business as usual?" If you achieve liberation from your addiction, is it still always going to be part of your identity (as in, "Hello my name is ___, and I'm an addict")? That's not "dropping dropped," as **Rujing**'s response to **Dogen**'s statement of enlightenment would have it.

If we are really going to transform society, and change the course of history (i.e., save the planet from a death caused by our own Anthropocene overdose), we'll need a new vision that rejects the "business as usual" goal in favour of something sustainable. That kind of "turning about in the mind" is not accessible within the status quo, or within the addiction/recovery model.

It is easier to work on a specific addiction, rather than an addictive personality. It is easier to work on an addictive personality, rather than a society whose engine is all about creating and pursuing addiction. It is easier to work on an addictive society, than to acknowledge that we ourselves are all addicts in one sense or another, no matter how functional we appear.

ADDICT RESOURCES
- www.psychiatry.org/patients-families/addiction/what-is-addiction
- drgabormate.com
- monoskop.org/images/4/4a/Susan_Sontag_Illness_As_Metaphor_1978.pdf
- www.wildmind.org/category/blogs/recovery-monday
- refugerecovery.org
- www.buddhistrecovery.org

BUDDHIST APPS

30 I confess to having an aversion to Buddhist apps such as Buddha Boxes, meditation timers, quotes-of-the-day, adjustable speed scrolling mantras with counters, ritual lunar calendars, mandala colouring collections, singing bowls, social networking for Buddhists, online dating for Buddhists, neuro-feedback trainers, classic Buddhist e-books from the public domain, swimming goldfish screen-savers where you can touch the screen and send ripples across the water, apps for drawing enso circles with your finger, Tibet- and Zen-themed online games, white noise sleep enhancers, lucid dream trainers, dream interpreters, chakra maps, aura interpreters, Tantric fitness guides, digital rosaries, and the like.

This cornucopia of Buddhist apps highlights our embrace of cyberspace as a dimension of daily life and personal growth. A lot of them have low star-ratings, few reviews, cost money, or have in-purchases. I wonder who is behind all these offerings and what their motivation is. Very very few of them are from recognized Buddhist organizations.

In a new book from April 2019, *Wish I Were Here: Boredom and the Interface*, **Mark Kingwell** explores neoliberal boredom in the inverted attention-economy paradigm where corporations profit from the big data derived from our endless scrolling, swiping and tapping. He describes how developers depend on the *Hotel California* effect (citing that hit song by **The Eagles**), where you can check out any time you like, but you can never leave.

This is the boredom and disengagement I see daily from students who would much rather play on their cellphones than engage in actual learning. Can Buddhist apps really elevate us beyond the ennui of insatiable desire for the next new digital thing? If boredom is merely the handmaiden of leisure and privilege (as Kingman suggests), the underlying premise itself must be deconstructed.

In **Gampopa**'s *Jewel Ornament of Liberation*, he notes that one of the unique benefits of human life is that it affords us the leisure and opportunity to study the Dharma. How does that leisure translate to boredom? Is our quest for "something more" out of life the very thing that leads us to Dharma practice? Can we find it in an app? And more importantly, for those already on the path, can digital experiences contribute to our learning?

Once in the 1970's, I attended a Chenrezigs initiation with **Kalu Rinpoche**. While we were in an anteroom waiting for the ceremony to begin, I overheard a conversation where a self-important Westerner was telling a newbie that Rinpoche would give him a mantra, and that he would have to repeat it 100,000 times for it to take effect, but not to worry because he had months to complete the task. The newbie was so upset by the prospect that he left right away, without attending the initiation. I found the exchange deeply disturbing and remember it vividly to this day. In a situation like that, a digital mantra counter would simply have added to the spiritual materialism of that mistaken view.

On the other hand, once in the 1990's, I was asked to assist a dying Chinese Buddhist man to cross over. His Christian family had no idea how to offer him spiritual care of that kind. Fortunately, I was able to obtain a Buddha Box (a small music player like a transistor radio, that plays Buddhist chants) for him to keep at his bedside as he sunk into unconsciousness. Nowadays, I can see how an app for that would be very valuable, in that right time and place.

I have a lot of magazine and newspaper apps on my phone. I find them to be more convenient and in-depth ways to keep up with the news than to watch regularly-scheduled broadcast news. *Buddhistdoor Global* has an excellent Buddhist news aggregator app.

My adult children swear by their podcast and e-book apps, allowing them to "listen and learn" as they drive to and from work. Theirs is a post-print generation. There are a number of excellent Buddhist podcasts, such as *The Secular Buddhist* podcast, hosted by **Ted Meissner**.

BUDDHIST APPS RESOURCES

- en.softonic.com/solutions/what-are-the-best-buddhist-apps
- www.cbc.ca/radio/spark/spark-437-1.5116618/canadian-philosopher-mark-kingwell-examines-the-idea-of-boredom-and-our-digital-devices-1.5116621
- greatergood.berkeley.edu/article/item/the_trouble_with_mindfulness_apps

BUDDHIST P2P

31

Every now and then, I find one of my Sumeru books being offered for free as a torrent on the web. As with the other shady neighbourhoods online, this one requires you to submit to a variety of probing identity questions before granting access to a valid file, or perhaps never presenting the file, which was spurious to begin with, or infecting one's computer with malware. Most torrents have been consciously designed or hacked with embedded malware.

Technological progress has merely provided us with more efficient means for going backwards.

Aldous Huxley
Ends and *Means*

So much for the peer-to-peer utopia envisioned by **Shawn Parker**, of Napster fame, and subsequent Facebook role.

On the other hand, when I asked **Eshu Martin**, abbot at Zenwest Buddhist Society in Sooke, BC, about the realities of maintaining a full-time resident teacher, he laughed: "Water may be free; but plumbing costs money."

Therein lies the dilemma. Shakyamuni said the Dharma should be given freely, without any desire for recompense. Nowadays, this does not give permission to those who would steal the intellectual property of others, for their own gain or to feign obliviousness to it.

In a discussion I had with **Glenn Mullin**, redactor of *Rimey Lama Chopa: A Tibetan Rimey Tantric Feast, A Rite to Invoke the Supreme Nectar of Wisdom*, by **Dilgo Khyentse Rinpoche**, with a foreword by **Ven. Matthieu Ricard**, we were talking about the proper distribution of royalties. Glenn insisted that half the profits would go to Ricard's Shechen Foundation for charitable works. However, when I suggested we donate the entire profits, he balked: "I put blood, sweat, and tears into this, and I would like recognition from that." We settled on 50 percent to Shechen, and 25 percent to each of us.

In the case of another Buddhist author, who shall go unnamed here, he was piously soliciting funds from all and sundry for the furtherance of his work, while a scofflaw in his rent, not returning loans, putting his main benefactor in financial jeopardy, and so on.

The usual template for intellectual property doesn't really translate all that well to Buddhist items. Books get translated, CD's get burned, movies get pirated, they wind up in a foyer display at some temple or (typically) Asian restaurant, and everyone is basically happy with the arrangement. It's a gift economy.

We could call this the reverence economy (cribbing a phrase from the attention economy), and certain monetary values could be deduced from the interdependent actions that were taken in making, and as a result of, their manufacture and distribution.

I am all for making the Dharma widely available. That is the prime motivation for The Sumeru Press. I try to do it in an environmentally frugal way. Hopefully, the authors feel their important messages are receiving the respect and commitment they deserve.

So this is what the Dharma business looks like in 2020: honouring the spirit of Buddha's instructions, while respecting the letter of copyright in a legitimate, transparent supply chain. Buddhists are generally a pretty sharing bunch o' folks. I tend to trust them.

There's more to this imagery. What, exactly, is a "peer" and why is the exchange lateral rather than vertical? Suddenly, the situation becomes more than a bifurcated decision in a win-lose proposition. The lack of demand for obligation is inversely proportional to the extent of the good will generated in such a mycelial network of tendrils.

As nameless monks of no rank, Chan masters after **Linji** roamed free, touching lives hither and yon. Nichiren wandered through Japan freely offering *The Lotus Sutra* and its wonderful mantra: NA MO HO REN GYO KYO.

Is this socialism? I don't know. That seems a superfluous classification after-the-fact. (No, that wasn't a typo.) As **His Holiness the Dalai Lama** notes, in *Ecology, Ethics and Interdependence*, you can have corrupt individuals taking advantage of the virtuous systems that employ them. By the same token, I suppose you can have virtuous individuals working within corrupt systems (and for more on that topic, see the section on Whistleblowers).

And then there's the ultimate P2P communication, when Shakyamuni showed the lotus to Mahakasyapa, who understood.

BUDDHIST P2P RESOURCES

- torrentfreak.com
- www.michaelgeist.ca
- www.theatlantic.com/ideas/archive/2018/11/what-should-america-do-its-empty-church-buildings/576592/
- www.meditationexpert.com/meditation-techniques/m_dharma_is_free_but_will_cost_you.html

BUDDHA STUFF

32 One premise of this book is that we live in an exchange economy of designed objects, relationships, and institutions. In this, I have been influenced particularly by two books, *The System of Objects*, by **Jean Baudrillard**, and *On Longing: Narratives of the Miniature, the Gigantic, the Souvenir, the Collection*, by **Susan Stewart**.

This stunning wrist mala bracelet of softly colored, pastel beads is suitable for mantra practice and for wearing as jewelry.

Online store

From this perspective, I have very mixed feelings about companies selling Buddhist stuff, such as meditation cushions, benches, shawls, statues, incense, jewellery, home and garden decor, giftware, rosaries, stickers, postcards, braided bracelets, and the like. I know there is a legitimate place for ritual objects, but when they are commodified, I get cognitive dissonance. On the other hand, I appreciate the efforts of Buddhist organizations to raise funds by selling things (even when it's at inflated prices), and I have purchased a significant number of objects from them over the years (not to mention cherished ritual artifacts I have received as gifts). So is the problem Buddhist stuff itself, or the intention of the folks who are selling it?

In China, a search on Alibaba tagged "Buddha" yields 37,849 items available from wholesalers. The vast majority appear to be plastic resin or cheap electroplated metal, and designed for the mass decor market. However, I admit, I perk right up whenever I see a solar-powered Kalachakra prayer wheel on someone's car dashboard!

As our experience becomes increasingly mediated and abstracted, souvenirs (not the same as decor) stand in for authentic experience in our private, nostalgic reverie of contact and presence. These objects evoke connection with the past but they also evoke longing for that which is distant, making them inherently incomplete.

Outwardly, our objects serve as talismans, projections of our identity. We all know how rich collectors fetishize famous works of art, rare cars, or antiquities. Most of us are unable to own originals, and so we must settle for simulacrums (knock-offs). Nevertheless, we fetishize these in the same way, and thus our objects become more about us than about their original use and materiality. Buddhist things would qualify here, as specimens of the exotic and as trophies celebrating our immediate experience of it.

This self-referential identity-building is a form of meta-consumption. You might say that Buddhist stuff is an ironic counterpoint to consumer culture, in the same way as *kitsch* or *camp*, virtue signalling our recognition and transcendence of the contradictions inherent in our late-stage capitalist exchange economy. However, I'm not buying it.

Buddhist stuff in museums takes it to an entirely different level. Stewart describes the collection as a paradise of consumption, where the object's intrinsic meaning is sublimated to a display value within the symbolic system of the collector. It's all about organization and classification, presenting that narrative as the normative representation of reality. Indeed, there is even a peer-reviewed *Journal of Material Culture*. This is why we feel the tension of seeing Buddhist relics and artifacts in a museum, consumed as art.

I experienced the effect on a grand scale at Borobudur. The dissociation of the world's largest Buddhist monument from its sacred function is viscerally inescapable as one experiences the decapitated statues (their heads looted during the colonial era), the throngs of Japanese tour buses, and the gauntlet of T-shirt and trinket vendors ringing the site. My solitary *Lama Chöpa* puja in a remote spot halfway up the Amitabha side of the mandala felt like a rebellious act of reclamation. (The T-shirt souvenir I bought on the site shrank and shredded long ago, but the memories remain.)

In 2015, after 15 years on the road, the Maitreya Loving Kindness Tour organized by **Lama Zopa** closed down and settled in for permanent display at two sites in India. The tour consisted of more than 3000 Sarira and ritual objects from Shakyamuni and 44 other Buddhist luminaries. I attended on several different occasions when it cycled through Toronto.

Like shards of the True Cross, or the Shroud of Turin, these relics were created, collected, and then "consumed" by visitors in an atmosphere of profound reverence and promise. I am reminded of the Buddhist text: *Awakening Faith in the Mahayana.*

BUDDHA STUFF RESOURCES

- egs.edu/faculty/jean-baudrillard
- www.nyu.edu/classes/bkg/tourist/Stewart-longing.pdf
- journals.sagepub.com/loi/mcu
- mbpkushinagar.org/maitreya-relic-tour-closing/
- www.lamayeshe.com/advice/advice-holy-objects

CITIZEN

33

To be a citizen requires, by definition, a shared identity with others; one cannot be a citizen in a society of one. Citizens together for a common cause is a fundamental principle of democracy, socialism, communism, and constitutional monarchies.

Canadians define "citizenship" as more than having a passport, obeying the law and paying taxes. These are widely seen as key aspects of citizenship, but just as important are being active participants in one's community, helping others and accepting differences.

Environics
2011 national survey

If you think of what it means to be a citizen, what images come to mind? There are certain inalienable rights (often under attack), responsibilities (often avoided), benefits (sweet), and challenges (bitter).

In reality, there are good and bad citizens. We all seem to be able to see the rotten apples among our fellow citizens: they usurp the rights of others, take more than they give, game the system, and maintain willful blindness to the plight of those they hurt. In the middle of the bell curve, most people are simply trying to get by, good to whatever degree they can manage and happy to be better citizens if given the chance. Then there are the celebrated model citizens, who (paradoxically) grow in stature by giving more of themselves to others. But there is yet another type of model citizen, comprising those who set themselves against normative society through civil disobedience: think of **Mahatma Gandhi**, **Martin Luther King**, or **Malala Youzafzai**.

Until the 1960's, citizenship was primarily conceived of as the individual within a city or state, but global citizenship is a trending concept. The problem is that global citizenship is so large, so complex, so amorphous, that it is hard to grasp. It is further complicated by the legal personhood of corporations and their transnational reach.

It's very easy to use global citizenship as a baffle, rather than dive in to local issues. So hats off to anyone who is an activist in their own community and has skin in the game. We shouldn't expect everyone to be a citizen superstar on a global stage; nor should we criticize people for being one-issue advocates. Every citizen has something to give, and the value is greater than the sum of the parts.

We used to say, "Think locally, act globally." Now we say, "Think globally, act locally." Global citizenship has brought with it a new, crowd-sourced version of citizen activism. Consider, if you will, coalitions of citizens united for a common cause, such as international associations, and charitable foundations, or fighting together against corrupt systems, through brand boycotts, #Occupy, #MeToo, or (most recently) Extinction Rebellion.

Buddhism has never made social relations its central premise. There is no canon law as in the Confucian code or Islamic Sharia. There are no longer any Buddhist theocracies. Yes, the Eightfold Noble Path provides guidelines for a well-functioning society, but the details of implementation (outside of the Vinaya code for monastics), are left to secular governments. Citizenship was not a concept of ancient times and the closest we might come to that idea would be the Bodhisattva ideal of Mahayana Buddhism.

In the pre-modern world, there may have been some justification for considering that Buddhist monks and nuns renounced their citizenship in taking vows, in the sense that they gave up secular society. Their allegiance was transferred from the secular state (in whatever form) to the lineage community that may have extended beyond the borders of that state. However, in modern society, one's Buddhist identity and one's citizenship are not seen as mutually obstructing. Yes, it is true some totalitarian governments have co-opted Buddhist leaders to serve nationalistic goals, but this is not the norm.

Which brings us to the current moment. How does the Bodhisattva Vow manifest itself as good citizenship in today's world, beyond simple *ahimsa*? Once we get off the cushion, how do we walk the walk? Compassionate acts of charity are one obvious answer, but our world currently needs Buddhists willing to be shit-disturbers. We need to afflict the comfortable as well as comfort the afflicted. And time is short, because we are at a global tipping point. Same old same old is simply no longer viable.

CITIZEN RESOURCES
- www.wikihow.life/Be-a-Good-Citizen
- ccla.org
- thekingcenter.org
- www.malala.org
- www.anonymoushackers.net
- rebellion.earth

SOCIAL

34

What does it mean to be social? To use social media? How is social media different from other applications we visit or use in cyberspace? And are these things compatible with Buddhist practice? These are the key questions here. Is our understanding of human relationships transformed?

> Privacy is dead, and social media hold the smoking gun.
>
> *Pete Cashmore,*
> *Mashable CEO*

I've already described how we are social beings, embedded in symbiotic relationships that are not only indispensable for our survival, but also add essential dimensions to our well-being and actualization. But that is not what most people think about when we talk about socializing. Instead, our minds turn to relaxation, enjoyment, entertaining conversation, a mood lift from "work," recreation. Granted, our ideas of socializing have changed a bit (as per the cartoon where one young camper says to another: "We're going down to the campfire to stare at our iPhones together. Wanna come?") but the motivation is the same.

With social media, we have the opportunity to interact with others on a mediated platform that allows us to curate ourselves, project customized personas, and build intentional online communities (even if only to be super-fans of running shoes or nail polish). I assume you are pretty familiar with social media, so I don't need to go into any detail.

For social media to work, there must be an assumption of open-source computing, and peer-to-peer (P2P) topography. The value comes from the aggregated exchange, rather than from something we do ourselves in private. Of course, that is not exactly how social media has evolved; we've seen how the platform operators wield enormous power to shape the dialogue, extract metadata, recognize patterns, apply heuristics, and monetize our interactions. Problematic issues of privacy remain unresolved. Nevertheless, the twin promise of disintermediation and egalitarian sharing remains a dominant leitmotif of social media. The appearance of "removing the middleman" and shattering the active-passive model of broadcast media is, paradoxically, backed by a voracious platform operator intent on pushing content of a commercial nature, or facilitating fabricated personas trying to influence our day-to-day decision-making.

In the Buddhist canon, there are plenty of dictums discouraging socializing as defined above. It's seen as wasteful activity, a locus for temptation, a karmically questionable decision, at best a distraction. However, the Sangha is presented as an intentional community where relationships are valorous and productive – a different kind of social contract. Integrity is posited as authentic, while curated personas are seen as false, unless applied by enlightened teachers as skillful means. And at the extreme (the exceptions that prove the rule?), we get outliers like Zen masters who hang out under bridges, living with homeless folk and fraternizing with hookers and drunks.

Could such categorizations be applied to social media as well? What would valorous and productive use of social media look like? A Google search for "Buddhist view on social media" yields more than 80 million hits. Lots of room for differing views, obviously. On one hand, pictures of bhikkhus holding cellphones seem very incongruous, and yet we know that much of Myanmar's Saffron Revolution was organized through social media. Have a look at *Burma VJ: Reporting from a Closed Country*, the 2008 documentary directed by **Anders Østergaard**. It's just really too bad that post-Saffron bhikkhus in Myanmar have been co-opted by the military junta in its goal of ethnic cleansing of Rohingya Muslims in Rakhan State. Now they use the same technology to whip people into frenzies of killing, raping, and burning.

Forums like *Reddit* have extensive discussion threads on Buddhism with hundreds of thousands of members. Others, like the *Dharma Wheel Forum*, have hundreds of users online at any particular time. I confess to having spent very little time in such forums. By the same token, I moderate a global EcoBuddhist Facebook group (*Plot to Save the Earth*) with a few hundred members. Very few of them are active posters, in spite of my frequent exhortations to put up relevant material.

We humans have an insatiable need to look at and interact with other humans, but it would seem that for the most part, this manifests as a passive and voyeuristic pursuit rather than an active Bodhisattva practice.

SOCIAL RESOURCES

- studybuddhism.com/en/advanced-studies/history-culture/buddhism-in-modern-times/applying-buddhist-principles-in-the-age-of-social-media
- thetattooedbuddha.com/2016/05/29/is-social-media-networking-a-hindrance-to-buddhist-practice/
- sumeru-books.com/products/burma-vj-reporting-from-a-closed-country
- dharmawheel.net

BUDDHIST GEEK

■■■■ Buddhist Geeks (*aka* Dharma in the Age of the Network) ran from 2006-
35 2016 as a podcast by **Vincent and Emily Horn** and **Ryan Oelke**. Then
it ran out of money and had to reincarnate itself as something more
modest after a bit of time in the bardo. It currently exists as a hub for a
variety of digital dharma projects, live retreats,
a conference, and training courses.

Jane McGonigal is an author
and game designer who
describes herself as "23%
Buddhist, 77% geek."
Buddhist Geeks website

Calling oneself a geek is something of
a humble brag, but the Buddhist Geeks idea
caught the public imagination, in much the
same way as TED Talks. It embodied a commitment to timeless wisdom in a Venn diagram
with cutting-edge technology and contemporary issues, weighing in as
much more than the collective output of Vincent, Emily, and Ryan. In
more than 300 podcast interviews, a broad swath of Buddhist luminaries,
tech titans, activists and innovators lent their voices to the conversation.
The guests included psychiatrists, psychotherapists, dharma teachers, environmental activists, a mindful cyborg, an eco-philosopher, a dharma
punk, a dharma brat, mindfulness educators, youth activists, contempla-
tive scientists, artists (traditional and digital), professors, a consciousness
hacker, leadership coaches, animal behaviourists, a subjective systems
analyst, authors, writers, poets and publishers, a social entrepreneur, an
embodiment coach, a neurologist, and more.

It would be interesting to track down all those podcast guests and ask
them how they feel about Digital Dharma now.

Funding insecurity is a familiar issue for Buddhist organizations.
Using digital platforms as teaching aids is also common for Buddhist
teachers and scholars these days. However, taking digital technology itself
as the subject for Dharma teachings is less common, at least in the sense
of really digging deeply into the cyber landscape.

In 2015, Routledge published *Buddhism, the Internet, and Digi-
tal Media: The Pixel in the Lotus*, edited by **Gregory Price** and **Daniel
Veidlinger**. (I only just discovered it. At $145 USD, it wasn't destined
to be a bestseller.) The title reminded me of a presentation I made at a
Buddhist conference in Vancouver in 2010: *Canadian Buddhists on the
Web: Push, Pull, and Practice*. The link to my slide deck is posted below.
Viewing it again almost ten years later, I only see one radical change: the
rise of secular mindfulness, its permeation of mainstream culture, and its

enthusiastic embrace of cyberspace as a realm of practice itself (through apps, mostly).

Today's Buddhist geek would do well to pay close attention to how online social justice, environmental action, and open source initiatives function. The focus is not on esoteric personal experience, but on ethics with a societal, if not planetary, goal. Buddhists here are not going to reinvent the wheel, or own the space; they have to be willing to give up some control and join in common cause with others. If they do, I believe they will find their participation is welcomed and respected.

In the world at large, many of our conversations about digital technology have evolved to focus on ethical dimensions, as opposed to the wow factor of features and functions. This burgeoning ethical awareness is a clarion call. Nothing energizes people like the awareness that their entire world is about to implode. Surely, Buddhist community leaders can claim some of the moral high ground here (in spite of some high-profile scandals), and humbly contribute something of great value.

This would be a new kind of Buddhist practice. It's not about digital technology, *per se*, but it does require a sophisticated understanding of how to leverage it for social good. What makes it new (as opposed to earlier forms of Engaged Buddhism) is being based on Universal Responsibility and not necessarily claiming itself as a "Buddhist" practice. It's not stealth Dharma either. The goal is neither to push Buddhism, nor to answer the pull of people looking for Buddhism. It's just what grown-ups do (or, more specifically, what some grown-ups do when other "grown-ups" act out in destructive ways).

In other words, if your computer skills rock, it's okay to put them to work for Dharma causes. They are not mutually obstructing goals. Whatever wisdom you glean along the way is yours to keep.

BUDDHIST GEEK RESOURCES

- www.buddhistgeeks.org
- www.slideserve.com/kamran/canadian-buddhists-on-the-web-push-pull-practice-john-negru-karma-y-nten-gyatso
- player.fm/featured/buddhist
- www.listennotes.com/best-podcasts/72/buddhism

BODHISATTVA

36

It is easy to feel rage and grief at the state of the world. As **Wanda Sykes** says in her 2019 Netflix stand-up special, "What the fuck? This shit ain't normal." It's merely the latest incarnation of the frustration expressed by **Peter Finch**'s character in the 1976 movie, *Network*, "I'm mad as hell, and I'm not going to take this anymore!"

Fall down seven times, get up eight.

Japanese proverb

One does not have to delve too far into popular culture these days to find expressions of climate nihilism, despair and giving up. Doomsday scenarios have a way of motivating diverse groups of people in very different ways. Some will seek escape in transcendentalism. Some will seek to profit from the momentum of destruction. Some will look for incremental paths back from the precipice. Some will focus on preservation of small pockets of light in the coming darkness. But most will simply try to make it through one more day.

We are reaching, or have surpassed, safe limits for many of the nine planetary boundaries needed to sustain life on Earth. As **Greta Thunberg** and the Extinction Rebellion crew are telling us: it's all up to us now.

In this book, I have repeatedly urged Buddhist community leaders to take up Manjusri's sword, if not Yamantaka's entire arsenal, against the ignorance and injustices all around us. However, no amount of speechifying or activism can substitute for working on ourselves to be the change we want to see in the world. That would simply be another instance of expecting other people to make the changes we ourselves are avoiding, and it's easy to see the results of such strident partisanship all around us.

I am trying to reduce my consumer footprint, to choose more wisely how I earn, spend, and invest my money, to devote myself to service, and to be a lifelong active learner. I am just not sure if that is going to be enough to solve the world's problems, in this critical time. As a result, I'm conflicted. All I can do is hope my efforts, activism and aspirations will be a positive contribution to the fate of the planet. But I want to do more. I feel I must do more. Faced with this existential unease, I can only proceed on the basis of no assurances. Good Zen approach, I think.

I read recently that Buddhists make up about 0.7 percent of the North American population. When we factor in the number who are not serious practitioners, we are left with a number that is statistically insignificant. This is the modern iteration of the paradox inherent in the first Bodhisattva Vow: living beings are numberless; I vow to save them all.

In other words, no matter what we do, we are guaranteed to fail, but we do it anyway. To say, "Oh, well there are no beings, so there is no one to be saved," is only half the picture, the reification of a dualistic view of Nirvana. Throwing ourselves into activism is the other half of the picture, in the misguided belief that we will actually make a difference. Finding the balance is a dynamic highwire act.

At this point, I think it is misguided to think we must be and act in a certain way, as if some metaphysical light switch has been turned on. A dynamic, fluid system requires us to be constantly vigilant and responsive to changing conditions and new opportunities. Perhaps **Shenxui**'s gatha for the Fifth Patriarch wasn't so bad after all, even if it lacked the timeless reach of **Huineng**'s. It captured something we could work with.

In talking with community leaders from various Buddhist lineages over the years, I've heard many positions on the need (or lack of need) for engagement, and many variations on what that engagement might look like. There is no doubt we are all acting in good faith, to the best of our vision. One is not better than another, just as diversity in agriculture is better than monoculture. But this does not mean those positions must remain static. Much as we may yearn for the perfection of Sukhavati, we're here on planet Earth. We are bound by the realities of our embodiment, yet liberated by our vows. The goal here is to make the vows, not to expect to be saved by the power of vows made by others.

Like **Dogen**, we can reflect that our efforts have simply been one mistake after another. And still, we persist:

I resolve to become Enlightened, for the sake of all living beings.

I will cut the roots of all delusive passions.

I will penetrate the farthest gate of Dharma.

I will realize the Supreme Way of Buddha.

BODHISATTVA RESOURCES

- tricycle.org/magazine/what-bodhisattva/
- www.buddhistdoor.net/features/humanistic-buddhism-in-australia-and-beyond-an-interview-with-venerable-dr-juewei
- posttraditionalbuddhism.com
- www.patheos.com/blogs/monkeymind/2019/07/never-again-is-now-a-letter-to-buddhist-leaders.html

VIOLENCE

KALI YUGA

37

If you're a bit bummed about the state of the world these days, it's not hard to figure out why. We are living in an age of intense violence, fake virtue, and rampant delusion. In ancient Hindu and Buddhist mythology, this state of affairs was called the Kali Yuga, or Age of Struggle.

If you want a picture of the future, imagine a boot stamping on a human face – for ever.

George Orwell
1984

For those with an apocalyptic bent, that may be enough to confirm any notions about how we've gone from the Age of Aquarius to the End of Days, all within our own lifetimes. Nevertheless, we have to play the hand we're dealt. Our path, like Ksitigarbha's, takes us through Hell.

As I have become old, I have had more occasion to ponder the koan of death. In the conventional realm, the suffering of death is portrayed as sadness at leaving all our family and friends behind, and no longer being able to enjoy the sweetness of life. It has been portrayed as an individual journey, and presupposes that the world we leave behind will remain. Sometimes, less frequently, when we hear of foreign wars or catastrophes, we try to imagine what it must be like for those for whom death includes the destruction of their society, of everything in their world as they knew it. For them, death is much more than a personal departure. Syria and Yemen come to mind.

The other day, I was apprised of a new book, a bestseller I'm told, *The Uninhabitable Earth: Life After Warming*, by **David Wallace-Wells**. It has been gleefully heralded as a profoundly grim view of our impending doom. This is only the latest in a series of jeremiads on the subject (to which I am no stranger, since I moderate a global ecoBuddhist Facebook group), but reading an excerpt really shook me.

And so, I have been contemplating how it feels to know with some degree of certainty that not only "I" am about to die, but that our entire world is on the same road. Embracing that larger death, I am drawn into the mystery of being, to experience a new awareness of loss and grief that my privileged upbringing has denied me.

The question then becomes, what is the Bodhisattva's path on death's road? It makes vivid the urgency of that question: "What if this day were your last?" What are the wisdoms I can only now enter? How must I prepare for the darkness? Of what value is my work (and this book) if we have already passed the tipping point? How do we Dharma in the End Time?

In this section of the book, I'm going to explore the brutality that characterizes much of our "news of the day" – and, hopefully, provide some engaged Buddhist social justice responses.

Finding the right balance between activism and disengagement is difficult. Situations are fluid and fast-moving. It's easy to get caught up in the current and difficult to stay focused on deeper causes and conditions. In the Kali Yuga, every problem is a wicked problem (or, as **Peter Herschock** would define it, a predicament over a clash of values). To put it another way, suffering is like a many-headed dragon. You can't cut off all the heads; but if you pick one and concentrate on conquering that one, you're more likely to see positive results.

Some say, for starters, be the change you want to see in the world. Walk the walk. Sometimes all that is needed is for someone to model a more enlightened way of life and a welcoming attitude. This does not necessarily mean retreating to a monastery, cave, or hermitage. It just means that sometimes, striving to create your own bodhimandala is more productive than arguing with idiots, who will drag you down to their level and then best you with their experience (as **Mark Twain** notably once opined).

Others can write more eloquently than me about the minutiae of death (of an individual, a society, or an ecosphere). Others can teach and preach about living our best lives. I'm still left with the koan of what it all means, knowing that when the Buddha said everything is impermanent, he really wasn't kidding or making some inspirational meme. And somewhere in all of that, it feels as though I have been handed a gift of immeasurable value: an invitation to an ancient ritual. It comes as a puzzle that must be solved in order to activate the empowerment. Ironically, it can only be solved in the last seconds of life.

KALIYUGA RESOURCES

- www.tibetanbuddhistaltar.org/the-nature-of-kaliyuga/
- en.wikipedia.org/wiki/Kali_Yuga
- dharmawheel.net/viewtopic.php?t=22154
- mommymystic.wordpress.com/2011/09/12/the-kali-yuga-working-with-your-speeded-up-karma/
- www.buddhistpeacefellowship.org

WAR

■
38

I'm going to start by admitting defeat on this one. I can't stop governments and non-state actors from war and its awful consequences. I can't
end the suffering, the machinery, or the rhetoric justifying it. I can't end the
glorification of it, the business of it, or the weaponization of cyberspace.

War. What is it good for?
Absolutely nothing. Say it
again.
Edwin Starr

In fact, if push came to shove, I'm not even
sure just how noble I'd be if my life or the lives of
my family were directly threatened. But for now,
I certainly can withhold my participation in any
push for war, and I can speak out against it.

Buddhism has always been portrayed as a
religion or philosophy of peace (in spite of recent history in Sri Lanka
and Myanmar). One has only to watch a few episodes of the old TV show,
Kung Fu, to get the gist of the normative myth. If you can imagine violent
Buddhist non-violence, fighting fire with fire, look to **Thich Quang Duc**'s
self-immolation during the Vietnam War as a touchstone.

My father fought in an actual war, but in my lifetime, wars have always been something far away in other countries, on television. As a young
adult, I learned about how our military-industrial complex exported war
and used other countries as profitable proxies for our larger international
conflicts. I learned about the complex issues of nuclear disarmament, sim-
mering brush-fire civil wars that would occasionally transform into con-
flagrations like Rwanda, and how **George Orwell**'s *1984* became a "how-
to" manual for many despots (**Donald Trump**, **Vladimir Putin**, and **Xi
Jinping** merely being the latest high-profile examples).

More recently, tactics of unconventional war – terrorist attacks, malware attacks on infrastructure, cybersecurity breaches, and massive disin-
formation campaigns by fifth column troll factories on social media, for
example – have added new leitmotifs to the symphony of conflict. In a
way, they have rendered our prevailing myths obsolete and ill-equipped to
deal with the modern face of warfare. What can you say when faced with
a robot attack dog from Boston Dynamics? Mu?

Nipponzan Myohoji, a Buddhist sect founded by **Nichidatsu Fujii**,
has devoted itself to building more than 80 Peace Pagodas around the
world since 1917, and participating in peace activism. **Jun Yasuda**, a
70-year-old nun who stands all of 4'11", is their well-known representative
in North America. **Dilgo Khyentse**'s Peace Vase Project has planted more
than 3,400 vases around the planet, and has the goal of planting 2,500

more. Both groups have forged strong relationships with other peace groups and indigenous social justice activists.

From time to time, Buddhist media run articles about Nonviolent Communication training. There have been NVC training initiatives incorporating mindfulness techniques rooted in Buddhist Vipassana traditions. Even police officers can now participate in mindfulness meditation workshops to help them with de-escalation techniques.

As wonderful as these initiatives are, they are basically soft responses in the free West, designed to nudge attitudes and develop skills through individual experience. They don't really address developments in the public sphere, like delegitimizing China's posturing on Buddhism, Myanmar's genocide, or India's abandonment of its Ambedkarite ideals.

I have yet to read an in-depth blog post, article or book about cyberwarfare from a Buddhist author. Indeed, I find most Buddhist writing about technology to be as fantastical as **Jules Verne** novels. On the flipside, other than Infowar Monitor's exposure of China's GhostNet espionage campaign against Tibet (among 102 other nations) ten years ago, I have yet to read anything at all in cyberwarfare literature that even mentions Buddhism beyond a passing reference to the fact that it exists.

In some ways, cyber is just a smokescreen. China's already won the war to be the world's next superpower. As **Michael Glantz** points out in his book, *One Belt One Road: China's Long March to 2049*, they did it by building ports, rail lines, dams, pipelines and other un-sexy low-tech infrastructure around the world through debt-trap diplomacy with all the money we've been giving them for years. Somehow China and Buddhism seem antithetical to me.

So perhaps I will not be saving the world, after all. But I can at least be that small bright spot in the yin-yang darkness.

WAR RESOURCES

- en.wikipedia.org/wiki/Black_swan_theory
- www.bostondynamics.com
- www.worldfuturefund.org/Reports/BWAR/buddhismwar.html
- sumeru-books.com/products/chinas-long-march-toward-2049
- peacepoleproject.org
- www.peacevaseproject.org

GUNS

39

There is no Buddhist justification for guns. There is no way to "normalize" gun violence. There is no karmic upside to the business of making and selling guns, and yet it goes on and on.

More than 1.5 million American civilians have died from gun violence in my lifetime. That is a staggering number and it doesn't even begin to consider injuries or deaths on foreign soil. Saying "guns don't kill people/people kill people" is a specious argument. Since it is unrealistic to expect an end to mental illness or criminal intent any time soon, making people safer by removing access to guns is a moral imperative. All you have to do to see that it works is to look at a graph of gun deaths comparing the USA with other countries where guns are banned, not glorified.

"On an average day in America, seven children and teens will be shot dead."

Gary Younge
Another Day in the Death of America

If you surf television channels, you're pretty much guaranteed to see a gun at least every three minutes; guns are central plot device in many shows, movies and video games. The toy department is full of Nerf guns, water pistols, and six-shooters. Paintball is a national pastime, an industry generating more than a billion dollars a year, and growing. Our gun culture is so ingrained we barely question it.

We lament the latest mass shooting tragedy (a school, a nightclub, a mosque here or there, some unarmed person caught living while non-white), but it seems nothing changes; the cultural momentum is overwhelming. Survivors still have no lawmakers willing to take down the National Rifle Association lobby. I live in Canada, where relatively few people own guns, but we have a thriving armaments export industry and weapons still saturate our media.

Mass shootings are statistically insignificant compared to the everyday mayhem of murder, injury and suicide by gun. However, they make for great political and news media theatre. Like reporting on a bus crash on the other side of the planet, they are there for their "entertainment" or propaganda value, not their news value. They were instrumentalized.

Sending thoughts and prayers, or standing with victims, is simply not enough. These are merely spiritual slacktivism. We need street protests, class action lawsuits, divestment, and creative ways to shift the conversation. I would be very curious to know how many Buddhists in America actually own guns.

VIOLENCE

One of the most interesting initiatives I discovered while researching this topic is an organization called LeadToLife. They melt down donated guns, turn them into shovels, and use them to ceremonially plant sacred trees in communities ravaged by gun violence.

The web has no shortage of material on Buddhist explanations for the emotional roots of violence, Buddhist ways to make sense of gun violence (as if that is even possible, and seems to me to be only another way of normalizing it), or Buddhist statements calling for gun control. You can read the Joint Statement by the Honpa Hongwanji Mission of Hawaii's Office of the Bishop and Committee on Social Concerns on Gun Violence and Mass Shootings, or the SGI-USA Statement on the Mass Shootings in Las Vegas to get a sense of what these sound like.

However, finding evidence on the web of specific actions, outreach and endorsements was much less fruitful. **Katie Loncke** of the Buddhist Peace Fellowship, **Ven. Thubten Chodron** from Sravasti Abbey, and **Joan Halifax Roshi** from the Upaya Zen Center have been stand-outs in participating in non-Buddhist organizations like LeadToLife and December-Sabbath. Nine local Buddhist organizations participated in the New York March for Life in 2018. But…Faiths United (a religious anti-gun coalition of more than 50 faith traditions) has zero Buddhist supporters! Ditto for CeaseFire and HeedingGod'sCall, both anti-gun coalitions of faith groups.

We need a sustained commitment to anti-gun activism as part of our Bodhisattva Vows. We need explicit anti-gun proclamations on Buddhist centre websites. And we need a much less insular stance from Buddhist leaders when it comes to joining in mass social movements for peace and nonviolence, in solidarity with the traditions of **Dr. B.R. Ambedkar** and **Dr. Martin Luther King**. More yang and less yin please.

GUNS RESOURCES

- www.buddhistaction.org
- www.decembersabbath.org/Buddhism
- www.buddhistpeacefellowship.org
- www.upaya.org/2015/09/if-i-used-my-voice-this-time-bearing-witness-at-a-protest-against-police-gun-violence/
- www.leadtolife.org

RACE

■ As **Shakyamuni Buddha** is quoted in **Dogen**'s *Shobogenzo* (circa 1250
40 CE): "All sentient beings have Buddha Nature through and through, And
the Tathagata continually dwells therein, ever constant."

The Platform Sutra of the Sixth Patriarch (circa 700 CE) has it that
when **Huineng** (the future Sixth Chan Patri-

Defeating racism, tribalism,
intolerance and all forms of
discrimination will liberate
us all, victim and perpetrator
alike.

Ban Ki-Moon,
former Secretary-General,
United Nations

arch) first met his teacher, **Hongren** (the Fifth
Chan Patriarch), **Hongren** doubted his ability
to attain enlightenment as "a barbarian from
the south." **Huineng**'s response was that "Although people from the south and people from
the north differ, there is no north and south in
Buddha nature. Although my barbarian's body
and your body are not the same, what difference is there in our Buddha nature?" The rest,

as they say, is history.

Be that as it may, tribalism and xenophobia are hallmarks of primate
evolution. Humans are no different; we naturally divide the world into
self, us, and other. Historically, this manifested in clan groupings and conflicts between clans over limited resources, with the consequent winners
and losers. Even in ecosystems where homeostasis is been achieved, the
power dynamic is in flux. Therefore, in the Anthropocene, transitioning
to global consciousness has been difficult.

There are many rationalizations for the dehumanization and objectification of others. These prejudices become encoded in social relationships, establishing a self-fulfilling feedback loop of societal stratification
and institutionalized oppression.

Objectification may be based on race, ethnicity, culture, faith, genea-
logy, gender, sexual orientation, physical or mental disabilities, or a
myriad of other, less easily identifiable traits. However, the most prevalent
criterion seems to be epidermal pigmentation – race. Ethnicity and faith
comprise the other two leading prejudices.

From a Buddhist perspective, this is samsaric thinking, the root of
much dukkha, and the cause for a lot of bad karma.

Racism is a virulent vestige of an outmoded mythology, as **Yuval
Harari** notes in his recent book, *21 Lessons for the 21st Century*. In other
words, it's not just bad from a Buddhist perspective, but from any global
sustainability perspective. The current predicament (remember, a clash of

opposing value sets) is that most of us still see the world as an us-versus-them struggle. This is simply not a viable way forward for all of us on planet Earth. It is the ultimate Pyrrhic victory.

There should be no discord between the Bodhisattva ideal and social justice. As **Cornel West** says, justice is what love looks like in public.

North American Buddhists have been struggling with how to incorporate modern, anti-racist awareness into their predominantly white Sanghas. Initiatives have included reflecting on privilege, aligning with anti-racism groups, promotion of Sanghas of colour, breaking down barriers between "convert" and "cradle" Sanghas, and adoption of explicit anti-racist policies. New organizations such as the North American Buddhist Alliance have sprung up with racial justice as keystone values in their mission statements. The Harvard Divinity School has been running an annual *Buddhism and Race* conference for five years (some videos and audio recordings available online).

However, tension between Dharma and racism is not exclusive to North America, as the Rohingya tragedy in Myanmar, the Tamil tragedy in Sri Lanka, or the Tibetan tragedy in China clearly illustrate. Indeed, even tensions between Theravada and Mahayana Buddhists can often be played out in racial issues.

There are a few humanist Buddhist organizations who have placed themselves firmly in the pan-human family and their benevolent activities are on behalf of all, regardless of race or religion. The Buddhist Compassion Relief Tzu Chi Foundation, Buddhist Global Relief, Fo Guang Shan, Shechen Karuna, and Soka Gakkai International are notable exemplars.

As fraught as discussions about race can be for Buddhists, those discussions are necessary, in the same way that discussions about sexual abuse by Buddhist teachers have come into the sunshine.

RACE RESOURCES

* northamericanbuddhistalliance.org
* tw.tzuchi.org/en
* www.buddhistglobalrelief.org
* www.fgs.org.tw/en/
* karuna-shechen.org
* www.sgi.org

WAR ON WOMEN

41 There is probably no more deeply-ingrained war than the war on women. Patriarchy is alive and well, in every mainstream culture and religion on the planet. This is pretty stupid. I would much rather see women running things than continue with the toxic masculinity that has gotten us into the mess we find ourselves in now. It's like playing doubles tennis, repeatedly whacking your partner in the leg with your racket and then blaming them for losing the game.

> I measure the progress of a community by the degree of progress which women have achieved.
>
> B.R. Ambedkar

One example of patriarchy I find particularly egregious is the "Pro-Life" movement. To my way of thinking, this is primarily a *Handmaid's Tale* domination scenario cloaked in sanctimonious verbiage. You can't be pro-life if you support guns, for starters. You can't be pro-life if you hobble women's education, healthcare, or employment opportunities. You can't be pro-life if you fail to provide the necessaries of life to millions of children (and let's not even start with the topic of the children of illegal immigrants).

One does not have to look far for examples of gender discrimination. Likewise, feminist voices are everywhere. The catch is, you have to be willing to look, listen and act. Giving up male privilege is scary.

Buddhists have fared no better in this regard. Female Buddhist leaders were traditionally rarer than Arhats, and even now female ordination (which I fully support) is a hotly contested idea. Why is it somehow better to have fewer dedicated Buddhist practitioners on the planet for the sake of upholding some ancient ideological purity? Don't we need all the help we can get? Do we really think that if women can become full monastics, Buddhism will suddenly lose its truth? Do those sexually abusive gurus and roshis get a pass? Is helpmate the best a female practitioner can aspire to? I wonder how many Sangha councils have gender parity?

Feminist critiques of Buddhism from scholars like **Rita Gross, Janet Gyatso, Miranda Eberle Shaw**, and **Tsultrim Allione** are still far from mainstream. Other female Buddhist scholars have achieved their "success" by avoiding feminist issues. Modern, accredited female Buddhist teachers are still considered outliers (although Wikipedia offers a pretty good list). Sakyadhita International Association of Buddhist Women and the Buddhist Women's Association (Jodo Shinshu) are fantastic organizations. **Bhikkhuni Cheng Yen**, who founded the Buddhist Compassion

Relief Tzu Chi Foundation, is a wonderfully inspiring role model for what modern humanistic Buddhism can do. The organization has more than 10 million members and is active in more than 47 countries.

At Sumeru, I have made a point of publishing books by and about Buddhist women (such as the anthology, *Lotus Petals in the Snow: Voices of Canadian Buddhist Women*, edited by **Tanya McGinnity**, the proceeds from which are all donated to Tzu Chi Canada). I believe this is clearly an aspect of Buddhist practice where we have to open up our thinking to voices outside the echo chamber. There is so much evidence that supporting the empowerment of girls and women has tremendous positive impacts on society.

Bhikkhu Bodhi gave the keynote address at a conference entitled "Buddhism and Women's Liberation," held in Bodhgaya in January 2019. A lightly edited version appears in the July 2019 issue of *Lion's Roar*, and it is available on the magazine website (as well as on his LinkedIn feed). The article is well worth reading. It is refreshing to see prominent male Buddhist teachers taking such a progressive stance, rather than expecting "the women" to go it alone.

Furthermore, evidence of the validity of his arguments is easy to find. For example, if you have the opportunity to screen the excellent documentary on population, *Don't Panic* (available on YouTube), featuring the late **Hans Rosling** (sadly missed) of the Gapminder Foundation, you will see the profound beneficial impact the empowerment of women can make. You will also see that the greatest impacts are felt in the developing world.

If Buddha Nature is neither male nor female, this is not exclusively a negation. My interpretation recognizes the vitality of Tathagatagarbha and an openness to the feminine divine. (Have a read of *Longing for Darkness*, by **China Galland**.)

WAR ON WOMEN RESOURCES
- en.wikipedia.org/wiki/Women_in_Buddhism
- www.sakyadhita.org
- www.buddhistchurchesofamerica.org/federation-of-buddhist-womens-associations/
- nakkbi.org/ibbf2018/
- www.womenwill.com

GENDER

I refuse to see the universe as cis-gender, where sex roles are defined by ideology and those who colour outside the lines are punished. We humans are dysfunctional enough. When natural inclinations are pushed into the shadows, it only creates further psychological dysfunction. From the perspective of harm-reduction, forcing people to hide from themselves and from others has no benefit. And isn't Buddhism about discovering your true face, before your parents were born?

> The Great Way is not difficult
> for those who have no
> preferences.
>
> *Jianzhi Sengcan,*
> *Third Chan Patriarch*

So, in that sense, I would rather be an LGBTQ ally than a hate-monger. However, I understand that our contemporary embrace of gender fluidity in all its manifestations can also be just another samsaric distraction. I would prefer to see a world where sexual orientation is simply a non-issue in public life, not taking up all the oxygen in the room. I'd like open Sanghas where LGBTQ practitioners feel at home, and where all of us can focus on more important issues. So today when the Anglican Church voted to not support same-sex marriage, I was disappointed.

There are not a lot of books from a gay Buddhist perspective. You've got *Queer Dharma: Voices of Gay Buddhists*, edited by **Winston Leyland** (Vol. 1, 1998; Vol. 2, 2000), *Sexuality in Classical South Asian Buddhism*, by **José Cabezón** (2014), *My Buddha Is Pink: Buddhism for the Modern Homosexual*, by **Richard Harrold** (Sumeru, 2019), and several other lesser-known options.

According to what you might find on the Internet, Buddhism is neutral and accommodating with regard to gay practitioners. The original Canon is ambiguous, medieval teachers were decidedly anti-, and modern teachers have been unclear. In reality, there is still a lot of marginalization, and I regularly hear stories about sexual abuse within monasteries (in addition to the #MyGuruToo scandals), but there appear to be fewer hard-line Buddhist ideologues denouncing homosexuality and gender nonconformism than in the Abrahamic faiths.

In an era when racism and sexism are under assault, homophobia seems to be a last refuge for the intolerant – a place where they can vent their rage and get away with it. That is a much more serious issue than whether or not LGBTQ people are "normal" or "subverting our children." Gay-bashing is a crime, as abhorrent as lynching. Normalizing that type of violence is just one symptom of pervasive social rot.

VIOLENCE

Being gender-nonconforming is neither a disease nor a lifestyle choice. It's just part of our diversity. The issue of sexual misconduct, to my way of thinking, is about objectifying and using others, to their detriment, more than about who does what to whom, when or how. In other words, it's about abuse, not sex. It is sexualized violence.

On the other hand, focusing on the sexual orientation of celebrities, be they politicians, pop stars or athletes, is sometimes just another example of misguided virtue signalling. Like other forms of slacktivism, it obviates the need for us to make real changes in our own lives, leaving the heavy lifting to our surrogates.

Feminists have been working long and hard to break free from the normative strictures of patriarchy, and thank goodness for that. Ever since **Rita Gross** published with *Buddhism After Patriarchy* in 1992, Buddhist centres have been evolving into new, more equitable, cultures. We know it can be done. Why not extend the same openness to the entire koan of gender?

Nobody is going to deny that sexuality is central to our sense of ourselves. The Vinaya has many rules about sexual renunciation for monastics, but even in historically Buddhist cultures, the laity had a much broader path laid out for them. Now, non-monastic practitioners are the majority, engaging in serious practice that was historically only for monastics.

Never mind the outliers; every one of us experiences our sexuality as fluid, transforming over time: it's always unfinished business. Aging and ill-health diminish us as sexual beings. Uncertainty in relationships leaves us in a constant state of second-guessing. Parenting is exhausting. And these are all in the sphere of the personal, not to mention the myriad of mixed messages about sexuality bombarding us every day.

Beyond all that, it's important to remember to breathe, and accept our sexual nature as a wondrous facet of our Buddha nature, just as we are.

GENDER RESOURCES
* www.wired.com/story/china-feminism-emoji-censorship/
* www.sgi.org/about-us/president-ikedas-writings/a-grand-declaration-of-gender-equality.html
* www.stephenbatchelor.org/index.php/en/is-gender-an-issue-in-buddhism
* fashionmagazine.com/culture/k-d-lang-on-buddhism-and-coming-out/
* www.mdpi.com/2076-0760/7/4/51/htm

WATCHER STATE

43 In **Franz Kafka**'s eerie fiction, we get our first glimpse of a malevolent surveillance state with seemingly all-powerful bureaucracy. In East Germany, before the Berlin Wall came down and re-unification occurred, the Stasi secret police perfected it in practice. In **George Orwell**'s prescient novel, *1984*, Big Brother used ubiquitous television cameras to monitor everything citizens said and did, in their quest for total thought-control. Does that sound like North Korea, anybody?

Authorities in western China's Sichuan province have further tightened controls at the Larung Gar Buddhist Academy...

Radio Free Asia, 4-19-2019

In **Aldous Huxley**'s *Brave New World*, citizens are led to believe their prison is the pleasure dome, with guilt-free sex and drugs for all.

Now, here in the Western Paradise of Surveillance Capitalism, we gladly buy in, give up as much information about ourselves as possible, and get upset if nobody is watching! Google wants to know our exact location all day every day? No problem. Facebook needs to see what you looked like 10 years ago, compared to now. Sure thing. At a protest rally? Just livestream it. Curious about your ethnic heritage? 23andme can help you with that. Want to save on insurance? Just plug this dongle into your car. Browse online for a bike, and be prepared for dozens of ads after.

The topic of Big Tech's incursion into our being, coupled with our loss of privacy, is clearly top-of-mind for many. *The Age of Surveillance Capitalism: The Fight for a Human Future at the New Frontier of Power*, by **Shoshana Zuboff**, is a bestseller, and this is hardly the only book on the subject. In fact, **B.F. Skinner** explored the totalitarian implications of governmentality in his 1971 behaviourist classic, *Beyond Freedom and Dignity*. What's changed is the arena, not the goal. As **Yuval Harari** notes in his newest book, *21 Lessons for the 21st Century*, you are the object, not the subject, and all that "behavioural surplus" data about you is being sold to corporations who want to hack your brain. You are indeed living in the Matrix. Privacy is a shining artifact of the past, as **Leonard Cohen** would say. (Incidentally, the Russian edition of Harari's book edited out all references to Russia and to his gay orientation.)

So what's a Buddhist to do? One obvious conclusion is to disengage as much as possible from digital media or at least to curate your online life mindfully. That's fairly congruent with simplicity, tranquillity, and groundedness.

How about funding privacy initiatives, supporting Net Neutrality, standing up for anti-monopolistic copyright legislation, holding social media companies accountable for their use of your data, and pressing for clear laws surrounding ownership of Big Data? Do those sound like they could be part of your Dharma?

We need to dig even deeper. The surveillance state is merely a subset of modern secularism's delusive paradigm. Trying to "fit" Buddhist practice into normative Western thinking leaves out much of why we practice. *Shifting the Ground We Stand On: Buddhist and Western Thinkers Challenge Modernity*, a free *Tricycle* e-book anthology of articles by **Linda Heuman**, explores this uneasy Venn diagram comprising religion, technology and secularism. It's another well-explored territory, but her book is focused specifically on Buddhist responses. In it, liberation, the main project of Buddhism, is ultimately a transcendent journey. Like Harari, her interview subjects return repeatedly to the need to find a new narrative that rises above the dialectic of control and resistance.

To me, that is analogous to "Taking Refuge." It is predicated on a radical disinterest in samsara, and the adoption of an entirely different set of values. Once we have some sense of what we are walking toward, it becomes easier to walk away from the past. This is not to say that living in a surveillance state has no relevance to Buddhists. Tibetans can certainly set you straight on that score. But at least here in the West, there are still some cracks in the totalitarian project. It's important to engage with these issues as skillful means, while remembering that they are not the be-all and end-all of our practice. Otherwise, we are surrendering to a vision of Buddhism typified by modern China: denatured and commodified, or corralled in "re-education" camps, tracked by facial recognition, genetic profiling, artificial intelligence, and a pervasive social credit system for enforcement.

WATCHER STATE RESOURCES

- www.shoshanazuboff.com
- www.bfskinner.org
- www.ynharari.com
- chomsky.info
- www.nytimes.com/2018/07/16/technology/china-surveillance-state.html
- tricycle.org/ebooks/buddhism-science/

TITANS

■ 44

Oh, how we love our captains of industry, our **Steve Jobs**, **Elon Musk**, or **Jeff Bezos**. Oh, how we follow the trials and tribulations of our superstars, our **Beyoncé**, **Simon Cowell**, or **Sean Hannity**. And oh, how we fawn over our gurus, our Rinpoches, Roshis, and Bhantes.

I have not failed. I've just found 10,000 ways that won't work.

Thomas Edison

These are the intimate strangers who provide us with the raw materials to build our narratives about reality. In many ways, they remind me of the Devas and Asuras of Buddhist cosmology. They exist in a parallel universe, affect our daily lives in a myriad of good and bad ways, display all the human foibles writ large, and rise or fall on the karma of their actions. Beloved one moment, reviled the next.

Our hunger for leaders, role models, celebrities, scapegoats, and surrogates is part of what keeps us stuck in powerlessness. It is easier to be a follower than to strike out on one's own. It is easier to live vicariously through the larger-than-life than to dwell authentically in our own lives. It is easier to spend our energy vilifying the unrighteous than in building a better world.

Most Buddhists would agree, I think, that the majority of society's plans for us are bullshit. Recent scandals in the Buddhist world have caused us also to question whether Buddhism's plan for us is any better. There is no doubt a sea-change underway. The Age of Gurus is giving way to egalitarian Sangha Councils and greater accountability for Buddhist teachers. That's a good thing, in my view. In the future, Enlightenment will be crowdsourced.

Don't get me wrong. I am deeply indebted to my teachers, and I try to spend each day in gratitude to them. It's just that, for me, service to society is the way to honour them and actualize their instructions.

In fact, it could be argued that dethroning the reigning monarchs of Dharma is quite in line with Shakyamuni's original deathbed instructions to his followers. Even the Dalai Lama has openly mused about abdicating his role, short-circuiting China's plans for their own puppet leader.

However, the issue here is not the purity of our teachers, or lack thereof. It is our propensity to hand control over our lives to others. As a technological design teacher, I've used a student-centred, project-driven, hands-on approach. I'm the guide on the side rather than the sage on the stage. Empowering students has worked quite well.

In pedagogy, we talk about **Vygotsky**'s Continuum, the goal of which is to empower students to manage their own learning. Like **Ivan Illich**, we need to deschool society. I'd like to see more of that in Buddhist communities. A variety of Buddhist teachers have, of late, bemoaned the loss of traditional guru-chela relationships. However, there is no getting back to Shangri-la, if indeed it ever existed. The headlong plunge that characterized Western Buddhist aspirants in the 1960s simply does not work now. I suspect that if Chögyam Trungpa (whom I first met in 1969) showed up today, he'd be laughed out of town.

One of the prevailing myths of Western civilization is that with hard work and a bit of luck, each of us can achieve Titan status. The reality of that happening, like fulfilment of teenage dreams of being an NBA star or rock legend, is infinitesimally small. Another part of that myth says we need billionaires to lead the fight for a better world. No. Billionaire philanthropy is an oxymoron.

A parallel in Buddhist practice might be striving for *satori*, or seeking *inka shomei*, or assuming that to practice Buddhism deeply one must have students. When I see the variety of wannabe's live-streaming their Dharma talks on the web, I cringe. They remind me of reality TV protagonists. The essential component is that they want to live their lives in public, not any specific aspect of their lives *per se*. Dwarves, polygamists, teen moms, trans people, unusually diseased, vegans, house hunters, it's all the same. This inverted funnel of celebrity should not become the default definition of the Noble Eightfold Path.

The number of Instagram followers, re-tweets, miles logged between speaking engagements, book deals, and such, are no more an indicator of holiness than being able to hold one's arm over one's head for years, or other extreme renunciate actions.

TITANS RESOURCES

- brobible.com/life/article/mark-cuban-billionaire-role-models/
- www.newyorker.com/news/john-cassidy/is-america-an-oligarchy
- www.businessinsider.com/a-message-from-us-rich-plutocrats-to-all-you-little-people-2012-11
- www.nytimes.com/2013/11/03/opinion/sunday/plutocrats-vs-populists.html

WHISTLEBLOWERS

45

"Everyone appreciates your honesty until you're honest with them. Then you're an asshole." **George Carlin**.

Whistleblowers: **Edward Snowdon, Julian Assange, Jodie Wilson Raybould, Chelsea Manning, Grigory Mikhailovich Rodchenkov, Deep Throat, Daniel Ellsberg, Karen Silkwood, Alyssa Milano**.

The consent of the governed is not consent if it is not informed.
Edward Snowden

Some Buddhist teachers about whom whistles were blown: **Chögyam Trungpa, Sogyal Rinpoche, Kalu Rinpoche, Joshu Sasaki, Eido Shimano, Sakyong Mipham, Lodro Rinzler, Noah Levine, Sangharakshita, Ashin Wirathu, Shi Xuecheng, Kai Hong**. Were they justified? No easy answers.

The role of the whistleblower in society is double-edged. On one hand, we value their insistence on speaking truth to power, transparency and accountability, and we enact laws to protect them. On the other hand, we accuse them of indiscriminate collateral damage, personal agendas, anarchism, or being snitches. In many cases, verifying the validity of the accusations is extremely difficult, a case of he-said-she-said.

On balance, I'm on the whistleblower side, but I recognize it means you have to have skin in the game. My last whistleblowing campaign cost me tens of thousands of dollars in legal fees, and three years of hell in multiple libel-chill lawsuits launched against me by the corporation in question (all eventually dropped). That gives me some street cred, I suppose. I've also had unpleasant experiences with leaving the Sanghas of more than one Buddhist teacher who turned out to be abusive.

The *Brahmajala Sutra* lays out ten Bodhisattva precepts, including four that relate directly to speech:

4. Not to use false words and speech, or encourage others to do so.

6. Not to broadcast the misdeeds or faults of the Buddhist assembly, nor encourage others to do so.

7. Not to praise oneself and speak ill of others, or encourage others to do so.

10. Not to speak ill of the Buddha, the Dharma or the Sangha (lit. the Triple Jewel) or encourage others to do so.

Breaking any of these was traditionally considered a major offence. Clearly, there is room here for modern re-interpretation, especially when we consider that secrecy is frequently the refuge of the culpable. Perhaps if we had a better process for dealing with accusations and allegations....

In the secular world, we know that those in power can work hard to create a culture of silence surrounding their misdeeds, corruption, ulterior motives, and doublespeak. Controlling the conversation is the natural corollary of that secrecy. We in Western democracies like to think we're better than the dictators, but whistleblowers repeatedly reveal to us that we too need checks and balances (and, seemingly, more than ever).

It has been harder to bring the culture of openness into the religious sphere. One has merely to look at abuse in the Catholic Church, residential schools for indigenous children, or any number of cults to see that. Aside from behaviour by "those in charge" that is so incongruent with the avowed goals of spiritual life that it must be concealed, there is the cognitive dissonance of "those in their charge" who find it difficult to come forward, not only because of possible societal repercussions such as shunning, but because to do so would destroy their own value systems. Fortunately, as we come to see that the benefits of transparency outweigh the risks, we are remaking the relationships in our Sanghas, and religious and public institutions.

In the best of all possible worlds, we'd get to a place where whistleblowers would no longer be needed. Meanwhile, mission statements by Buddhist organizations that explicitly define the ethical terrain for teachers and students are a huge step in the right direction. We also need clear conflict resolution guidelines too, like restorative justice.

Dealing with scandals such as how opioid manufacturers and distributors have gamed government regulations, or how Nestlé has obtained extravagant water rights, or how Bayer-Monsanto controls 90 percent of the world's agricultural seed stock, is going to require a bit more than some heroic loner going out on a limb. The acid test is not how we treat whistleblowers, but how we change society based on their revelations.

WHISTLEBLOWERS RESOURCES

- www.lionsroar.com/bdwinter2014/
- andreamwinn.com/offerings/bps-welcome-page/
- assets.documentcloud.org/documents/602812/report-on-joshu-sasaki-allegations.pdf
- www.theatlantic.com/national/archive/2014/12/the-zen-predator-of-the-upper-east-side/383831/

WORK

CONSUMER

46   According to Buddhism, desire is one of the three poisons that makes the world go round. Like Hungry Ghosts, we have a neverending thirst for something new that will quench our appetites. In our current world, this means shopping – for material goods, experiences, status, or lifestyles.

When we see the world through this lens, we surrender our power to those who would

> A cynic is a man who knows the price of everything but the value of nothing.
>
> *Oscar Wilde*

hold us in their thrall through diversions – the proverbial bread and circuses.

I think that Buddhist teachings are pretty good at outing materialism and consumerism as poor personal choices, as well as at pointing out the illusory promise of satisfaction proffered by marketers of every stripe.

However, I think that Buddhist teachers have done a pretty lousy job of explaining the systemic problems stemming from our neoliberal, free market, late-stage capitalist, transnational corporate paradigm.

As a result, we lack the tools to engage with that ideology in a meaningful way for change. We have much to learn from progressive activists such as **Annie Leonard** (*Story of Stuff*) or **Naomi Klein** (*This Changes Everything*), and from progressive organizations like the Post-Growth Alliance.

There is lots of room here for Buddhist voices, from Buy Nothing Day, to Change Your Mind Day, to activism around pesticides, fossil fuel divestment, GMO intellectual property, greenwashing, e-waste, social justice in global supply chains, conflict minerals, human trafficking, girls' education in developing nations, and a host of other consumption-related challenges facing us.

It's important to note here that Right Livelihood isn't just about our own spending and saving. It's also about investing in organizations that themselves are guided by the dictum: "Not to commit evil, but to do all that is good, and to purify one's mind – that is the teaching of all the Buddhas." Organizations that seek and obtain B Corp status are good examples. (B Corps are for-profit companies certified by the nonprofit B Lab to meet rigorous standards of social and environmental performance, accountability, and transparency. I'm currently applying for certification.)

Another area where engaged Buddhists can play a meaningful role as change agents is in creating better workplaces. Bringing real value to our activities in the world of work means we are reducing suffering and increasing happiness, on balance, for the greatest number of people.

When we engage in Right Livelihood in the workplace, we are creating the opportunity for others to actualize their Right Livelihoods too. It is a win-win situation, rather than the zero-sum game that is the normative paradigm of competition and accumulation. Greyston Bakery is a great example.

I recently read a meme that said: "Poverty exists not because we cannot feed the poor, but because we cannot satisfy the rich." I think many of the world's problems, and not just food insecurity, from overwhelming refugee flows, mass extinctions, and plastic pollution, to climate change, can all be linked to that quote. It is a thread that runs through every aspect of work, which is arguably the most significant way each of us engages with public life.

As our consumption becomes increasingly digital, emerging technologies become critical factors in the dynamic. Data is the new El Dorado. Consider, if you will, that **Jeff Bezos**, founder of Amazon, is the richest man in the history of the world. Does that make him the *Chakravartin*? Are the titans of industry, like **Mark Zuckerberg**, **Elon Musk**, **Larry Page** and **Sergey Brin** the new messiahs or the new conquistadors?

The algorithms of artificial intelligence already run most of the financial services industry, as well as many critical components of our national infrastructure. Disruptive new technologies like blockchain are poised to render many professions and livelihoods obsolete.

What is the meaning of work, when meaningful work is unavailable to most people? What is the value of investing, when the lion's share of profit goes to those who can mark to market in milliseconds with supercomputers, leaving the losses to retail investors? Are we what is consumed?

Being an engaged Buddhist means a lot more than buying organic local produce at the market!

CONSUMER RESOURCES

- storyofstuff.org
- www.naomiklein.org
- www.postgrowthalliance.org
- www.bcorporation.net
- blogs.dickinson.edu/buddhistethics/files/2013/09/Harvey-Consumer-final1.pdf

MAKER

▬
47

In this world of mass production, we have nostalgia for the age of craft that preceded the Industrial Revolution of the 1800's. We shop for unique handmade items on Instagram, Pintrest, etsy, eBay, and the like. We build our uniqueness with customization. We get the urge to make stuff ourselves. Here's a way out of consumerism: we reframe ourselves as makers. In fact, entire industries have sprung up to satisfy this quest for a new form of self-made identity.

Craftsmanship means dwelling on a task for a long time and going deeply into it, because you want to get it right.
Matthew B. Crawford

There is much value to this transformation. By opting out of the normative role of passive consumer, we're empowered to be creative, to make and sell and share with peers directly. Maker culture is now a real thing, not just the exclusive enclave of nerds and geeks in the shadows.

Somehow, this new approach has become associated with Buddhism. Mindful physical work (*samu*, in Japanese) has always been an essential component of Zen training. How did it come to be a meme in the West?

It began with an appreciation for the painstaking artistry of Japanese artisans. **Robert Pirsig** distilled the ethos of it, in *Zen and the Art of Motorcycle Maintenance*. **Malcolm Gladwell** explored the psychology of it in his thematic 10,000-hour Rule, in *Outliers*. More recently, **Matthew Crawford** purified it into a bit of a manifesto, *Shop Class as Soulcraft*.

Most of the time, we are caught in relative powerlessness as cogs in a giant assembly line, endlessly checking our TO DO lists. I think what's romantic here is the sense of agency and escape from discursive thought.

These visions of a path to our natural liberation are enticing: Make Making Great Again. The reality is somewhat more complicated.

Consider 3D printers (*aka* fabjigs), P2P, open source, citizen science, makerspaces, crowdsourced problem-solving (e.g., Innocentive), the gig economy (e.g. Fiverr or Amazon Mechanical Turk), and other attributes of this new realm. This brave new world looks a lot like a chaotic dystopia bearing a greater resemblance to the musings of **Marc Andreessen**, or the science fiction of **Neal Stephenson** (especially in *The Diamond Age*).

I'm going to try to deconstruct the "maker" identity and tease out what is or is not an appropriate perspective for an engaged Buddhist. Let's start with some things a maker is not...

A maker is not a prosumer, a Luddite, a Bangle Buddhist, a social media influencer, or an evangelist for the new economy. Making something does not end the quest to make something else. Controlling the means of production does not mean a maker controls the full spectrum of business and work. Being mindful of the fact you're shovelling shit doesn't transform it into sugar.

In fact, in our capacity as workers participating in livelihood activities, all of us are makers. The mode of work has changed; that's impermanence. Yes, for the nimble, opportunity awaits. For most, however, work is still a means to an end that lies in another facet of life. The changing rules of work may simply be stressors creating more harm than good, particularly for the precariat class.

Those of us in the privileged classes have the leisure to self-actualize, beyond the world of work. We might eat right, practice yoga, volunteer at a local charity. Compassion is bigger than that. As Bodhisattvas, we've got to figure out how to alleviate the suffering of others, and a lot of that suffering takes place in the world of work. We need to make change, not stuff.

Let's make Fair Trade certified supply chains, gender pay-equity, social entrepreneurship, guaranteed minimum wage, open hiring, employee cooperatives, housing-first urban policy, walkable cities, restorative justice, impact investing, and the like. Let's respect all makers.

This is not to say that mindfulness in relation to physical tasks is bad. Chopping wood and hauling water are not part of our everyday lives in our hyper-digitized modern world, but we can still benefit from gathering our thoughts and engaging in acts that have immediate, palpable consequences. Conceiving and completing creative projects bring a value to our lives that is not simply defined by monetary rewards, especially when they involve peer-to-peer networks. These are components of a healthy spiritual practice. I am just saying they are not the be-all and end-all of that practice.

MAKER RESOURCES

- www.theguardian.com/books/2017/apr/25/robert-pirsig-obituary
- en.wikipedia.org/wiki/Outliers_(book)
- www.innocentive.com
- a16z.com (Marc Andreessen's website)
- en.wikipedia.org/wiki/The_Diamond_Age

MONEY

48

According to the Vinaya, a monk may not accept money himself, cause another to accept money for him, or consent to having money placed near him or kept for him. These rules were subsumed under the larger directive that monks should not own property. Perhaps that was a viable code 2500 years ago when barter was the primary mode of value transfer, but it doesn't really work today when so much of what we do is mediated by currency (be it fiat, local, or digital).

> Too many people spend money they earned...to buy things they don't want... to impress people that they don't like.
> *Will Rogers*

Money has value as a means to an end, but no value in and of itself. The value comes when we spend it on something else. Every time we spend money, we are casting a vote for the kind of world we want. I think the spirit of the Vinaya rules around money is like saying we shouldn't mistake the finger pointing at the moon for the moon itself.

To put it another way, Right Livelihood acknowledges our need to earn money and encourages us to do so without harm to others. We also have a moral obligation to avoid becoming a burden to others. If we can earn money by benefitting others, all the better. When our basic needs are met, money may help us acquire the education and skills to self-actualize. Beyond that, acquiring money to set us apart from others by virtue of exclusive possessions becomes toxic.

All of the world's wars have been about conflicts over resources: land, water, fuel, food, and so on. They may have been gussied up as manifest destiny, triumph of the supermen, jihad, liberation of the oppressed, or defence of national security, but basically it's all about winners and losers. There is, however, a parallel history of cooperation as the real engine of survival and prosperity.

Things have changed since our agrarian days. We've had the Industrial Revolution, the Information Age, the Personal Computer Age, the Networking Age, the Age of Convergence, and the Biotech Age; we are now approaching the threshold of the Singularity. We've got online banking, high frequency trading, the attention economy, digital wallets, banking APIS, microfinance, crowdfunding, P2P parallel economies, blockchain, cryptocurrencies, offshore tax havens, cybertheft, and so much more.

With all this disruption, it's no wonder we are in a state of confusion about the value and role of money in our society. It's a wicked problem.

WORK

Most religious teachers in America have a hard time making a living. Like untenured professors, they are part of the precariat. One big-city Zen abbot I know was forced to leave his role and become a clinical hypnotherapist because his Sangha could not afford to employ him full-time. He said to me: "The Dharma is like water. It may be free, but plumbing costs money."

The dialectic: Buddhists as noble paupers and renunciates, on one hand, and Bauble Buddhists on the other, buying their way to bliss. Philanthropy is the new *dana*. And just to mix it up a bit, let's throw in the news stories of fake Buddhist monks begging in one town or another. There are lots of pernicious myths about Buddhism and money.

A new perspective, Buddhist Economics, is emerging from this fog. Here are a few books worth reading on the topic, from Western authors... **E.F. Schumacher** –*Small Is Beautiful: A Study of Economics As If People Mattered*; **Clair Brown** – *Buddhist Economics: An Elightened Approach to the Dismal Science*; and **Vaddhaka Linn** – *The Buddha on Wall Street: What's wrong with capitalism and what we can do about it*. They all offer food for thought, yet they are but humble beginnings. For a more in-depth analysis of what Right Livelihood looks like in the modern age, **Rod Burylo** has written *The Wealthy Buddhist*, exploring what earning, spending, saving, and investing look like from a Buddhist perspective. As an ethics expert in the financial services industry, he teases out the nuances very well with some very positive suggestions.

This highlights one of my main motivators for writing this book. If Buddhist teachers are out of touch with the realities that their congregations face, they will be unable to provide meaningful guidance. We cannot stand apart from the fray, leaving it for the technocrats, anarchists, or profiteers to steer spaceship Earth.

MONEY RESOURCES
- www.envisioning.io/legacy/money
- www.envisioning.io/work/cryptonomy
- adbusters.org
- www.buynothingday.org
- degrowth.org
- www.centerforneweconomics.org/buddhist-economics

WORK 4.0

■ 49 It's hard to imagine what the future is going to look like. Looking at past visions of it from the world's leading thinkers of their day often leaves us slack-jawed at how badly they got it all wrong. Everybody was thinking flying cars, but nobody saw the Internet coming.

We shape our tools and thereafter they shape us.
Marshall McLuhan

One would be hard-pressed to find a job today that does not involve the Internet in some way. It may not be the the substance of what you do, but it will be booking your appointments, paying your bills, controlling your thermostat, ordering your supplies, and so on.

There are many excellent resources available to predict our near future work with some precision, at least in regard to emerging technologies. *MetaScan 3* is one such document, published by the Canadian government.

In terms of work, 1.0 involved direct production, 2.0 involved using data to facilitate that production, and 3.0 involves using data as the means and substance of production – the digital economy. In terms of the workplace, 1.0 involved physical proximity, 2.0 involved distributed collaboration, and 3.0 involved a gig economy. In terms of agency, 1.0 involved human cogitation, 2.0 involved human cogitation enhanced by access to computers, and 3.0 involves artificial intelligence, machine learning, neural nets, and robotics. In terms of autonomy, 1.0 involved individuals, 2.0 involved management, and 3.0 involves ubiquitous, omnidirectional connectivity. Can we extrapolate from all of this to Work 4.0?

In all of these facets, ethics are the ghost in the machine. Whether tomorrow is a utopia or a dystopia depends more on the heart than the mind. In other words, a Buddhist perspective (avoid harm, do good, purify the mind) remains the ideal touchstone.

For individuals, it's very difficult to maintain focus in a world of information overload, multi-tasking, pervasive connectivity, and zero wait time. Designer **Richard Saul Wurman** calls it *Information Anxiety*. This anxiety has been the impetus for many mobile apps promoting mindfulness, tranquility, and so on. They may be a panacea, but hardly a systemic upgrade. As sci-fi writer **Bruce Stirling** notes, we suffer from an aversion to cognitive loading and we demand of our technology: "Please don't make me think." On the flip side, **Kevin Kelly**, founder of *Wired* magazine, has written extensively about how we rewire our brains to conform to the paradigm our technology demands. He calls it *The Technium*. In short, our work has become less about relationships with others and more about relationships with semi-intelligent machines that are becoming increasingly intelligent while you are reading these very words! What will Work 4.0, the Fourth Industrial Revolution, look like? I've included a few prognostications in the Resources section below.

In all of this, one thing seems clear to me: Samsara is not going away. The rich will continue to crave riches, and class warfare will increasingly beome the defining feature of the future of work. It's anybody's guess how successful the pushback will be, and that success will not be uniformly felt.

Like Gautama before his first awakening, a privileged few will enjoy the good life while pondering First World problems such as when they might get a self-driving car or when Amazon will begin delivering their butter knives via drone.

The best lesson of history is that people don't learn from the lessons of history. Storm's a-comin'.

Amidst all this turmoil, at least one positive new Work 4.0 has emerged: social entrepreneurship. Think of it as companies whose mission is to develop, fund and implement solutions to social, cultural, or environmental issues, as opposed to making profits for shareholders. In many cases, the focus is on appropriate technology rather than advanced technology. **Muhammad Yunus** (Grameen Bank) and **Bill Drayton** (Ashoka) are two well-known pioneers in the field. Grayston Bakery is probably the best-known North American Buddhist example of this type of enterprise.

A Buddhist model for economic activity cannot simply be a negation of worldly work, because that would be cruel to literally billions of people. Buddhist economics must simply put healthy lives and a healthy planet at the centre of its economic model. That's the kind of Work 4.0 I'd like to see.

WORK 4.0 RESOURCES

- www.horizons.gc.ca/en/content/metascan-3-emerging-technologies-0
- work4-0.eu/wp-content/uploads/2017/11/Jobs-for-Work-4.0_ Awareness-Raising-Guidelines_v24112017-2.pdf
- www.weforum.org/agenda/2016/01/the-fourth-industrial-revolution-what-it-means-and-how-to-respond/
- www.ashoka.org

PROGRESS

50

It gets better, right? That's the mantra of human evolution. It is the founding myth of progress and secularism. We can't read the future, but we can construct a narrative of what happened in the past and then extrapolate. Civilization has matured; social constructs have become more democratic; we are more prosperous; we are healthier; less of us suffer from war and violence. Even the poor Africans all have cellphones....

[I]f everything that we observe in the world around us honors limits to growth as a means to sustain itself, why is the underlying foundation for our current paradigm of progress ever-increasing growth?

Tom Wessels
The Myth of Progress

We'll just keep progressing until we reach the end of history. Some say we're already there.

Some say this linear, eschatological view of progress stems from a Abrahamic mindset, comparing it to the traditional cyclical cosmologies of Eastern religions. The irony is that this end of history – neoliberal capitalist society – is decidedly secular and has rejected its spiritual roots. Furthermore, since it was proclaimed by **Francis Fukuyama** some 25 years ago, it has been under assault from all sides. More on that later.

Martin Luther was instrumental in the development of notions of personal growth and progress in the West, with his emphasis on the perfectibility of the human soul, in contradistinction to the Original Sin of Catholic dogma. The corollary guilt in the Protestant Work Ethic, for those who fail to achieve that perfection, is the assumption that they simply didn't try hard enough. This puritanical judgementalism has turned deviation from the normative myth of progress into moral downfalls, rather than simple manifestations of diversity (in the case of gender identity), or illnesses (in the case of addiction), and a kind of toxic individualism that considers communal interdependence to be something abhorrent. Furthermore, evangelists for this paradigm of linear progress see only exponential material growth and expansion – a clearly unsustainable model. **Tom Wessels** and **James Lovelock** have each explored this in depth.

And by the way, I am not advocating Communism here. That ideology is just the flip-side of Capitalism, sharing the same underlying blind faith in progress and perfectibility. Just as the *devas* need the *asuras* in the Wheel of Life, these two economic models are codependent.

I think one thing that draws westerners to Buddhism is a motif that identity is fluid, our afflictions adventitious, that we can opt out of the materialist dialectic, and that we can achieve happiness attainable through stages of practice. It looks a lot like progress from our vantage point, and it seems sustainable because our True Nature is not eternally constrained by Original Sin. On the surface, Buddhist notions of progress may appear similar, but looking at progress from a Buddhist perspective is tricky.

Remember: **Huineng**, the not-yet Sixth Patriarch of Zen, defeated his rival, **Shenxui**, in a poetry debate by kicking the legs out from under Shenxui's progressivist stance.

Until we jettison our addiction to progress, we will never be able to see a different model for a sustainable future. When I look at the global debate about the shape of the future, it is largely based on how we can come up with new technology to plug the ever-increasing holes in our leaky vessel. **Buckminster Fuller**'s Spaceship Earth and all the other post-growth models still languish in the margins of serious investigation while we attend our hot yoga classes and read *Elephant Journal*.

The truth is out there. It's not too hard to find if you start looking. Consider, if you will, *Buddhist Technology: Bringing a New Consciousness to our Technological Future*, a 1997 keynote address by **Arthur Zajonc**, to the Seventeenth Annual E. F. Schumacher Lectures.

I am a bit of a geometry nerd. I am fascinated by geodesics, tensegrity, and discoveries of geometric forms like the scutoid. To me, they evoke the inner energy and cohesive interbeing of mandalas. Couldn't this be the basis for a more sustainable vision of Gaia?

Until post-growth solutions to the problems we see all around us are routinely filling broadcast media and trending on social media, our new mandala will remain but a design, and not an edifice. Buddhists should be instrumental in bringing post-growth vision into the mainstream. It has to be an integral part of our practice, a cornerstone of our engagement.

PROGRESS RESOURCES

- fukuyama.stanford.edu
- www.antioch.edu/new-england/faculty/thomas-wessels/
- www.jameslovelock.org
- www.bfi.org
- www.centerforneweconomics.org/publications/lectures/zajonc/arthur/buddhist-technology

PERFORMANCE

51

Holistic digital assistants have come a long way in just a few years. Meet the digital humans on the Soul Machines website to see what the state of the art looks like. Follow **Lilmiquela**, a virtual social media influencer, on Instagram. Search "deepfake video" on the web and read about what is just around the corner. Or stream that ancient (1999) movie, *The Matrix*, again.

> Every designer ought to have an intuitive sense of the practical limits of the performance of moving machinery and a broad sense of the adequacy of materials and the fabrication process.
>
> *Eugene Ferguson*
> Engineering and the Mind's Eye

Could you imagine an AI digital Bhante, Rinpoche, or Roshi? Just go visit one of the Buddhist "temples" in Second Life for a hint.

All of this begs the question: what is the relationship between performance and function?

When **Eugene Ferguson** wrote in 1993 about how engineering design had moved foolishly away from authentic, gut-level, personal experience to mathematical models, he was talking about fixing elevators and building locomotives. This is the same kind of experience praised by **Robert Pirsig** and **Matthew Crawford**. How far we have come!

Much as we may decry the relentless onslaught of a digital economy, we cannot deny the benefits of it. We may yearn for the tranquility of the monastery or the yogi's cave, but only for a vacation. In fact, the Zen Masters are in our midst and are online with the rest of us.

We humans love our rituals. We've got the fancy hats, the secret handshakes, the rites of passage. On the other hand, when we see demagogues using spectacle to overturn reason, or the degradation of civil debate into sloganeering and objectification, we see the danger of the excesses of ritual.

In the political sphere, performance becomes the handmaiden of tyranny, as **Timothy Snyder** so eloquently points out. In the religious sphere, performance becomes blind faith, Inquisitions, and persecution of those who do not confess the same creed. In either case, people are killed.

As Buddhists, we can not, should not, must not succumb to empty ritual, collusion with tyranny, or looking the other way. Authentic practice demands that we confront ignorance, hunger for power, and hatred.

Regardless of the mode of expression, whether we embrace digital forms of representation and performance or not, this is the touchstone by which Buddhists are rightly judged: do they walk the walk, or just talk the talk?

I am not saying our public *persona* must be perfect. Indeed, to claim we are perfect is already disingenuous. Our True Nature, yes. Our realization and actualization? Not so much. What I <u>am</u> saying is that what we do in the world is the necessary complement to our discovery of successive layers of meaning. There is no sound to one hand clapping.

In the "real" world, authenticity is well understood. It is recognized, storied, and lauded, in both mundane and extraordinary situations. When mediated by digital environments, facing the ethical dilemmas of emerging technologies, or grappling with phenomena that dwarf the personal and private in scale, authenticity is more elusive.

It is easy to raise up heroes; it allows the rest of us to be spectators. It could be a first responder, a dog who saves a child, a human rights activist. The phenomenon is merely the flip-side of the dynamic between a bully, a victim, and the bystander. In either case, being a bystander is the "safe" place. Bodhisattvas do not get to hang out in that place, but they do not need to act alone.

"Lone Wolf" is an epithet we usually ascribe to heroes and villains. It has nothing to do with how wolves really act; they live in tight-knit communities of cooperation, in balance with their ecospheres. Read **Jiang Rong**'s wonderful novel, *Wolf Totem*, or **Nate Blakeslee**'s book, *American Wolf*, for inspiration on that front.

Like wolves, Bodhisattvas are always building community, empowering others, and leading from consensus. It is here that our investment in gaining experience is of most value. We are stronger together. Old Eastern models of Sangha don't work in the West. We need to build new social structures that do, and that reflect an activist spirit. **Ken Jones** wrote about that in his revised edition of *The New Social Face of Buddhism* in 2003. I haven't seen anything like it since.

PERFORMANCE RESOURCES

- findingaids.hagley.org/xtf/view?docId=ead/2249.xml (Eugene Ferguson archives)
- www.soulmachines.com
- secondlife.com
- timothysnyder.org
- www.kenjoneszen.com

CORPORATION

52

The debate over whether or not a corporation is, can achieve the same goals as, or is entitled to the same rights as, a person or group of persons, has been a hot topic in recent years. **David Loy** tackled the question from a Buddhist perspective in his 2001 essay on whether corporations can become enlightened.

> As long as corporations remain the primary instruments of economic globalization, they endanger the future of our children and the world they will live in.
>
> *David Loy*
> Can Corporations Become Enlightened?

For a more detailed explanation of the way corporations work, see **Duncan Green**'s 2016 book, *How Change Happens.*

What I want to explore here is how the vector of transnational corporations has impacted our world since the dawn of the twenty-first century, how it is evolving, and how Buddhists may act meaningfully now.

As I write this, Apple has just become the first company worth a trillion dollars, and **Jeff Bezos** is the richest human in history, with a worth of $150 billion. On the radio, the new paperback edition of **Franklin Foer**'s 2017 book, *World Without Mind: The Existential Threat of Big Tech,* is being hailed as one of the 100 *New York Times* notable books of the year.

There is no doubt that technology companies are at the centre of much of our modern global economy, but they are hardly the only player. Transnational corporations have been around since the ancient days of empire, and in the past few hundred years have been a favoured method of colonization. You may remember that **Christopher Columbus** was under contract to the Spanish Crown to pillage the New World. Much of Britain's history under the House of Hanover is inseparably linked to the Hudson's Bay Company and East India Company.

Thinking of the world's large transnationals, such as Exxon, Nestlé, Monsanto, Barrick Gold, and the like, it's clear that neither ethics nor compassion are at the top of their priority lists. In fact, they seem to have no compunctions about putting profit over the impact of their actions. Ten of the world's 50 largest banks are Chinese, and that country's "One Belt, One Road" initiative is all about wielding financial power abroad.

In fact, the North American stock market is shrinking, smaller by 25 percent from the number of publicly-traded companies in 1976. Power and profit have been increasingly concentrated among the largest corporations, whose value is increasingly about their intellectual property.

Like the growing differential between CEO salaries compared to those of front line workers, this is yet another example of the increasing inequity between the rich and not-rich, and the diminished options presented to the not-rich for changing the rules of the game.

My Buddhist conclusion from all of this is that small is indeed beautiful and the less support I can give to these behemoths the better. I would much prefer a decentralized, diversified ecosystem to the economic equivalent of monoculture.

Nevertheless, I recognize that this world order is not about to go away any time soon. While Buddha's inclusion of Right Livelihood in the Eightfold Path provides us with some general direction, it requires considerable updating before being applicable to the intricacies of today's nuanced labour markets. What to do?

For starters, opt out; wake up from the hypnotic consumer coma that corporations are spinning. By the same token, don't expect much from government; the same corporations and oligarchs have the inside track on lobbying for legislation for their own benefit. They're in bed with the politicians who are beholden to them for campaign funds. If you're Buddhist (or really following any religion seriously, for that matter), you can't be complicit in this stuff. Constructive engagement is the way to go.

Using the Buddhist triad of body, speech, and mind: with our bodies, support local businesses wherever we can, and starve greedy companies by not buying their stuff (like guns, products with toxic additives, products from companies who don't respect human rights or the planet); with our speech, let corporations and government know we expect better of them (over and over again, I'm afraid); with our minds, put our energy into other forms of communal endeavours that strengthen the fabric of society and the planet.

CORPORATION RESOURCES

- enlight.lib.ntu.edu.tw/FULLTEXT/JR-MISC/101784.htm (David Loy's essay)
- how-change-happens.com
- www.theatlantic.com/author/franklin-foer
- en.wikipedia.org/wiki/Facebook–Cambridge_Analytica_data_scandal
- www.newyorker.com/magazine/2012/10/22/boss-rail

SHARE

53

The sharing economy was going to be the great equalizer. From Napster and torrents to Uber or Airbnb, app-enabled peer-to-peer networks were going to give us the power to free ourselves from greedy corporations. And as we know, that didn't go exactly as planned. Sharing became just another sector to be co-opted by corporations, relying on a bottomless pool of under-employed, unprotected gig workers.

> As people's access to the Internet grows we're seeing the sharing economy boom – I think our obsession with ownership is at a tipping point and the sharing economy is part of the antidote for that.
> *Richard Branson,*
> *estimated net worth $4.1B*

Uber and Airbnb have been in the news repeatedly for ethical lapses and unintended negative consequences to the communities where they operate.

E-books, music, and films have been another battleground in the sharing economy. It turns out that digital rights management means you don't actually buy a book, record, or film, but merely pay for the privilege of accessing them. Hence, you can't share them the way you would with a physical product. They illustrate a deeper principle at play: in the sharing economy, ownership is indeed being replaced, but by an even more precarious model of subscribership to a streaming service that could be cut off at any time.

For a comprehensive overview of the sharing economy, you can listen to an excellent panel discussion from the *Ideas* show by the Canadian Broadcasting Corporation, noted in the Resources section below.

A Buddhist model of sharing is quite different from what you might think. For starters, it is based on the principle that we share this planet with the entirety of other living beings. We are not apart from it, and it is not there for us to dominate: we need the planet more than it needs us.

Buddhist sharing is built around public good.

From toy and tool libraries to communal gardens and rummage sales, projects can be hyperlocal. These initiatives are often aimed at repairing damage created by corporations or governments who have abandoned the community. Aside from their physical presence, their primary goal is to build positive community relationships.

Sometimes, community-based initiatives take on a larger life, become movements, and radically transform urban planning, as illustrated in **Gary Hustwit**'s wonderful documentary, *Urbanized*, showcasing how good ideas can become physical realities in shared spaces.

At a global scale, challenge sites like Innocentive and Openideo crowd-source solutions to local problems from across the planet. Open education sites like Khan Academy and MOOC's (Massively Open Online Courses) put the power of knowledge in the hands of everybody. Organizations for social entrepreneurship empower millions.

Even more fundamentally, sharing must begin with initiatives that are designed to care for our planet, with no hidden agenda saying it is for our own personal benefit. What does that look like? Sri Lanka's Sarvodaya Shramadana organization is a great model.

Perhaps you might consider a conservancy organization dedicated to enhancing wilderness and wildlife. Perhaps you might get involved in re-wilding degraded ecosystems, cleaning up pollution. Perhaps your passion moves you to reduce your carbon footprint. The locus of your efforts is less important than your willingness to get involved, and to put your sweat equity into a healthier planet. Simply put: volunteer.

There is another way to see the future. **Stewart Brand**'s Long Now Foundation hopes to provide a counterpoint to today's accelerating culture and help make long-term thinking more common. They hope to foster responsibility in the framework of the next 10,000 years.

Huayan Buddhism talks about the simultaneous interpenetration of the three times and the ten directions. Seeing ourselves in the context of time through this lens can liberate us from the insistent clamour of our brief lives. We need not be concerned with our own idea of individual eternity in the afterlife if we become the present manifestation of a Gaia that is so much more precious. This is how Pure Lands are made, one lotus pond at a time.

The Three Jewels can be shared, and like love, they are undiminished by giving them away.

SHARE RESOURCES

- CBC Ideas - The Sharing Economy and the Public Good, Part 1 / www.cbc.ca/radio/popup/audio/player.html?autoPlay=true&clip-Ids=2634376305
- www.karuna.org
- www.sarvodaya.org
- longnow.org

GIVE

54

Volunteers are the heroes of society. They remind us that it is better to give than to receive. In fact, their contributions to society are the secret sauce making countries great. Governments may try to glorify volunteerism simply to avoid investing in the public good themselves. Corporations may play on the volunteer efforts of their employees. Tyrants may quash any individuals who promote grassroots collectives counter to the regime's agenda.

> The purpose of life is to discover your gift. The work of life is to develop it. The meaning of life is to give your gift away.
>
> *David Viscott*

These do nothing to take away the value of volunteerism, for the volunteers themselves, or for the organizations who benefit from their involvement. These relationships strengthen the bonds of communal well-being. It's safe to say that pretty much any volunteer activity (short of helping out at the gun range) is a good thing.

What about idiot compassion? This happens when we give people what they want because we can't stand to see them suffer. We throw the bum a dime rather than solve the systemic problems that put them on the street. We coach the softball team but never confront locker-room trash talk. We never say no.

These are all forms of enabling; they are situations where we dose ourselves with "compassion" rather than deal with uncomfortable feelings.

Caregiver burn-out is a common consequence of this behaviour. We give and give until we collapse. Insofar as organizations are reflections of the same types of dysfunctional relationships we see in families (see **John Bradshaw** on this topic), they are not necessarily going to help us. That is why self-care has become a popular topic in the caring professions of late.

As a designer, I recommend *Design for Care*, by **Peter Jones**, as a way to view the challenge from a foresight and strategic planning perspective. It's not about you; it's about the system. Design a better system and empower caregivers to deliver superior service without burning out.

Philanthropy is another aspect of giving that has been disrupted by technology. Aggregators, portals, open databanks, and grant proposal apps have simplified the process of finding money. Crowdfunding platforms have enabled pretty much anyone to reach out to everyone, using the same microfinance tools that allow you to buy a song for 99¢ online and get the receipt in your e-mail. But this doesn't mean that philanthropy is now a slam dunk.

Not too long ago, I read that the Zen Hospice Guest House in San Francisco has closed because of a lack of donations. Many Buddhist communities suffer from underfunding. The problem is endemic.

People are frequently accosted on the streets of North America by earnest young canvassers pitching one charitable cause or another. They are working on commission. Many charities take an unconscionable amount out of their donations for "operating costs." And then, of course, there are the tele-evangelists of all faiths who preach that helping them amass huge fortunes buys us a golden ticket to some paradise or another.

Questioning the nature of our giving, the motives of those to whom we give, and the end result of our giving, are essential if we are to remain true to the intent.

Similarly, it is important to remember that sweat equity is always worth more than cash, petitions, and slacktivism in its various forms.

One last point: our society does not do enough for caregivers. I don't mean the first responders, hospital staff, coaches, and so on. I mean those individuals who are caring for an infirm family member or children whose parents are absent for any number of reasons (and perhaps most tragic of all, children who are caring for adults). Our neighbours may be living lives of quiet desperation because the social safety net does not value their service, even while relying on it. They may be reluctant to reveal the depths of their struggles. This is where Buddhist chaplains can make a real impact, to a degree even greater than Buddhist teachers in Sangha settings. For a sense of what that looks like, see *A Thousand Arms: A Guide to Caring for Your Buddhist Community*, by **Daniel Clarkson Fisher** and **Nathan Jishin Michon**. Another excellent book on the subject is *Kalyanamitra: A Buddhist Model for Spiritual Care*, by **Rev. Monica Sanford**, to be published by Sumeru in 2020.

GIVING RESOURCES

- www.johnbradshaw.com
- rosenfeldmedia.com/books/design-for-care/
- sumeru-books.com/products/a-thousand-hands-a-guidebook-to-caring-for-your-buddhist-community
- sumeru-books.com/blogs/news/how-buddhist-chaplains-are-trained

PLAY

#NOWTRENDING

55 Are you #woke to what's going down in digital culture? Nyan Cat did this, that, or the other.... But they weren't expecting THIS. What happens next will shock you. This is hilarious. Click here....

From #sexynude to #entrepreneur to #FakeNews, the Internet has no shortage of titillating clickbait for us. It's a nonstop digital burlesque show – a kinetoscope of hashtags.

> Figuring out what the next big trend is tells us what we should focus on.
>
> Mark Zuckerberg

From its humble beginnings in 2007, the hashtag now pops up literally billions of times each day, encouraging us to like or follow a vast array of subjects. Like Oroboros swallowing its own tail, hashtags have even become self-referential meta-tags where the content is largely irrelevant. We do it for the 'gram. How did self-expression become self expression?

For a sociologist of popular culture, hashtags are the rosetta stone for our ever-shifting *zeitgeist*. You can check rankings on a daily basis, to find out, for example, the top ten Buddhist hashtags. (Hint: #dharmaburger didn't make the cut.)

Why do we click? Is it for instant tribal membership? Do hashtags somehow arouse our ancient hunter-gatherer brains by promising some form of nourishment? Are we scanning for potential threats, ignorance of which might exclude us from the tribe? Or is this some new form of play.

According to the *Oxford English Dictionary*, the definition of *play* is to "Engage in activity for enjoyment and recreation rather than a serious or practical purpose." Puritans hate such displays of impulsive joy. Since social media has become the addictive time-waster of choice for so many of us, one could argue that our fascination is a form of passive play. This passivity has many well-documented negative consequences.

What does healthy play look like? Psychologists say when children play, that is their work as they learn about how the world functions. They role-play different scenarios and relationships, as well as testing the laws of physics. In fact, we all play in this way. Our brains are constantly running simulations: what would my life be like if...? Like computer modelling, we are testing out alternative futures. We're wired for it. Several hours on a meditation cushion will demonstrate our natural capacity for getting lost in our own simulations, and this is perhaps why digital media are so appealing to us: they allow us to run through life's algorithms at top speed. The problem is that, like algorithms, we are playing with a limited ruleset.

In Vajrayana texts, reference is often made to the way accomplished teachers will play with elemental forces, as a demonstration of their liberation and also as a teaching tool for their students. For example, the **First Panchen Lama**'s *Lama Chöpa*, a practice manual written about 400 years ago and still very much in use today, contains the lines:

> OM...
> I visualize myself as a Guru Yidam
> with a nature inseparable from the three Vajras.
> AH...
> This nectar of uncontaminated, pristine awareness
> HUM...
> Without moving from a state of Bodhicitta,
> I play with, to satisfy the deities within my form.

I interpret those words as an invitation to engagement, rather than as a rejection of worldly activities. However, engaging in this play is very different from being a captive of trends and pop culture. It embodies the truths of the *Prajnaparamita Hridaya* or *The Platform Sutra of the Sixth Patriarch*. It's called timeless wisdom for a reason. It's a meme generator.

On a lighter note, I love **Kusala Bhikshu**'s frequent Buddhist cartoons on Facebook, as well as those archetypal *New Yorker* cartoons involving Zen monks or mountaintop sages. As **Arthur Koestler** noted in his 1964 book, *The Act of Creation*, humour can often take us out of our habitual thought track and, crucially, show us a new perspective. Koestler, no stranger to Eastern religion, clearly had Zen koans in mind, and he deserves a round of one-hand-clapping applause for his insightful book on the subject.

#NOWTRENDING RESOURCES
- www.wired.com/2017/05/oral-history-hashtag/
- www.vice.com/en_us/article/7xegk4/thailand-buddhist-monks-video-games
- www.encyclopedia.com/children/encyclopedias-almanacs-transcripts-and-maps/theories-play
- ftw.usatoday.com/2019/04/poker-scott-wellenbach-buddhist-donates-winnings

@TROLL

56

Many ancient mythologies embraced animistic belief in spirits of place who manifested elemental forces. These beings were normally inimical to humans, perhaps because they represented threats in the natural world. In Norse mythology, these elemental beings were called trolls, and they often made it their business to harrass all who passed their way, demanding propitiation and threatening violence.

"Who's that tramping over my bridge?" roared the troll.
Three Billy Goats Gruff
Norwegian folk tale

In the Anthropocene, trolls have taken on a different meaning. Now, instead of being forces of nature, they embody malevolent human agents. We typically find them fomenting dissent on the Internet, where their preferred *modus operendi* includes cyber-bullying, shaming, surrogate rage, flamewars, and comment threads that seem always to end with somebody being compared to Hitler.

There are, of course, many varieties of troll (as darkpsychology.co enumerates), from those who viciously attack individuals (to the tragic degree that some victims commit suicide), to those who attack our social fabric (such as **Alex Jones** at Infowars, or Russian trolls and bots out to destabilize liberal democracies), to "white hat" trolls who call out duplicitous leaders for lies and oppression.

There is definitely evil in the world; an entire chapter of this book is dedicated to the subject of violence, but in our focus here, I am talking about the means. Trolling is a form of harmful speech, in direct contravention of one of the five primary Buddhist precepts for ethical conduct.

Engaging with trolls is a tricky business; very often any attempt to counter their attacks simply whets their appetites for more. As **Mark Twain** famously said: "Never argue with stupid people; they will drag you down to their level and then beat you with experience."

Human nature has not changed in the brief time we have inhabited this planet, but our technology certainly has. Cataloguing the morass that is the Internet, we see the three major swamps: for desire, the bottomless pit of clickbait; for anger, the flaming gas of trolls; and for ignorance, the spam that chokes off 90 percent of its bandwidth. Together, they are the weapons of mass distraction.

With regard to trolls, cyber-bullying of vulnerable young people is perhaps the most appalling instance, specifically because of the vulnerability of the victims. Unlike the sophisticated statecraft of cyber-warfare amongst vigilant governmental protagonists, cyber-bullying is often the work of "relatively decent" youths who descend into mob savagery in a process well-documented by **William Golding**'s 1954 novel, *Lord of the Flies*. By relatively decent, I mean that these bullies are redeemable. Yes, our ape heritage is brutish. But we have enough experience to know that abusive attitudes and behaviours are taught, and we have the resources to mount credible diversion and rehabilitation programs.

I am not sure why reactionary forces in our society wish to prevent young people from having the understanding of what cyber-bullying is, its consequences, and tools to protect themselves from its malevolence, but in many school districts, there is strong pushback to such programs. For young people just coming into their adult identities, gender politics are foundational, and thus often a focus for trolls. I believe in the idea that knowledge is power. As a teacher and as a Buddhist, I support sex education that addresses Internet issues such as consent, cyber-bullying, sexting, privacy (or lack thereof), safe space, and so on.

Indeed, ministering to those who have suffered the trauma of Internet attacks and countering the culture of toxic masculinity should be key planks in any Buddhist welfare program. There can be no place in Buddhist practice for trolling others, whether they are collectively the members of an oppressed group (such as Myanmar's Rohingya), individual whistleblowers who have called out abusive, coercive behaviour by Buddhist leaders, or Sangha members who are gender non-conforming.

Buddhists who ride the energy of anger must be extremely careful that they are not under the spell of Mara's demons. They don't just come in dreams; they come in memes. This is why non-violent dissent such as civil disobedience is safer than a call to arms. In the personal realm, remember the *Dhammapada*: hate cannot drive out hate.

@TROLL RESOURCES

- darkpsychology.co/troll
- www.psychologytoday.com/us/blog/better-living-technology/201408/why-the-online-trolls-troll
- www.alternet.org/media/Internet-trolls-explain-why-they-do-what-they-do
- www.newyorker.com/magazine/2018/08/20/alex-jones-the-first-amendment-and-the-digital-public-square

CELEBRITY

57

In our society, it pays to be a celebrity. In fact, it pays so well that celebrity has become a career in and of itself, a goal many entrepreneurs and other up-and-comers strive for. Whether it is YouTube ad revenue, deals for product endorsements, spokesperson TV ads, spin-off businesses, breaking the Internet, or simply making it into life on the D-list, fame has become our obsession. There's even a whole genre devoted to infamy, with sites like FailBlog and the Darwin Awards. We've got to stop making stupid people famous.

> Every time I say something that's extremely truthful out loud, it literally breaks the Internet.
>
> Kanye West

In this age of personal branding, it all begs the question: what is an authentic life?

There is something inherently human about putting others up on pedestals. We do it with **The Dalai Lama** and **Thich Nhat Hanh**. When it comes to Buddhist teachers featured in the media, or Buddhist writers, there is definitely an A-list. Meme-worthy Buddhist quotes are regularly dangled as clickbait. And yet, the advice we receive from **Ayya Khema**, founder of the Sakyadhita International Association of Buddhist Women, is that we should be nobody, going nowhere. The *Dhammapada* says the track of a wise man is like that of a bird in the sky. What's up with that? It's enough to give you cognitive dissonance.

Although our fascination with celebrities has roots far back through history, the advent of mobile computing (*aka* smartphones) has really been a transformative enabling technology, even for Buddhist monks, according to many pundits. Those pundits are often invested in spreading the connectivity gospel. Google "monks and mobile phones" and you'll get almost 7 million hits. It's not about the device.

I would contend that the addiction is with screens of all kinds, and the virtual world they offer in lieu of living in the material world. I would also contend that our digital dossier has significant repercussions for us in the surveillance state. That was covered in a previous section of the book.

How does one become a cult leader? What is the mix of charisma, genuine good intentions, inspirational impact on those around us, and personal failings that get acted out on others? It is so easy to be seduced. Perhaps *failings* is too weak a word. Perhaps these character traits would better be described as narcissistic, sociopathic, Machiavellian, defilements. It's hard just to call them failings when they are so destructive to others. As the saying goes, "Power corrupts."

I believe that trust in the broader Sangha is a counterweight to demagoguery. Institutionalized accountability is necessary to prevent rogue teachers from gaining unhealthy dominance, and it is the responsibility of those institutions to ensure that policies to protect their Sanghas are actively employed. Sadly, religious institutions are often more concerned with covering up scandals, or they are content to serve as functionaries of cultural genocide (as was the case of Canada's residential schools for aboriginal children, as well as it is in Myanmar today).

This is why understanding the psychology of cults is essential. Each of us must trust our gut feelings when something smells fishy or walks and quacks like a duck. Rather than second-guessing our instincts, and engaging in doublethink, we need to remember the maxim of Ockham's Razor: the simplest explanation tends to be the right one.

For those individuals who are truly called to be teachers, or who find themselves in that role, I pray that they have the integrity and the wise preceptors to guide them on that very dangerous path.

For the rest of us, an ounce of prevention is in order. Recognize the fame game for what it is, and step off the celebrity merry-go-round. The vertigo will quickly pass. Renunciation is not an all-or-nothing practice. We can pull back from aspects of worldly life that harm or hypnotize us, without the need to shave our heads and become forest monks. We don't need to turn everything we do into some entrepreneurial opportunity.

As **Alexander Berzin** says in *Wise Teacher, Wise Student*, "Relationships with spiritual teachers need to be built slowly. This allows for the natural growth of trust on both sides. Students need confidence in teachers' qualifications, to trust that they will not mislead them. Teachers need confidence that students are serious, to trust that they will not misunderstand or misuse the teachings."

CELEBRITY RESOURCES

- sociology.iresearchnet.com/sociology-of-culture/celebrity-culture/
- hackspirit.com/master-buddhist-thich-nhat-hanh-reveals-brutal-truth-happiness-less-2-lines/
- studybuddhism.com/en/advanced-studies/lam-rim/student-teacher-relationship/matching-the-level-of-teacher-with-the-level-of-student/different-levels-of-spiritual-teachers-and-students

MEDIA

58

The quest for more knowledge is baked into our evolution as humans. We seek information to better control our situation, find resources, avoid threats, and advance our possibilities. Sometimes that information came to us orally in the form of stories and myths, evoking in us not just knowledge but an emotional connection to the ideas we were receiving.

This program contains scenes that may be disturbing for some. Viewer discretion is advised.
Standard content warning

With the advent of writing and printing, our connection to the stories became defined by the medium through which they were conveyed. A plethora of writers, scribes, playwrights, reporters, authors, editors, typesetters, printers, and the like sprang up to fill the need. The fifth estate was born.

With the advent of radio and television broadcasting, the paradigm changed again, bringing an immediacy and holistic quality to storytelling that both harkened back to our oral roots and propelled us forward into virtual reality. The role of television in shaping culture was a particularly passionate topic of debate during its heyday. **Marshall McLuhan** wrote eloquently on the subject in the 1950's and 1960's, and his books are still very relevant. *Four Arguments for the Elimination of Television*, by **Gerry Mander**, was a bestseller in 1978. We can only imagine what these thinkers would have made of the 500-channel universe or the Internet.

On a parallel timeline, the evolution of audio-visual recording technologies brought more choice to audiences, a move from broadcasting to narrowcasting with cable television further segmenting audiences, and the advent of geostationary communications satellites connected us to the global village. All of this was pre-Internet, and one cannot fully contemplate the state of media today without understanding all the issues involved in the way we got here. For example, the entwined history of media and celebrity in the last millenium was well-documented in the 1985 classic, *Intimate Strangers: The Culture of Celebrity in America*, by **Richard Schickel**.

So, when we talk now about our relationship to media, the Internet, streaming, sampling, interactivity, intellectual property, social media, gaming addiction, fake news, the digital divide, clickbait, the ephemeral nature of digital archives, the industrial ecology of devices, VR, privacy, consent, data mining, screentime, or a host of other contemporary issues in media studies, history is lurking in the shadows. And yet, the paradox of our fascination with crime and punishment, killing, sex, police, doctors, sports, disasters, celebrities, and bad news remains unresolved.

Ultimately, our relationship with media is not about technology. As the saying goes: "Believing is seeing." We make our own reality and then populate it with experiences that reinforce our perspective. But there is another dimension to this dynamic: our shared experience and the very real impact of choices others make and how they affect us. **George Orwell** made the role of media in that very clear, in his 1949 book, *1984*.

Buddhist leaders have been all over the map on how to deal with media, from abstinence to passionate embrace. Where is the Middle Way?

Certainly, waking up from the group sleepwalk of mainstream culture is a necessary component of liberation. That means maintaining a sensible media diet. However, I advocate neither the social media asceticism of **Jaron Lanier** nor the digital hedonism of **Buddhist Geeks**. I do recommend a skeptical frame of mind when evaluating what we consume, a preference for documentaries from a broad range of sources, and, since so many of us now are creators as well as consumers of media, a conscious ongoing effort to follow Buddha's advice: not to do evil, but to do all that is good, and to purify the mind.

In light of the many recent scandals concerning the abuse of power by Buddhist teachers and governments, it's also important to remember that Buddhists are not immune to manipulation of media to hide their crimes, promote debased agendas, or oppress others.

The same skepticism that reveals the pernicious or shallow nature of most samsaric media content can and must be applied to Buddhist groups to evaluate whether cult mentality is at play. Dis-illusioning ourselves is an essential component of practice and that also involves protecting ourselves from our own gullibility. This revolution will not be televised.

MEDIA RESOURCES

- nook.cs.ucdavis.edu/~koehl/Teaching/ECS188/Reprints/Mander_TV_78.pdf
- www.kirkusreviews.com/book-reviews/richard-schickel-5/intimate-strangers-the-culture-of-celebrity/
- www.researchgate.net/publication/250172309_Why_Are_Buddhists_So_Nice_Media_Representations_of_Buddhism_and_Islam_in_the_United_States_Since_1945

MOBILE

59

Let's not call it a phone any more. Not a cell phone, mobile phone, or smart phone. It's a super computer in your pocket that happens to make phone calls along with a hell of a lot of other important stuff. You're more likely to use it for browsing the Internet, shopping, keeping up with your social networks and emails, playing games, listening to music, taking pictures, doing your banking, watching TV, getting driving directions, hailing an Uber, or reading a book. Phoning people is way down the list. It's all about the cloud now.

Every once in a while, a revolutionary product comes along that changes everything.
Steve Jobs
iPhone introduction, 2007

Mobility has introduced us to the world of ubiquitous computing (ubicomp, for short). In the infinitesimal decade since the launch of the iPhone, so much has changed. The number of mobile phone users in the world passed the five billion mark in 2019. We are now cyborgs in all but flesh.

Mobile has been a tremendous boon, but it is not without its costs. All those batteries ravage the environment. The thirst for coltan has plunged central Africa into conflict, chaos, and extinctions. Our devices and their infrastructure are frying us with microwaves. Our brains are rewiring themselves. Texting and driving is a killer. Students in school are compulsively addicted; they can't put their devices away and be fully present. With every answer at our fingertips, we've lost the ability to ask the right questions. We can't spell, can't write, and can barely type. We've surrendered our privacy and autonomy, exposing ourselves ever more to the surveillance state. Since we reached smartphone market saturation in 2012, negative emotional states in adolescents have spiked. The sheer complexity of it all leaves us vulnerable to being taken advantage of, and to all manner of crimes. Yet there is no putting the genie back in the bottle.

Futurist **Don Tapscott**, author of *Growing Up Digital* (1997) and *Grown Up Digital* (2008), has written effusively about the Net Generation. Literally millions of articles have been written about how cell phones are changing society (and our brains). As a high school teacher, I've had a front row seat at the revolution, and I am not particularly encouraged.

Disclaimer: I have a mobile phone and I use it a lot. I like to think it's mostly for work, but I recognize that I waste a lot of time with it too. There's a definite addictive quality to those screens, and in the attention economy that is critical. Sticky eyeballs are currency for app developers and they freely admit to baking in obsessive qualities that keep us hooked.

Ask your career Buddhist teacher about mobile phones, and most of them will tell you they don't know much. They didn't grow up with a phone. If you see pictures or cartoons of monks or nuns with mobile phones, the captions usually refer to some cognitive dissonance: hey, those two things don't go together! Even the **Buddhist Geeks**, self-professed acolytes of digital Dharma, had no podcasts on the topic of mobile phones. In fact, their organization went belly-up a while back and was only recently reborn with a different monetization framework. That means not many Buddhists find this stuff mainstream.

To me, that sounds like a lot of Buddhist teachers are out of touch with current realities, and certainly out of touch with the lived experience of young people today. We like to talk about how Buddhism changed as it moved from culture to culture, but we usually mean from country to country. Buddhist adaptation to global digital culture is still in a very nascent state. What do you say to the duct-cleaning phone pitch from Dacca?

As a high school teacher, I'm constantly telling my students they have to be lifelong learners. I too am constantly learning new skills and applications, adapting to my changing circumstances. That's how best to respond to impermanence.

Somehow, we have this idea that Buddhist teachers are on a Path of No More Learning. We set them up in stasis. That's no good.

Every organization requires comprehensive policies to function effectively. A communications management plan is one such policy. Does your temple, dojo, or monastery have one? Are you actively pursuing initiatives to learn more about the rapidly-shifting landscape of mobile computing, and to respond with engaging programming for your Sangha members? Rather than just banning cell phones, or ignoring them, or embracing existing apps willy-nilly, what's your plan?

MOBILE RESOURCES

- dontapscott.com
- wearesocial.com/blog/2019/01/digital-2019-global-Internet-use-accelerates
- newbuddhist.com/discussion/23907/can-monks-use-smart-phones
- studybuddhism.com/en/advanced-studies/history-culture/buddhism-in-modern-times/applying-buddhist-principles-in-the-age-of-social-media

PORN

60

There's that old joke, where the sex-worker says, "It's a business doing pleasure with you." Whether it's sex porn, food porn, cabin porn, gun porn, or some other addiction, the dynamic is the same: the commodification of desire. We all have thirsts we cannot quench, we look for ways to sublimate our emptiness or dull the pain, and we struggle with shame. It stands to reason that since sexuality is so primal to our being, it is the locus for much of our dukkha.

> Sex can be renounced – but sexuality cannot. We can't avoid sexual issues by avoiding sex, or by dismissing its importance, or by showing disrespect to our own or other people's sexual feelings.
>
> *Sallie Tisdale*

In other words, fascination with engaging in sex, looking at sex, or reading about sex, or fantasizing about sex, is hardwired into us. Have a read of Buddhist author **Sallie Tisdale**'s early book, *Talk Dirty to Me*, or clinical psychologist **David Ley**'s book, *Ethical Porn for Dicks*, for a bit more on that subject. Everybody has an opinion.

We tend to be very proscriptive about what is and is not acceptable to our tribe. Much of the public discourse about porn is really about negotiating a shifting sexual landscape among consenting adults, or how young people just beginning to explore their own sexuality may be misled by divergent cultural narratives to which they are exposed, putting them in dangerous situations.

I see two problems. The first involves exclusive truth claims by tribal leaders that do not permit expression of the true range of healthy sexuality by criminalizing it. The second involves those who use others for their own sexual fulfillment, in a way that is dehumanizing, abusive, and coercive.

In other words, it's not about sex, but about violence toward others. Of course, violence is a topic of great importance to Buddhists, and in this case it happens to be sexual violence. The problem, as **Richard Pryor** pointed out, is that "You can't talk about fucking in America, people say you're dirty. But if you talk about killing somebody, that's cool."

If you're going to deconstruct that, you've got to take on everyone from the National Rifle Association to Harlequin Romances.

My best translation (or modernization) of the Buddhist precept about sex is: "Don't be sexually irresponsible." It's not an absolute demand for celibacy, and it must be considered contextually. Non-violence (*ahimsa*) is the underlying principle that should be guiding one's evaluation. Of course, there a million shades of gray, but domination and control are antithetical to enlightened sexuality, however they are gussied up.

From a neurological perspective, our response to porn (focused on sex or any other desire) is like all addictive thirsts we are unable to slake – we want the dopamine rush. No amount of ideology is going to master our unruly hormones.

This is particularly relevant to teen-agers, insofar as access to sexual porn is easy, and we are deluged daily with other forms of porn (fashion, food, experiences, etc.) encouraging us to consume with a gusto that would make a hungry ghost blush. Given that our prefrontal cortex (the brain's Executive Functioning control centre) isn't fully developed until we are about 26 years old, young people represent a highly susceptible target.

In the "just say no" camp, we have the absolutists who are convinced the solution is anathema to any other expression of sexuality apart from their own circumcised definition of what's divinely approved.

In the "harm reduction through education and decriminalization" camp, we have the relativists who are convinced the solution is sex education that includes topics like sexting, gender identity, rape culture, STI's, sex crimes, human trafficking, and consent, as well as the mechanics of sex presented without euphemisms.

I'm definitely in the latter camp, but I would go further to say that if we don't understand sexual consumerism in the context of society's larger problems around materialism, misogyny, abuse in all its forms, intolerance, and so on, then our discussions of porn will lack enough perspective to dismantle its dependent origination. That would be like arguing for tighter automotive gasoline emission standards, without discussing our addiction to fossil fuels.

We need more openness to alternative ways of thinking.

PORN RESOURCES

- sallietisdale.com
- shessomebodysdaughter.org
- maggiestoronto.ca
- www.tandfonline.com/toc/usac20/current (*Journal of Sexual Addiction and Compulsivity*)

GAMES

61

There is a list of games that Shakyamuni Buddha would not play, and that his disciples should likewise not play, because he believed them to be a cause for negligence. That is certainly not how we think of games today.

For videogame designer, popular author (and self-identified Buddhist) **Jane McGonigal**, games represent a fun way to learn, get healthy, and enhance our skills. For architect and futurist **Buckminster Fuller**, the World Game was a tool that would facilitate a comprehensive, anticipatory, design science approach to the problems of the world. For those who study game theory, the study of mathematical models of strategic interaction between rational decision-makers helps to predict behaviour. For sociologists and for anthropologists, games reveal deeper truths about our civilization.

> Reality is broken. Game designers can fix it.
>
> Jane McGonigal

In spite of precepts in pretty much every major world religion against gambling, we have no shortage of lotteries, casinos, sports betting, bingo halls, childrens' card and board games, dungeons and dragons, and gaming consoles. Games are a trope in our movies, music, and books. It is the platform for much of our human interaction, and a lens through which we evaluate politics, business, education, and so on. We put on our game face and we play the game.

In many instances, games act as social glue. The goal is not to win, but to enjoy the experience with others. However, that function is increasingly being mediated by interactive digital technology. For example: we are eagerly awaiting the arrival of fully immersive virtual reality (such as the holodecks portrayed on Star Trek); we debate the relative merits of Oculus Rift versus Google Glass; we suffered through the media frenzy around PokémonGO (an augmented-reality geo-tagging game); we watched the Watson supercomputer beat humans on the Jeopardy quiz show; we "play" sports at home with our Wii consoles or "brain games" to stave off dementia; and our government-run gambling consortia encourage us to "play responsibly."

There is an entire field of design devoted to UX (user experience), known as interaction design. As our gaming increasingly involves role playing and simulations, where experience is the commodity and the goal, it has become a key battleground in the attention economy. With the advent of artificial intelligence, chatbots, and humanoid robots, we are edging closer to the uncanny valley. Like all battlefields, it is shrouded in the fog of ambiguity. On one hand, we are enchanted by the possibilities offered by our own intelligence, objectified, externalized, and enhanced. On the other hand, we see a world in which real life is extraneous, and in some ways irrelevant. We ponder a future of cute robot companions for old folks, sex robots for the lusty, and Westworld robots we can kill for sport, all without ethical qualms. We even have Buddhist funerals for robots (not to mention Buddhist monk robots you can order online to officiate at services).

Back in the real world, sports commentators and runners speak of a Zen-like flow where players are "in the zone." Buddhist commentators ponder whether or not there is a place for contact sports in Buddhism, while others make movies about the soccer obsession of young Buddhist monks. Magazine articles and documentary films explore the "mind games" that abusive gurus use to build their cults.

Suffice it to say, there is no shortage of hot topics involving games and Buddhism.

Back in the 1960's I read *Magister Ludi (The Glass Bead Game)*, by **Hermann Hesse** (who also wrote the immensely popular *Siddhartha*), a wonderful novel presenting the protagonist's early spiritual journey as a process of interdisciplinary harmonization, a vision that still resonates for me. I find his vision much like that of Huayan Chinese Buddhism, or the concept of Namgyal in Vajrayana Buddhism.

The big questions here are: how do we navigate through mainstream contemporary ideas about games to reach a truly Buddhist understanding? How do we wean ourselves off samsaric involvement in games (especially the violent ones) with relevant Dharma teachings? And how do we incorporate positive aspects of our gaming nature (*Homo ludens*) into our Dharma practice?

GAMES RESOURCES

- www.superbetter.com
- www.bfi.org/about-fuller/big-ideas/world-game
- gamestudies.org
- zen-athlete.myshopify.com
- www.buddhistdoor.net/features/is-there-a-place-for-contact-sports-in-buddhism

INFORMATION

62

"Information wants to be free." The 1960's phrase is attributed to **Stewart Brand**, founder of The *Whole Earth Catalogue*, quoted in his talk at a 1984 hacker conference, and again in a published conversation with **Steve Wozniak** from 1985 regarding the tension between that view and the view that information wants to be expensive because it is so valuable (according to *Wikipedia*). We search for new alternatives for intellectual property, like Creative Commons, a third way.

> Water may be free, but plumbing costs money.
> *Eshu Martin, Zenwest*

That tension is still unresolved, and it is strikingly analagous to the debate around whether Dharma teachings should be free, as well as how Buddhist precepts can or should be applied to the consumption of information.

As a "product," the Dharma is certainly information. Some might say it is the world's heritage and shared intellectual property. Nevertheless, when pirate editions of Dharma books appear on peer-to-peer torrents sites, it is a perversion of that trust. Those authors have worked hard to bring their books into the world and deserve the remuneration that would allow them to continue their work.

Once upon a time, people read animal tracks and clouds. More recently, we distilled information into printed words to augment experience. But symbolic information has increasingly become the focus of our our work, in ways that bear little obvious connection to lived experience. Our heads are filled with passwords, algorithms, or menu sequences, multitasking and grinding metacognitive gears like crazy. We suffer from information overload.

After work, we suffer information hangovers. We find people (and real life) much harder to relate to than the world in our screens. Empathy is an increasingly rare commodity. Some lose themselves in infotainment. Others go post-literate.

Buddhist teachers call out this spectator ethos as but a simulacrum of authentic living and that somehow becomes pop shorthand for what Buddhism (Zen, especially) is all about. It's a rather reductionist view.

In our topsy-turvy world, we forget the facts but remember where to find them. For example, what's the atomic weight of Iron? When we let the algorithms do the heavy lifting for us, our critical thinking skills wither away. It's not easy to make sense of this new situation. We worry that students know how to find the right answers, but not how to ask the right questions. We experiment with educational concepts like the flipped classroom. We abhor cellphones in the classroom and at the same time struggle valiantly to incorporate them into our lessons. Such ambivalence.

We ponder the future of educational technology. The Internet of Things (IoT) keeps us up at night. Is there a mindfulness app for that? Well, yes, of course there is. In fact, your entire physical condition can be quantified and displayed on your smartwatch.

In this era of fake news, a war on science, online trolls, bots out to subvert rational decision-making, and a tsunami of superficial messages, even information itself dissolves into a churning miasma of uncertainties.

For those who yearn to return to the mythical simplicity of the forest monk, to abandon themselves to a guru, or to be happy in the midst of everyday life, information is the enemy. However, it is like the tar-baby in the *Uncle Remus* story from 1880; the more Brer Rabbit fought with the tar-baby, the more entangled he became. Or, to use a more contempory analogy, Dr. Strange makes his way to the mountain monastery, but his unfolding "woke" story is still all about fighting. True escape becomes co-opted by worldly paradigms again. It is an infinite labyrinth in the pattern of **Jorge Luis Borges**' *Garden of the Forking Paths*.

The Buddha said it is extremely difficult for one to encounter the Dharma – the instruction manual for liberation – in this degenerate age. No kidding! When you add untrustworthy Dharma teachers into the mix, it gets even more difficult. No wonder we feel paralyzed when purveyors of Dharma are themselves #metooguru examples of spiritual materialism.

At the same time, brave Bodhisattvas deconstruct the false premises of samsara – privilege, inequality, and oppression – by bringing information into the open, sharing, and showing a different way. They are infused with the spirit of Ksitigarbha.

INFORMATION RESOURCES

- creativecommons.org
- www.knewton.com/infographics/flipped-classroom
- www.envisioning.io/legacy/education
- www.lionsroar.com/mindful-media-consumption/
- www.cjr.org/innovations/mindfulness-media-buddha.php

ART

63

Clearly, art is an integral component of humanity. The contours of art are porous – embracing the sheer joy of creativity, expressions of sacred yearning, all aspects of design, or propaganda. We enjoy being in its presence, communing or consuming it. We lionize the artists (or fear them) for revealing deeper truths about existence. We doubt our own artistic abilities, but cherish the experience of making art. We recognize its role in the education of children. The history of art, and our relationship with it, is complicated.

The world's earliest-known cave painting of an animal has been discovered on Borneo in Indonesia. It dates back to at least 40,000 years ago, a new study says.

USA TODAY, 11-7-2018

Neuroscience tells us that the two sides of our brains function in different ways. The left side is logical, linear, verbal, and organizational. The right side is associative, nonlinear, pictorial/musical, and lateral. We usually associate art with those right-side functions: the flash of insight; the surprise connections; the fugue; the immediacy. Still, most artists will tell you that left-side capabilities are also essential if one is to be successful. As the saying goes: Success is 1% inspiration and 99% perspiration. And since Dharma is the Middle Way, we don't want to favour one mental mode over another.

Arthur Koestler famously explored how artistic process works, in his book *The Act of Creation*. He describes it in a fashion that reminds me of the Zen portrayal of Enlightenment as a "turning about in the mind." Unfortunately, like mistaking the pointing finger for the moon, many of us have elevated art to a religion, while others simply see it as hedonism, characterizing artists as leeches at worst or cultural workers at best. I would say that art shows us how malleable reality really is: believing is seeing.

Separating art from politics is impossible. All politicians want art to serve their political agendas. We're familiar with how "enemies of the state" were airbrushed out of photos in revisionist history; it's so much easier now with Photoshop. We're familiar with the memes and tropes of "fake news," the banned books, the show trials of artists like **Ai Weiwei**. We've seen the campaigns to return art to its country of origin from the museums of the colonial explorers, like **Sir Aurel Stein**, who plundered it; we've also seen museums and galleries presenting "foreign" art as if it is the last trophy from a lost civilization. The obscene auction prices for "masterpieces" give us a vicarious frisson for the plutocrats at play. Outrage at the vandals who destroy world heritage sites like Bamiyan or Palmyra unites us.

PLAY

Separating art from business is impossible too. Whether we're streaming the Victoria's Secret fashion show, grooving to the hit parade, shopping for a mobile phone, planning a vacation, or playing a first-person shooter video-game, we are participating in the ecosphere of art and design as consumer product. We must, perforce, consider the broader implications of our actions. Is there an ethical supply chain? Are we supporting militarism, imbibing the cultural Kool-Aid, or chasing a straw man? Can we draw a line between "pure" art and "commercial" artisan? Who's **Banksy**?

The technology of art continues to evolve at a breakneck pace. The paradigms keep morphing. As a society, we invest billions of dollars and hours in technology designed to facilitate the delivery of art. Our relationship with that art technology spans the gamut from passive spectator to immersive interactor, from owner to renter, from solitary to communal. These days, it seems the central issue is not the evolution of aesthetics (Romantic vs Baroque, Modern vs Post-modern, etc.), but rather the evolution of media (Broadcast vs Narrowcast, Augmented vs Virtual, etc.).

Can art be part of our Buddhist practice? Have you ever taken a Zen Photography course? Done Ikebana? Made a sumi-e brush enso? Sewn a Rakusu? Prepared an Oriyoki meal? Attended a tea ceremony? Written a haiku? Why are all these Japanese arts so closely associated with Buddhist practice, while those of other traditions have failed to capture the imagination of Westerners? Can arts we don't normally associate with Buddhist practice still be part of it? Is there Zen blacksmithing?

Perhaps the koan of art as practice is better answered with a Bodhisattva view: does it alleviate suffering? Is it inclusive? Does it deconstruct constrictive views and challenge us to "Go Beyond" as the *Heart Sutra* instructs in the final gatha?

ART RESOURCES

- bigthink.com/robby-berman/a-tibetan-monk-gives-us-a-peek-inside-the-wonder-of-buddhist-art
- www.buddhistdoor.net/features/the-trendy-buddha-skillful-music-for-propagating-buddhism
- qz.com/835253/leonard-cohens-tortured-love-affair-with-zen-buddhism/

COMPUTERS

REALITY

■
64

Buddhists love to talk about reality. The entire project of Buddhism has the direct realization of reality as its goal. It's supposed to be experiential, but the collections of Abhidhamma and Prajnaparamita are enormous. For most of the history of Buddhism, the focus was on the interface of objective phenomena, perception, and consciousness. The methodology was to reveal the emptiness of imputed inherent nature through the quadrilemma of fourfold dependent origination, following **Nagarjuna**'s logic.

In my opinion, there is no aspect of reality beyond the reach of the human mind.
Stephen Hawking

In the digital age, in common parlance, reality is an entirely different beast. We talk about virtual reality and augmented reality, while we ponder the nature of reality in the probable near future. This brave new world is decidedly ambiguous and our feelings about it are decidedly ambivalent. More and more of it seems to exist within the computer screen, robotic process automation, or the screenless, haptic Internet of Things. Our avatars play in Massively Multiplayer Online Role Playing Games (MMORPG's), our workgroups collaborate in the cloud, and algorithms manage the minutiae of our public life. **Ray Kurzweil** envisions a time, in our lifetime, of cyborg singularity. The definition of reality is up for grabs, and we're all busy curating our personas.

In this modern age, we certainly understand that reality is a consensual group experience, and that it is subjective. Pharmacopia has allowed us to regulate mood and see the connection between brain chemistry and "reality." We have also developed a healthy skepticism about fake news, marketing propaganda, and being manipulated for the benefit of other people's agendas. That is quite congruent with the Buddha's message. However, humanity's absorption in screen-time and addiction to digital modes of thinking have led to an alarming dysphoria and narrowing of cognitive brain function, particularly among young people. Buddhism, mindfulness, and spirituality in general, have been recast as a yellow brick road back to nature and reconnecting with our authentic selves.

This reality is just like clay and we are the potters. These days, we use computing as our model and cast reality in its image. The paradigm of augmented reality is flipped: computing is the reality and it is augmented by what? Lived experience?

The entire Mahayana project is about subverting our habitual notion of reality. Isn't that what the narratives of dream, bardo, Sambhogakaya and deity yoga are all about? They're all virtual. Criticisms of Yogacara by the Modern Consciousness Only School reject its function as a training vehicle, but true Consciousness Only is not solipsism. However, I digress.

Some, like **Vincent Horn** and the Buddhist Geeks collective, are working to bridge the gap and find ways to integrate digital thinking and language more explicitly into Buddhist investigations of reality. Neuroscientists are working to articulate the physical bases of brain function as influenced by meditation, as if Buddha's message can be distilled into some objective scientific reality. Others find these efforts missing the mark: a case of fiddling while Rome burns. The bottom line is that nobody owns reality. Who gets to write the narrative? Why, you do, of course.

New Agers like to talk about other dimensions of reality, citing the visions of mediums, oracles and healers, life beyond death, and so on. They're searching for The Secret. Buddhists do it too, as in the Cyborg Buddha Project. A Zen Roshi would slap them in the face.

I believe the link that ties all these disparate perspectives together is the probable near future. Whatever our digital predilections, our lifeworld is decidedly biological. If we cannot solve the eco-crisis, we will be editing ourselves right out of evolution very soon (earning a species-wide Darwin Award in the process). No amount of streaming movie channels, no app, no video game level, no spectacular number of YouTube views, no 3D printer, no blockchain or bitcoin, no Singularity, none of it will save us. Unless we focus on the crisis at hand, these digital advances will, at best, benefit a privileged few, or, at worst, be pleasant music playing at an execution.

Just as wisdom is meaningless without compassion, just as cognition is meaningless unmoored from ethics, so too any holistic discussion of reality must consider implications beyond philosophy or financial gain. In the remainder of this section, I'll try to show what that might look like.

REALITY RESOURCES
- www.accesstoinsight.org/tipitaka/abhi/index.html
- www.buddhanet.net/pdf_file/abhidhamma.pdf
- plumvillage.org/news/thich-nhat-hanh-new-heart-sutra-translation/
- ieet.org/index.php/IEET2/cyborgbuddha
- www.broadinstitute.org/what-broad/areas-focus/project-spotlight/crispr-timeline

NETWORK

65

While **Charles Babbage** is credited with the original conception of a computer in the 1820's, and his contemporary, **Ada Lovelace**, with inventing the world of programming, it took **Alan Turing** and others during the 1940's to create the first electronic computers, ushering in the Information Age. Stand-alone mainframes dominated the world of computing for the next 30 years. **Bob Metcalfe** invented the Ethernet Local Area Network (1973), and ushered in the Network Age. The invention of Personal Computers early in the 1980's ushered the PC Age, putting digital computers on anyone's desk. In 1996, **Tim Berners-Lee** introduced the Worldwide Web.

> There is no reason anyone would want a computer in their home.
>
> *Ken Olsen, founder of Digital Equipment Corporation, 1977*

The next ten years saw more and more technologies mediated by networked digital tools and the introduction of the Internet of Things. More recently, this trend has continued with an increasing number of applications transforming from stand-alone programs to cloud-based subscription services. In our current Age of Convergence, data is created, accessed, reconfigured and repurposed without barriers except for the paywall. Now we are poised on the tipping point of a new Biotech Age, where networked digital tools allow us to visualize internal biological processes in real time, print 3D organs, edit genes with CRISPR, and explore unforeseen futures.

Networks are a double-edged sword. While offering many benefits, they also leave us unable to function effectively when they are down, and open us up to new types of threats. (For example, the school board where I work fights off literally thousands of network attacks each day!)

As more and more physical assets evaporate into virtual surrogates, much of our knowledge base is going the way of the buggy whip. Our technological progress comes with a different kind of cost as well. **Kevin Kelly**, founder of *Wired* magazine, calls this the Technium, as outlined in his book, *What Technology Wants*. It locks us in to a particular, self-fulfilling way of thinking. Technology begets more technology, and there is, as yet, little in the way of an alternative perspective that has been able to slow it down.

Of late, three themes have emerged in the debate around networks. The headlong rush to 5G networks, in spite of the controversies around their surveillance state capabilities, the dubious economics of implementing them, and the possible health hazards of their microwave frequency, shows the momentum of the Technium. The emergence of a digital divide, between those with access to the network (i.e., opportunity), and those without (i.e., a new underclass), shows the central role of digital networks in our identity. Malfeasance by the rich and powerful has also emerged as a pressure point in the Age of Convergence, as per a T-shirt slogan I saw the other day: "Make George Orwell fiction again."

I don't see a direct Buddhist response to the dilemmas of our digital evolution. Clearly, this was not something that any Buddhist teacher prior to 1940 would have even considered. So we are making it up as we go along and any guidance will have to be through extrapolation.

The path of awakening has always been portrayed as a solitary affair, even if followed in the company of others. Traditional Buddhist understanding of society is as a collection of individuals, and places the emphasis on individual transformation. Re-visioning our task in society as an open-source, collaborative team effort is difficult, but necessary; and whether or not we see that network as digital is really beside the point. Besides, most Buddhists will tell you, abandoning one's self is difficult. The difference here is that this is not just an example of Buddhism adapting to a new (digital) culture; it is a matter of networked life and death.

What is the alternative? Acknowledgment of the intractability of samsara, the inevitability of our impermanence as a planet (Now? Really? Right now? In this very lifetime?), and individual "salvation" amidst the impossibility of altering the course of world events? Such pratyekabuddhahood was rejected by Shakyamuni and every Bodhisattva thereafter.

As pervasive and profound as our "reality as information" or "society best understood with computer network topology" paradigms currently appear, they are still ephemeral manifestations of impermanence. The true path lies outside of the dialectic posed by computer culture.

NETWORK RESOURCES

- dpworkshop.org/dpm-eng/timeline/popuptest.html
- www.youtube.com/watch?v=-eWxUWJgfzk (IBM 100 Years)
- www2.deloitte.com/insights/us/en/focus/tech-trends/2019/future-of-connectivity-advanced-networking.html
- www.buddhanet.net
- www.prisonmindfulness.org/projects/network-directory/

ARTIFICIAL INTELLIGENCE

66

Much of our modern, First World lives are run by algorithms. Our financial system, electrical and water grids, traffic lights, and communications networks are all semi-autonomous. Self-driving vehicles, AI diagnosis from medical imaging, and Personal Digital Assistants with Internet of Things agency are just around the corner. People don't seem to have a problem with that. But those hearing aids ads you see on your browser for weeks after reading an article about hearing loss are a creepier example of AI intersecting with daily life.

OK Google, what is Artificial Intelligence?

In its current iteration, AI exists in silos that can't communicate with each other, because we haven't programmed them to do so. The *Terminator* scenario we fear is still a long way from reality, in spite of being a Hollywood mainstay. True, those robot dogs from Boston Dynamics are pretty damn scary. Still, AlphaGO is not going to cross-breed with the robotic hamburger flipper to create a new super-intelligent dominatrix sex robot with machine-learning skills any time soon.

In Japan, there have been stories of Buddhist temples installing robot priests to officiate at funerals, holding funeral services for robot dogs, and now inaugurating a new AI Kannon statue. Cute. But these are really just pandering to the masses. Do you really want a machine as your roshi?

By the same token, the thought of a sentient AI (another sci-fi trope) has spawned discussions of whether a robot can become self-aware, like some reboot of Pinocchio. **Steven Speilberg**'s movie, *Artificial Intelligence*, comes closest, I think, to illustrating the possibilities of sentient robots with emotional lives. Others ponder whether or not a robot can become Enlightened. In 1985, **Masahiro Mori** published *The Buddha in the Robot: A Robot Engineer's Thoughts on Religion and Science*. And that leads us to the question: what IS Enlightenment, anyway? Shakyamuni holding up a lotus is rather cryptic.

It should seem self-evident that Enlightenment is more than a cognitive event, even if it is "a turning about in the mind." There are motivational, emotional, and moral dimensions to be transformed as well. Furthermore, *kensho* is merely the beginning of practice, in my view, and certainly neither the final destination nor *sine qua non* of Buddhism. In other words, Enlightenment is not an event, but an ever-expanding union of realization and engagement. Maybe that's how we Buddhists see ourselves, but it is certainly not how society at large sees us.

It would seem that our societal love affair with artificial intelligence means abandoning our own common sense. It is true that most people function quite well in managing their own lives, sometimes in spite of overwhelming odds. It is at the societal scale that things begin to break down. The real challenges come in the commons, where wicked problems and predicaments emerging from clashing values create such overwhelmingly complex systems that most of us simply retreat into our small, personal lives rather than engage. We may lament how some exploit the chaos for personal gain at the expense of others, but what is there to be done? This very disengagement and disempowerment is fostered by those in privileged positions, and AI is often their tool.

Devices capable of machine learning (AI artilects) are still the creation of their designers, in spite of fiction about free-thinking bots. The danger is not in the device, but in the intentions of those who make it (or hack it). For the foreseeable future (the one that really matters), decisions made by machines will only be within the ethical framework of humans; robots are not going to spontaneously invent a new one. They may pass the Turing Test, but they're not going to pass the Tokyo Test any time soon.

There's a Buddhist parable, about the Bodhisattva who kills a pirate to save him from the karma he would incur by killing 500 passengers aboard a ship (as opposed to the Bodhisattva finding another way to save the 500 intended victims). It's analogous to the trolley-car problem. Until artilects can grapple with the trolley-car problem like humans, narratives of their taking over are probably just smokescreens for the Titans who actually run things, and use AI to amplify their efforts. I'm not proposing that type of action, but I do think that the hype about AI is a sideshow, compared to the ethical challenges our world faces. We need a change of values, not a change of software.

ARTIFICIAL INTELLIGENCE RESOURCES
- www.telegraph.co.uk/technology/2017/08/24/japanese-robot-trained-host-low-cost-buddhist-funerals/
- www.japantimes.co.jp/news/2019/02/23/business/tech/robotic-kannon-unveiled-kyoto-temple/#.XLiC7ejYr8k
- newbuddhist.com/discussion/23235/ai-could-a-machine-become-enlightened

CYBORG

67   In the beginning of this book, I made the point that we tend to overlook the many non-digital technologies we use on a daily basis to enhance our functioning. Whether it's band-aids or high heels, we are constantly employing mechanical or analog devices as body modifications to exceed our limitations. On that basis, you could say we have already been cyborgs since the moment we first picked up a stone tool.

Late twentieth-century machines have made thoroughly ambiguous the difference between natural and artificial, mind and body, self-developing and externally designed, and many other distinctions that used to apply to organisms and machines. Our machines are disturbingly lively, and we ourselves frighteningly inert.
Donna J. Haraway

Our modern devices are obviously more sophisticated than wooden peg-legs and Captain Hook's hand. We have cochlear implants, pacemakers, insulin pumps, robotic exoskeletons, corneal transplants, and the like. Enhancements can also be extra-corporeal and they aren't only for the disabled. Just ask Siri. All these things are different by degree, but not qualitatively different.

In his book, *The Singularity is Near*, **Ray Kurzweil** talks about medical nano-robots in our blood. Fantasy, perhaps. Other cyborgian futures melding humans and machines are closer than they appear. A new technology – CRISPR – not strictly speaking digital, but enabled by digital tools, cuts closer to the bone.

Genetically modified organisms have been around for a while, but the technology recently took a giant leap forward with CRISPR gene editing. Now we are on the precipice of a substantially different enhancement that is qualitative, not just quantitative: we are altering the very genetic code that makes us us. However, as with many technologies, our capabilities extend beyond our ethical comfort zone. Advocates tout a cornucopia of miracles; detractors warn of doomsday scenarios.

This is not a topic you can look up in the *Nikayas*. **Shinran Shonin** had nothing to say about gene editing or cyborgs. Ditto for **Tsong Khapa** or **Ajahn Chah**. We'll have to address the problem from the general perspective of Buddhist ethics: intention, non-harming, and the possibility of unintended consequences.

To me the possibility of unintended consequences looms largest. The history of GMOs in agribusiness is a litany of empty promises, spin, contrary outcomes, increasing economic inequality (which is directly related to decreasing quality-of-life outcomes), and corporate aggression. Our government agencies seem powerless to enact regulations as simple as labelling GMO foods as such.

Since it is virtually impossible to separate GMO and cyborg technologies from the business in which they are embedded, any full discussion must include voices from the field of Buddhist economics (and I don't mean just the fluffy generic kind, but actual policy platforms like *The Leap Manifesto*). I think it is fair to say that even from the limited data we have about GMOs as patented Intellectual Property (IP), coupled with our vast ignorance of the synergistic functioning of genes (let alone the larger synergistic functioning of biospheres), we can see that gene manipulation has so far resulted in many more negative than positive consequences. In this realm, past performance is a pretty good indicator of future outcomes. Of course, others will disagree; however, it would be safer to err on the side of caution.

Nobody wants an outbreak of some antibiotic-resistant superbug spawned by human tinkering gone wrong. Nobody but a few very sick individuals wants the weaponization of CRISPR. The more insidious, creeping problem (like the invisibility of creeping climate change until it reaches the tipping point) is about privatization of what was, until very recently, considered our shared inheritance. One has merely to look at the evolution of the current price of insulin (patent sold for $1 by **Banting** and **Best** in 1923) for evidence.

Perhaps if one could reify Enlightenment, it could be a thing you could program into a device. But it is an awareness, not a thing. Conversely, if one could definitively identify how that awareness exists in our consciousness, one could ostensibly create a tool that would enhance it. However, individuals are simply too individual to be able to do that.

CYBORG RESOURCES

- humanityplus.org
- www.wired.com/1997/02/ffharaway/
- web.archive.org/web/20120214194015/
- www.stanford.edu/dept/HPS/Haraway/CyborgManifesto.html
- www.dekaresearch.com/
- online.sfsu.edu/rone/GEessays/gedanger.htm.org

SINGULARITY

68

In physics, the Singularity exists in a celestial black hole, beyond the event horizon, where space and time are deformed to such a degree that it is the antithesis of the physical laws under which we normally operate. It is unknowable. At the same time, it is thought to be the vital wellspring from which our entire universe is created, over and over. That sounds to me like a very good metaphor for Tathagatagarbha!

> When you talk to a human in 2035, you'll be talking to someone that's a combination of biological and non-biological intelligence.
>
> *Ray Kurzweil*

However, in common parlance, the Singularity has come to be equated with something entirely different: a melding of human and AI neural networks, in which our intimate and immediate access to troves of digital data and machine learning will somehow bootstrap us into a qualitatively different, enhanced level of evolution. The exact date of this leap is a hotly-debated topic, but 2040 seems popular – just far enough away to be unverifiable, but just close enough to be believable. It's rather like Zeno's Paradox.

Returning once again to business, the push to 5G networks relies heavily on this narrative. Somehow, a boost in ubiquitous computing (ubicomp) is seen as a prerequisite to the promised benefits of the Singularity. Never mind the loss of net neutrality as a hint of what's to come. Never mind the potential health implications of blanketing our cities with microwave transmitters. We want it all, and we want it NOW, dammit. (And if we don't, corporate shills are here to convince us otherwise.)

Many studies have shown that societal inequality is inversely correlated with well-being. In the realm of the Singularity, this manifests as what is known as the digital divide. Whatever benefits do come from advances towards it will be disproportionately enjoyed by the privileged few, while the externalized costs will be borne disproportionately by the poor, in spite of the fact that the poor will have the least access to those benefits.

As a cultural narrative, as opposed to a realistic technological goal, the Singularity epitomizes our compulsive attraction to new technologies, our wilful blindness to collateral damage, and our willingness to gamble with our future. It's an example of the three poisons: greed, aversion, and ignorance.

At this point, our gamble seems to be in a race to the 2040 finish line: a race between extinguishing ourselves as a viable planet or transforming our relationship with the climate and each other. I fear that the dire warnings, coming from the likes of **Bill McKibben** in his new book, *Falter: Has the Human Game Begun to Play Itself Out?*, will be lost in the cacophony of public discourse. The Singularity won't mean much when we're all in a struggle for our very existence.

So, as a Buddhist, I don't care much for the Singularity. It is not going to get me closer to Enlightenment. It is not going to ease the suffering of beings in samsara. It is not going to solve other, much more pressing problems. Being able to download a two-hour movie in five seconds does not sound like much of an upside to me. Ditto for turning our educational system over to AI teachers in flipped virtual classrooms where students purportedly will direct their own learning. Ditto for 24/7 quantification of my biometrics via nano-robots in my blood.

Back in 1990, after His Holiness **the Dalai Lama** won the Nobel Peace Prize, I was commissioned to make a commemorative poster for the Tibetan Community of Ontario on the occasion of his visit to Toronto. The quote chosen for the poster was: "I pray for a more friendly, more caring, and more understanding human on this planet." That is still my watchword. If somebody can explain to me how the tech singularity can help with that, I'm all ears.

Fictional portrayals of life post-Singularity such as *Neuromancer*, by **William Gibson**, or *The Diamond Age*, by **Neal Stephenson**, or *Ex Machina*, by **Alex Garland**, highlight the paradox that the Singularity does not result in homogeneity. In real life, merging with smart machines may happen, but I do not believe it will change our fundamental human search for meaning through direct experience. It may, rather, provide another layer of noise preventing us from hearing that small, still voice. Siri and Alexa cannot provide a trap-door escape from our current ethical crisis.

SINGULARITY RESOURCES

- en.wikipedia.org/wiki/Transcendent_Man
- en.wikipedia.org/wiki/Hugo_de_Garis
- nomosjournal.org/2016/06/technological-singularity-and-robot-buddhas/
- dhammawheel.com/viewtopic.php?t=9407
- www.forbes.com/sites/cognitiveworld/2019/02/10/the-troubling-trajectory-of-technological-singularity/#22b6c4506711

UBICOMP

69

The premise behind 5G technology is ultra-fast wifi connectivity for mobile devices, everywhere. It is the key to ubiquitous computing (ubicomp, *aka* pervasive computing). The speed (10-20 times faster than current technology) will allow self-driving cars to communicate with each other easily, allow your health monitoring device to communicate with medical centres in real time, allow for broad implementation of the Internet of Things (IoT) in applications like drones, enable screenless and haptic Internet applications, or (more prosaically) download a two-hour 4K HD movie in seconds from your bicycle. You'll need a new generation of mobile device to access it.

> Next comes ubiquitous computing, or the age of calm technology, when technology recedes into the background of our lives.
> *Mark Weiser*

In order to achieve efficient 5G service, firms offering the service will have to install a network of short-range microwave transmitters blanketing service areas. They will be "hidden" in lampposts, under manhole covers, on sides of buildings, etc., in quantities far greater than the cell towers we now live with. This roll-out is expected to take place within the next five years. Right now, the major players are fighting for the inside track.

There are, of course, many promised benefits from 5G technology. For the purveyors, it represents a huge new market and mega-profits. For consumers, the cost/benefit ratio is less clear. Putting aside the economic issues, there are two problematic issues: health and privacy concerns.

The 5G networks will work on a microwave bandwidth we have not used before. The effects of exposing all of us to an exponentially greater amount of EMF radiation than we currently endure are unknown. I, for one, do not wish to be personally microwaved further, nor do I expect it will be healthy for my grandchildren. Brussels has banned 5G for health reasons. Needless to say, studies supporting implementation, paid for by the purveyors, will show otherwise.

The privacy issue is highlighted by the brouhaha around Huawei's 5G technology. Multiple media outlets are reporting on how the Chinese government is monitoring citizens in Xinjiang Province with algorithms based on their cellphone use, and how they are selling that technology to other countries. The intrusive nature of 5G means that everything you do, everywhere you go, will be available to Big Brother, and it won't just be the Chinese government listening in. So far, privacy laws lag far behind the push for new, invasive applications for communications technology, as we can see from recent court battles involving Facebook. **Michael Geist**, a Canadian pundit on all things IP, has lots of great material on this subject, as does the Electronic Frontiers Foundation (EFF).

OK, so what does all this mean for Buddhists?

The premise behind Buddhism is to find out who you truly are, and how to be in the world in the most positive way. When your identity is manufactured by government fiat and reinforced by corporate interests, that is very hard to do. Instead, you get an ersatz construct designed to enrich others and entrench the status quo privilege of the ruling class. For this reason, Buddhists should be strong, vocal supporters of organizations like the Electronic Frontier Foundation, and any other organization that extends the struggle for Human Rights into the digital arena, works for net neutrality, and so on.

Buddhists can decline to have their centres or organizations participate in implementation of 5G networks. Centres can brand themselves as surveillance sanctuaries, and institute digital-device-free zones where and when cellphones, smart watches, fitness trackers, and so on, are turned off and out of sight. We can also support initiatives designed to thwart the efforts of purportedly Buddhist of "Buddhist-friendly" totalitarian governments seeking to control their citizens (for example, in Tibet, Xinjiang, or Myanmar).

Lastly, we can promote a healthy lifestyle that embraces escape from the tyranny of digital addiction in all its forms.

The quote for this topic comes from **Mark Weiser**, considered the father of ubiquitous computing. I find his use of the term "calm" (with all the Buddhist harmonics and resonances that summons) to be the polar opposite of what is actually about to engulf us.

UBICOMP RESOURCES

- en.wikipedia.org/wiki/Mark_Weiser
- www.michaelgeist.ca
- www.eff.org
- www.envisioning.io
- www.forbes.com/sites/zakdoffman/2019/04/25/huawei-xinjiang-and-chinas-high-tech-surveillance-state-joining-the-dots/#6ec407afcd52

CODE

70

I remember how in the mid-1990's, my Board of Education promoted initiatives around character education that were swiftly replaced with multiple intelligence, that were swiftly replaced with differentiated instruction, that were swiftly replaced with yet other programs. No chance for consolidation. Onward and upward.

The most valuable asset a coder has is a clear mind.
codingmindfully.com

On the other hand, computer skills have been touted for quite some time as the make-or-break key to 21st century success.

Learning how to write computer code has become increasingly emphasized in schools. Children as young as five are being initiated into the realm of if-then logic, for loops, iterative design, and debugging, to augment their already prodigious UX skills acquired from years of playing with cellphones and tablets in their strollers! We have large-scale initiatives like "Hour of Code," "Digital Literacy," "Girls Who Code," and guidance departments pushing computer courses. Coding is the new life hack paradigm. But it's a bit of a zero-sum game, because there are only so many hours in the school day.

The underlying logic of this is that while you don't need coding skills to use applications, you do need them to create new ones, and in the new digital economy, that's where the money will be. Never mind that those coding jobs will likely be shipped out to India or some other country where there are millions of coders willing to work for low rates in a gig economy, or that lots of coding will be done by AI.

Meanwhile, vast swaths of our knowledge about how to thrive on this planet are going the way of how to recognize edible plants. I'm not just talking about touchy-feely things like civility (Communities of Character), or connectedness to nature (NatureSacred); I'm talking about basic stuff like how to feed ourselves. Granted, I'm unlikely to need masonry skills to build a new Borobudur in the near future, but I would like to think that being a keyboard monkey is not my only future. There is a fundamental difference between Lifeworld and Codeworld.

For Buddhist teachers, geek skills are similarly in demand. From *Tripitaka* digitization and AI translation, to YouTube teachings and Facebook Watch Parties, Sangha leaders are increasingly expected to master new media. Indeed, there is a subtle bias upvoting celebrity teachers who offer omni-channel output versus those who don't. By extension, they might be expected to delegate some of those responsibilities to Sangha members who are enlisted for the cause. Buddhist coders are in demand!

I am not immune. I've been looking for someone to take on the tech responsibilities for the web directory of 600+ Canadian Buddhist organizations that I have been running for 10 years. I want to take it to the next level of interactivity with a mapping API, user-created input for program changes and the like, infrastructure for pictures of places of worship (inside and out), reviews (or at least comments), etc. I've made repeated requests to the community. No takers.

When I taught grade 9 students about binary mathematics for coding, I explained its value to students as being like a second or third language. If you are multilingual, you are at an advantage; it's not that one language is better than another. The same applies for math. Reality is bigger than the labels we impose on it; being flexible is the transferable skill.

Likewise, coding is valuable, but it exists within a larger context. Consequently, I spent less time on binary or coding in the senior courses, and more time on systems thinking and the project management skills (see *PMBOK*) needed to design and implement new computer applications.

What would happen if we applied the same kind of meta-cognitive thinking to Buddhist practice? Buddhists understand the graduated path, and the need to build on fundamentals. But when I hear Buddhists adopt the language of digital technology and culture to express Dharma truths, I feel they are clumsy graftings. The real advance of computer culture is in the cybernetic understanding of systems. That grand overview is what is missing in modern Buddhism's embrace of the future.

I know Buddhist teachers will tell me that Buddhism is indeed about understanding the totality of reality, and that Engaged Buddhism is about healing the world. What would a rigorous, systematic application of that core ideal look like for you in the arena of urgent modern problems?

CODE RESOURCES

- hourofcode.com
- www.ic.gc.ca/eic/site/102.nsf/eng/home
- girlswhocode.com
- www.asianclassics.org
- www.zenprogrammer.org
- codingwithempathy.com/2016/03/29/the-mindful-developer/

HIVE

71

When Shakyamuni died, early Buddhists consolidated their understanding of his teachings through a series of Councils in the years that followed. These gatherings were designed at first simply to reiterate the Suttas, Vinaya, and Abhidhamma (the Three Baskets). Later, Councils were tasked with resolving sectarian disputes, but their lack of success signalled the end of pan-Buddhist councils as the teachings spread to other places and cultures. Subsequently, Buddhism has always relied on the Refuge of the Sangha Jewel in its local embodiment, in conjunction with important teachers and community leaders. That is important to remember, as we lose more lineage holders to death or imprisonment, and as we lose our trust in others embroiled in scandal.

Can collective intelligence save the planet? It's the only hope we have.
Patrick Joseph McGovern

You know the old saying, "Two heads are better than one." As eusocial beings, we participate in realms of understanding that surpass our own individual knowledge. This why I say that in the future, Enlightenment will be crowdsourced. It is another way of looking at anicca, anatta, and dukkha: reality as a social construct. Intentional communities are nothing new; there have always been attempts by groups of people to fashion a structured way of living that empowers members to withstand the chaotic winds of the larger world. Nevertheless, it seems that most North American Buddhist centres do not have democratically elected leaders, clearly defined policies on transparency and accountability, or even much sense of common purpose amongst members. That does not bode well.

Increasingly, we have come to understand that our relationships extend beyond humanity to entire ecosystems and the planet as a whole. You could say we are like a planetary hive, and our planet is suffering from imminent hive collapse disorder. (The analogy is particularly apt, because the extinction of bees will vapourize much of the world's food supply. It is a real and present demonstration of the larger metaphorical crisis.) It will require the coordinated efforts of humanity as a whole to solve the problems we face. There will certainly be community leaders around whom we will rally, but they alone will not save us. Each of us has a role to play. As another old saying goes: "United we stand; divided we fall."

I see these two levels of membership as related. By practicing our commitment to the former (our home team, so to speak), we prepare ourselves for action in the latter (the big game).

It doesn't take a lot of work to discover the world's problems. Dukkha is always here, and it can seem entirely overwhelming. Much of our courage to go on with life each day comes from our commitment to bettering the world in which we find ourselves. That commitment becomes much easier in the company of kindred spirits.

It is time for Buddhists to once again break out of their silos and support intrafaith (not to mention interfaith) initiatives for this common cause. The narrative that Buddhists pay less attention to sectarian divisions, compared to their Abrahamic brethren, is only a half-truth. We may not be killing each other, but we don't pay much attention to each other either, let alone the larger faith community.

I hate to harp on the subject, but I recently contacted the Interfaith Rainforest Initiative to be put in touch with their Buddhist member organizations. Turns out, there are none. Case in point.

These times demand activism, and activism demands group cohesion. There is strength in numbers. If you are dismayed by the direction the world is taking, speak up.

Many Buddhist lineages use mandalas as symbolic representations of the universe as a Pure Land. These mandalas are not just pretty shapes, but are populated by enlightened beings, peaceful and wrathful, vibrant with the vitality of the Tathagatagarbha. Perhaps this is a more motivational image than a beehive, if we imagine ourselves as denizens of such a Pure Land. However, actualizing ourselves at the pinnacle of Maslow's Hierarchy of Needs won't be so easy if the real beehives are gone and we have no food. Don't be hard on me; I'm a highly-initiated Vajrayana practitioner. It's just that in the Generation Stage, Yidams are the beginning of practice and not the end. We don't get to realize the Completion Stage unless every being is there with us.

HIVE RESOURCES
- sos-bees.org
- www.collectiveintelligence.info
- realitysandwich.com/1207/next_buddha_will_be_a_collective/
- www.stephenbatchelor.org/index.php/en/creating-Sangha
- www.buddhistdoor.net/features/what-is-the-role-of-the-buddhist-sangha-in-the-21st-century

LOVE

■ 72

Love is a word so overused that it has come to mean practically anything while justifying practically everything. Whether evoked in online dating sites, advertisements glorifying the simple pleasures of the nuclear family or bemoaning the plight of strays and orphans, popular songs, rom-coms, calls to arms, sex robots, the Ashley Madison data breach, invitations to honk if you love _____, BDSM bestsellers, or that animatronic Kannon statue, in fact, the only things we truly love are serotonin, oxytocin, and dopamine.

> One is not called noble who harms living beings. By not harming living beings one is called noble.
>
> Dhammapada, 270

Within this maelstrom, it's hard for people to understand what Buddhists mean by "love." We can only equate it to what we already know. For clues, I turn to Christian *Agapé*, Jewish *Chesed*, and other artifacts from my Abrahamic past. Not much help, and certainly not deeply understood notions within the public sphere. Maybe it's even hard for Buddhists. I know that's the case for me.

At the moment, I'm in a school staff room surrounded by copies of *Glamour* magazine. The teaser on one cover says, "LOVE! 18 Stories of lust, loss & trust in 2018;" another says, "Sex without shame." We are adrift in some very challenging waters. This is clearly not the type of love Buddha had in mind. However, navigating these shoals is high priority for each of us when we first enter the sea of love. They can't simply be dismissed.

Finding love in the world of online dating is the topic of some debate these days: just how do we get the algorithm right? How much do we really know about what makes folks connect? It can't be reduced to a single metric. Is it just about making sure our dysfunctions match?

Older folks know romantic love fades, even though it is one of our prime cultural narratives. It may mellow into our most profound friendship if we are lucky, or lead us into one relationship illusion after another. After the "joys" of parenting, we join the sandwich generation caring for aging parents, and then becoming those aging parents ourselves, caregiving our partners through yet another passage in the journey of love. Love is a many-splendoured thing, as the song goes, but it comes with a lot of complicated downside too, and those take centre stage in many lyrics too.

Another cultural narrative tells us we should be good citizens. Consider the maxim: Love thy neighbour as thyself. It's easy to love members of your own tribe, not so easy to welcome the stranger, especially when the stranger arrives in numbers that threaten to strain the social safety net. This is clearly a higher order of love, and perhaps closer to what Buddha had in mind.

When we get to a spiritual love, the message is no clearer. Religious leaders talk the talk, but finding those who walk the walk is very difficult. And when we do, we tend to put them on a pedestal we deem to be more elevated and removed than we could hope to inhabit ourselves. For all too many of us, our expressions of divine love are manifested in cyberspace as incentivized outrage, coordinated harassment attacks, and virtue signalling our tribal affiliations. Probably not what Buddha had in mind.

Perhaps we don't really ever know what love is. We just have a lot of experiences with it, and try to create some composite mental image from them. Like memory, it is our attempt to organize chaos into a recognizable narrative after the fact. In Madhyamaka we sometimes talk about the non-nature of the remainder. In other words, once we've stripped away all the false truths about the nature of love, we are left with something defined by what it is not. Perhaps our openness and unknowing are the key to the type of love Buddhists talk about when we say *metta*, or *karuna*, or compassion. It's more a thing we do than a thing we understand.

In other words, we learn to love through our actions as *kalyanamitras* (spiritual friends). As with meditation, the benefits come from actually doing love, and there is no substitute.

I read recently that the advent of more female Zen teachers has nudged mainstream Rinzai Zen practice in North America out of its militaristic, hellbent-for-leather pursuit of "The Enlightenment Experience" towards a gentler focus on Compassion. They're still outliers; perhaps those majority male community leaders need to occupy that space too.

LOVE RESOURCES
- www.amazon.ca/Love-Time-Algorithms-Technology-Meeting-ebook/dp/B008EKMDWG
- utopiaordystopia.com/2015/02/14/sex-and-love-in-the-age-of-algorithms/
- www.dharmamatch.com
- tisarana.ca/metta-in-action/
- www.wildmind.org/metta/introduction/outline

ACTION

GLOBAL

■ 73

In our global village, each action has implications that pervade the entire system. Eventually, those ripples become waves and those waves circle round to affect us too. What goes around comes around.

I really like the analogy that each of us each of us is a cell in the unified life of the planet. Science tells us that more than half of our own bodies is composed of foreign organisms living in symbiosis with us. When we all get along, things go well. That's a narrative I can work with.

> A spiritual voice is urgently needed to underline the fact that global warming is already causing human anguish and mortality in our nation and abroad, and much more will occur in the future without rapid action.
>
> *Bill McKibben*

The thought of being a Buddhist teacher has never appealed to me. I don't think my personal experience is repeatable or even relevant for others. But I'm willing to do my part, and willing to meet in the agora to discuss issues of vital importance to all of us, bringing the perspective of my experience as a long-time Buddhist practitioner.

It is not sufficient for Buddhist teachers merely to quote scriptures. They must be able to address the applications of those scriptures in the real world, and to do so they must be credible. In a sense then, this is really a book for Buddhist teachers, to give them the tools they need to participate in the conversation. The resources presented in this book are, I hope, a good beginning for that education. I think Buddhist teachers are usually very good at understanding human nature and in nurturing personal transformation. Translating that into societal transformation can prove to be much more difficult.

Communications technology has brought the entire world into our homes, and not merely in the passive way that was described in the last century by **Marshall McLuhan**. We now interact directly with our far-flung family 24/7. Global e-commerce is commonplace, and ubiquitous computing of all kinds will soon be the norm everywhere, with the advent of 5G networks. On the flip-side, we have all become widgets in the attention economy, quantifying every aspect of our lives and relinquishing our privacy to data miners for their financial gain or political control.

Recent events in the world of politics have shown that populism, protectionism, and pugnaciousness are very much alive and well. Engaged Buddhists have been active in resistance, and must continue to align themselves with the oppressed rather than the oppressors.

Resistance, however, is not enough. We must also embark upon positive initiatives for the common good. There is no shortage of ways to get involved (as you can see by the breadth of topics in this book).

It should come as no surprise that doing good makes us feel good. According to psychologist **Martin Seligman**, this dynamic is called the PERMA model. PERMA stands for:

- Positive Emotion
- Engagement
- Relationships
- Meaning
- Accomplishments

Within a context of Mahayana Buddhist ethics, this "positive psychology" perspective can be a gateway to something more than individual fulfilment. In fact, individual fulfilment without engagement is a chimera. A noted critic of modern Buddhism, **Slavoj Žižek**, puts it as a question: "Is the goal of the Buddhist meditation nirvana as the shift in the subject's stance towards reality, or is this goal the fundamental transformation of reality itself, so that all suffering disappears and all living beings are relieved of their suffering?"

The really important message is that we need to see the larger system, both in terms of the global implications of our actions and in terms of the long view over time, to make wise and compassionate decisions about our shared future. The Bodhisattva 4.0 is active in the ten directions and the three times. Putting our sandals on our head and walking out of the room, or performing some complex liturgy are, by themselves, far from demonstrations of deep understanding of the Buddhadharma. We need to make our voices heard and lend our sweat equity in the larger world outside the Buddhist bubble chamber.

GLOBAL RESOURCES

- positivepsychologyprogram.com/perma-model/
- connections.ucalgaryblogs.ca/2018/01/21/the-perma-model-strategies-for-promoting-workplace-flourishing/
- www.nantien.org.au/sre-web/threeactsforwellbeing.php
- bigthink.com/postcards-from-zizek/slavoj-zizek-on-buddhism-and-the-self

ENGAGED

▬ 74

What exactly is an Engaged Buddhist? Is it more than simply being a socially engaged citizen? **David Loy** of the EcoDharma Center thinks so.

Does it embrace more than an environmental focus? **Ken Jones**, who founded the Network of Buddhist Organisations in the UK, thinks so.

Is all Buddhism "Engaged?" **Thich Nhat Hanh** thinks it should be.

> Engaged Buddhism is just Buddhism. If you practice Buddhism in your family, in society, it is engaged Buddhism.
>
> *Thich Nhat Hanh*

Is Engaged Buddhism easy? Certainly not. Aside from the obvious push-back from powerful forces committed to maintaining the status quo, this is a path with many pitfalls. Consider, for example, the rose-coloured spectacles of privilege, slacktivism, bangle Buddhists, the shallow consumerism of experiential philanthropy, the commodification of compassion, the false logic of caring for far-off causes at the expense of those suffering on our own doorsteps, the Lady Bountiful complex, the ease with which we are enthralled by ideology, subversion of our actions by what we perceive as our righteous indignation, and so on.

Nevertheless, we persist. Why? Because this is a path of incremental improvement. As the saying goes, "If at first you don't succeed, try, try again."

In the design world, very few things are truly new inventions. The vast majority are incremental improvements on existing ideas, mash-ups of existing technologies, or off-label applications of stuff. In the Buddhist view of how things work, everything is in a state of flux – including our path.

I recently attended a Dharma talk where the presenter was talking about Seven-Point Mind Training. She talked about recognizing life as a dream-like illusion, with the goal of waking up and leaving it behind. I don't see it that way. All through the talk, I kept thinking of **Stephen LaBerge** and his work in lucid dreaming. Why not apply the same perspective to our waking life? Isn't this forward motion, this dreaming ourselves into the beings we wish to become, our *Sambhogakaya*, a more compelling interpretation?

There are so many people doing good work in the world. We always like a solitary-hero story, but measuring success by one person's biggest numbers (most people healed, most animals rescued, most acres protected, most money raised) misses the point and devalues their work. We need to join hands.

176   BODHISATTVA 4.0

Leaning in with like-minded individuals shifts the focus. It's about the community rather than the individual. We often hear that the traditional relationship between Buddhist monastics and lay people doesn't work any more. The Sangha Jewel has become cloudy and needs to be re-cut.

The paradigms of neoliberal capitalism, free market economics, and state socialism are dictatorships. Of course, every dictator describes himself as benevolent, but there are better ways to organize our society.

I've had many conversations with Buddhist leaders about the financial difficulty of running a centre if they don't have Asian donors. Western Sangha members usually don't have the wherewithal to support full-time resident teachers. This is not a uniquely Buddhist phenomenon; many religious teachers these days need to find other work to sustain themselves and their families. Leading a congregation has become an avocation, even in mainstream religions.

Some communities expect their members to give their all for love of the community's perceived core beliefs, or for a charismatic teacher. That's not a very sustainable model. You get a community of poor people with no resources. Some communities start businesses to sustain themselves, and there have been some very successful examples such as Grayston Bakery. But for most people, their engagement is going to be in organizations beyond a temple, practice group, or community; these are organizations that already exist and welcome volunteers. And they don't expect you to drain yourself dry or give up your entire life to help. Engagement, carried to an extreme, operating like a pyramid scheme, is not the Middle Way.

The notion of a wealthy Buddhist is an oxymoron to most people. But what about the notion of a well-funded organization that is empowered to bring about change? The B Corporation movement is an excellent example of Right Livelihood in action. Employee cooperatives are another.

ENGAGED RESOURCES

- www.nbo.org.uk
- www.mindfulnessbell.org/archive/2015/02/dharma-talk-history-of-engaged-buddhism-2
- northamericanbuddhistalliance.org
- inebnetwork.org
- bcorporation.net

REVOLUTION

75

Buddhist teachers like His Holiness the **Dalai Lama**, **Thich Nhat Hanh**, and **Dr. Ambedkar**, and others like **Martin Luther King**, have always managed to speak out about injustice in an entirely non-violent way. Yet they have each transformed society in revolutionary ways. I would venture to say that in the instant that any one of us turns from a path of violence and exclusion to a path of peace and acceptance of diversity, we are ourselves revolutionaries.

> Life's most persistent and urgent question is, "What are you doing for others?"
> *Martin Luther King*

This is not to say we should be devoid of anger when we see the mistreatment of others, animals, and our planet. Anger is part of our nature; the question is: how will we channel it? On this topic, Vajrayana Buddhism has much to say, while other lineages give less explicit instructions on how to work constructively with such negative emotions.

Within the larger social context, acting as a mahaSangha, we saw the Saffron Revolution in Myanmar, where non-violent protests by monks precipitated the fall of a brutal military regime. The 2010 movie, *Burma VJ: Reporting from a Closed Country*, documents that struggle. Sadly, a subsequent chapter in that saga has turned those same Buddhist monks against their Rohingya compatriots in condoning the government's horrific ethnic cleansing, but the story is not yet over.

We are also seeing the ongoing effort by female Buddhist practitioners around the world, working tirelessly to re-awaken full ordination for women. What a gift to the world that would be!

Meanwhile, in North America, the late **Arun Likhati**'s *Angry Asian Buddhist* blog reminded us again and again to broaden our perspective. Buddhist leaders of colour are similarly pointing out a way forward in terms of race. Gay Buddhists like **Richard Harrold** (*My Buddha is Pink*) are bringing gender issues into the spotlight as well.

Modern non-violent revolution depends on digital technology to a high degree. Information and communications technologies have enabled intentional cyber-communities, mobile citizen reporting, the ability for anyone to upload content to the Web, and crowdsourced initiatives for change. Understanding the power of this, reactionary forces seek to control and confine our access to them, or to subvert them by any means necessary.

By limiting access to the Internet, governments hide alternative perspectives from their citizens. By using trolls and bots to populate whatever cyberspace is left, they undermine faith in independent media, foment antagonistic emotions that can be manipulated, and disrupt civil discourse. The Dalai Lama has been a repeated victim of this type of attack.

Cyber attacks on Buddhist organizations are an ongoing concern. For example: the *burmavjmovie.com* website has been hacked and now contains "reviews" of corporations like Home Depot and KFC!

Corporations choke our bandwidth with their gospel of consumerism. Spammers, hucksters, clickhole baiters and their ilk dominate the attention economy. Internet service providers, search engine giants and social media portals render Net Neutrality a unicorn.

We also see how totalitarian governments monitor our every online search or exchange with our peers, sniffing out and snuffing out any hint of dissent.

So what is to be done? Complete liberation will not come about on the cushion alone, and very definitely not from the Internet.

Maybe my opinions are informed by my being Canadian. Maybe I have no aspiration to be a rock star Buddhist. But I do believe that if each of us simply works on one or more positive initiatives in our own local sphere, regardless of how many followers, likes, retweets, sales, or podiums we get (and, indeed, if we do not even consider those as our goals), good will come of it.

On one hand, many Buddhists recommend turning away from our obsession with digital media. Psychologists back them up in highlighting the deleterious effects of screen addiction. But on the other hand, digital media presents us with a remarkably powerful tool if used wisely. Unlike weapons, which can only bring harm, communication does have the potential for bringing people together. Anger tempered with a wish to find win-win solutions is ultimately the only way forward in that regard.

REVOLUTION RESOURCES

- www.crisisprevention.com
- buddhaweekly.com/the-importance-of-ahimsa-non-violence-in-buddhism-buddha-ghandi-and-dr-king-showed-us-nonviolence-is-the-weapon-of-the-strong/
- www.pbs.org/thebuddha/blog/2010/apr/12/buddhas-revolution-sharon-salzberg/

SCANDAL

76

In the secular world, scandal is the dark shadow of name and fame. Just as bystanders who are complicit in bullying by saying nothing, so too as spectators in the media circus of scandal, we reveal our eagerness to take pleasure in the punishment of others. So one aspect of scandal has to do with our participation in the picture of reality fed to us by the media. Given that nothing on the Internet is private or ever goes away, much of our knowledge of the transgressions of others comes through "gotcha" tweets and the like.

These days there is a lot of poverty in the world, and that's a scandal when we have so many riches and resources to give to everyone. We all have to think about how we can become a little poorer.

Pope Francis

According to American psychologist **Jonathan Haidt**, who specializes in the psychology of morality and ethical leadership, "Scandal is great entertainment because it allows people to feel contempt, a moral emotion that gives feeling of moral superiority while asking nothing in return." It is a kissing cousin to the self-justified "righteous indignation" so prevalent in online flamewars. (You know the kind: the scornful meme, sarcastic rejoinder, or comment thread usually devolves into "send her back where she came from" in no time at all, the "no, that's not what I meant," and so on.)

Our addiction to outrage is one of the three poisons Buddha revealed as the cause of human suffering. It blocks our ability to see other paths, to act in other ways, such as with forgiveness or harm reduction.

There are no tragedies in nature; tragedy is a human concept. However, when we see abuse we must act. Sometimes, it is abuse by a person in a position of power over others. Sometimes it is an institutional system that oppresses entire groups of people. Sometimes it is the attempt to remake society in the image of an aggressive ideology. Sometimes it is desire for short-term gain over long-term sustainability.

According to self-help pioneer **John Bradshaw**, since our institutions are made up of people, our dysfunctional institutions merely reflect the kinds of dysfunction we see in any family. We act out the patterns we know. Ultimately, we need to heal ourselves in order to escape this type of toxicity, but it cannot be separated from our need to reform society.

Buddhist institutions are no strangers to scandal, but it is only recently that Buddhists behaving badly have come under wider public scrutiny. Yes, some of that interest has been motivated by a desire to say, "See, you're no better than us." But part of it is an important reckoning for community leaders and role models who hide behind "crazy wisdom." How to deal with this abuse is still a work in progress for those involved. America's crime-and-punishment model of morality, with its focus on the individual, doesn't leave much oxygen for alternative pathways such as restorative justice or Aboriginal-style Healing Circles. How to deal with Buddhist scandals in the modern world has little precedent in the Vinaya: sexual abuse, addiction, misuse of funds and the like had remedies (usually expulsion from the ordained Sangha), but those were simpler times. There is much to do in this regard. Fortunately, lineage leaders are beginning to formulate and publish comprehensive guidelines for their teachers and students. Explicit guidelines such as the ethics statement of the Soto Zen Buddhist Association are wonderful models.

There are larger institutional scandals involving Buddhists, such as trolling of the Dalai Lama by the NKT, genocide of the Rohingya in Myanmar by Buddhists, China's fake Panchen Lama and their continued occupation of Tibet, the destruction of Bamiyan by Muslim fundamentalists, or the destruction of Mes Aynak by a Chinese mining corporation.

Beyond that, there is no shortage of causes for engaged Buddhists to address, and every voice is needed. Healing ourselves and healing our world go hand in hand. This is not mercy in the conventional sense. It is a co-created, shared journey.

The immediate challenges are to get beyond being stuck in the minutiae of each scandal, to avoid succumbing to scandal fatigue, or to ignore what is going on around us because "it doesn't concern us." Finding an appropriate positive response is the second step: truth and reconciliation, forgiveness and rehabilitation, not punishment. Sticking with it is the third. We may not see the results in our lifetime, but we will know we acted in a noble way.

SCANDAL RESOURCES
- people.stern.nyu.edu/jhaidt/home.html
- www.justiceeducation.ca/about-us/research/aboriginal-sentencing/restorative-justice
- www.accesstoinsight.org/lib/authors/bodhi/wheel259.html
- szba.org/szba-ethics-statement/

SILK ROAD

■
77

The ancient trading route, known as the Silk Road, connected civilizations from Greece to Turkey to India to China and back again. It was the Information Superhighway of its era. All along its path, Buddhism found places to take root and flourish over millennia.

A people without the knowledge of their past history, origin and culture is like a tree without roots.

Marcus Garvey

Many of those places are still with us, like treasures rediscovered in a latter age: Nalanda, Taxila, Ajanta, Swayambhu, Bamiyan, Mes Aynak, Shwedagon, Doi Suthep, Khotan, Serindia, Mogao, Angkor Wat, Borobudur. Some, like the Swat Valley or the Tsangpo Gorge, remain inaccessible and are more the stuff of legend. Some, like Wutai, Emei, Jiuhua, and Putuo, are centres of pilgrimage. Some, like the Potala and Borobudur, have been stripped of their spiritual power and exist re-cast primarily as tourist attractions. Some have been lost to wind and sand. Even those that are physically present are metaphysically mysterious and opaque.

Reading of the exploits of early travellers, like **Xuanzang** or even **Marco Polo**, can give us a perspective we can't find in the biographies of **Bodhidharma**, **Marpa**, or others who travelled great distance to propagate the Dharma. Reading books by and about early Western explorers who travelled the Silk Road and wrote about their adventures, such as **Sven Hedin**, **Sir Stamford Raffles**, **Sir Aurel Stein**, **Alexandra David-Néel**, and **Joseph Rock** (to name but a few), adds another facet, as does study of more recent archeological research projects in the field.

In all these places and times, Buddhism was a long-term, communal, diverse, and engaged endeavour existing within dynamic societies. We must remember that the path within to wisdom is only one half of the practice of Dharma. Our interest in mindfulness, self-care, meditation apps, self-improvement, and so on, will only hobble us if we do not take our place in the larger society and model our Buddhist values. Conversely, activism without reflection is no liberation.

Beyond even that, the lessons of history show us that impermanence is the rule. Experience shows us that not all change is for the better. Wisdom shows us that our legacy has value and provides a compass; we are not the first to tread this path.

In each of the UNESCO World Heritage Site descriptions listed in the resources to this topic, you will find much more than just Buddhist images. The examples show urban planning, architectural and infrastructure technologies of great sophistication, and other enduring characteristics. To fully understand the message of the Buddha, it is not sufficient to live in the present with no thought of the past or future. We could say there is no self without society, just as in a gestalt there is no figure without the ground. If engagement is a given, the critical factor here is the nature of that engagement. As a Buddhist, reading this book, you are in the unique position of imagining what form that engagement might take.

When Buddhist teachers refer to this life as something disappearing even as it comes into being, like a dewdrop, a rainbow, or flash of lightning, and indeed something without inherent substance, that can be hard to reconcile with the gratitude we feel towards those countless ancestors whose good fortune allowed us to be here today. It is a debt that can only be paid forward. Would that we could peer forward in time an equal span, to see what Buddhism might be in another 1000 years.

On another note, the Silk Road has become cultural shorthand for a few ideas that have nothing to do with Buddhism. For example, it is the name for a particularly seedy outpost on the dark web where a variety of criminal enterprises were facilitated. Another example involves China, who have used the Silk Road metaphor for their hegemonic efforts to build their world power through infrastructure loans to developing countries at what are often terms that put client states at a disadvantage – an extremely effective form of debt-trap diplomacy. In yet another example, it has become a tourist marketer's destination (as in The Orient Express).

One has merely to look at the international efforts (discretely out of the normal public eye, but still intensely competitive) around "ownership" and bragging rights for the future development plans in Lumbini, to get some sense of how the geopolitical game plays upon Buddhist tropes.

SILK ROAD RESOURCES

- whc.unesco.org/en/list/1442. *See also 121, 139, 140, 200, 208, 242, 243, 322, 440, 450, 524, 561, 574, 576, 592, 660, 666, 668, 707, 736, 737, 779, 886, 912, 913, 1003, 1039, 1056, 1277, 1279, 1444, 1502*

- www.savingmesaynak.com

- artsandculture.google.com/partner/xuanzang-memorial-nava-nalanda-mahavihara

GOOD WORKS

■ 78

There is no shortage of humans behaving badly. The supply is endless. Ditto for the greenwashers who spin their quest for self-gain into Good Works fantasies. If you go by the bell curve, half of people are stupid, greedy, and violent. If you go by the Pareto Principle, eighty percent of the problems we face spring from the most egregious twenty percent of us.

Protecting and saving water, together. [PR slogan, 2018]
Maurizio Patarnello, CEO of Nestlé Waters

Right Livelihood may have looked very different 2500 years ago in an agrarian society, but human nature hasn't really changed at all.

Every religion has a version of the Golden Rule, and even in secular society the humanists tell us to "do no harm." In Buddhism, compassion and universal responsibility are the driving themes underpinning our efforts to heal the world, starting with ourselves.

In the Anthropocene, it has become clear that our faith in our own cleverness has led to extensive negative outcomes. We have repeatedly failed to discern the complex cybernetic feedback loops in the systems we seek to "improve." Some humility is in order. We need to figure out how to live sustainably within the world as it is, rather than bending it further to our short-term, imperfectly visualized future.

Enough with the self-driving cars. Enough with GMOs. Enough with ordering something from the other side of the planet by drone, just by talking to a device on the kitchen counter.

Enough with the 30-day mindfulness challenge. Enough with the rhyming love poem about yoga. Enough with "The Modern Self-Love Trap & What Loving Ourselves Really Means" magazine articles.

How much renunciation is each of us willing to accept? We say the Middle Way does not endorse excessive renunciation, but finding the middle point on the bell curve is not easy. Can we renounce a bit, please?

This is the point where I really have to start reflecting on my own behaviour, my own attitudes about what is important, and figure out how to scale back my own appetites. In other words, either with or before any attempts at helping others, I have to opt out of so much of normative culture, as hard as that is to do. And what do I find? Renunciation is a path that progressively reveals new onion-like layers of how I collude with society in entrapment. It turns out that while ultimate reality may be stainless and immutable, Buddhist practice requires constant vigilance. **Huineng** was wrong and **Shenxui** was right: we have to keep polishing the mirror. As a white, Canadian, educated, healthy, left-wing Buddhist man, I think I can say that whatever my current state of renunciation is, I could certainly go a bit further. I'm going to have to work on that! Damn.

In the Huayan metaphor of Indra's Net, from the *Avatamsaka Sutra*, there is a deep interconnectedness throughout each and every element of the universe. Surely, then, my small individual acts of renunciation, and not just my consumption, will have ripples in the cosmos.

Renunciation is not a popular word these days. We are programmed for self-indulgence. But if we really want to get to a post-growth, sustainable planet, we're going to have to sacrifice something (okay, a lot).

For starters, we're going to have to reprioritize our toxic value system. Pivoting from a benchmark of Gross Domestic Product (GDP) toward Gross National Happiness (GNH) is a great start. Contemporary discussions of this topic in Buddhist economics highlight the values of social equity, community, and connectedness. That's healthy, because you can't heal a sick individual within a sick system. (See **Michael Moore**'s documentary, *Sicko*, for a great example.) On the other hand, our efforts can't just be to graft this new dimension of compassionate outreach on to our old beliefs. That's a bootstrap scenario.

In Vajrayana initiation ceremonies, we become the Bodhisattvas we dream ourselves into being. We are all emanations in Indra's Net; there is no inherent true nature to our self-concept, and so nothing stopping us. Actualizing this requires a balancing act, a Dharma dance of stillness and movement – renunciation and good works. With one but not the other, we topple over. Like designers, we work with this incremental change over successive iterations to improve. That's easier to do if we have a plan.

Even making a plan is a giant step. I'm a Certified Associate in Project Management and I heartily endorse project management skills.

GOOD WORKS RESOURCES

- americanhumanist.org
- humanistcanada.ca
- skoll.org
- tzuchi.org
- blogs.dickinson.edu/buddhistethics/

PETITIONS

79

In the early history of petitions, they were requests to a person in power to right a wrong. Today, a similar application would be to petition the Court.

In our modern world, petitions have come to mean something entirely different from these more formal, legal precedents.

Please sign and share.

Social media is full of petitions: save the whales; impeach Trump; redesign a dangerous intersection; don't redesign our popular snowmobile trail.... The list is endless and we are likely to become jaded, numb, or fed up with them. The backlash calls them #slacktivism. According to the *New Statesman*, a British progressive liberal magazine, they simply don't work. The *New York Times*, profiling petition aggregator change.org, concludes that raising awareness makes petitions successful, not their ultimate acceptance or rejection.

So what is the value of petitions? Are they a valid form of activism?

A distinction can be made.

A petition about a specific topic, with a local focus, sent to an administrative body that is really in charge of that local jurisdiction has a good chance of passing. That seems worth investing in.

A petition about a general topic, with a global focus, shared amongst peers, is really a group identification marker that has little downstream impact. That does not seem worth investing in, or at least it should not be the terminus of our activism. There has also been a disturbing trend of using petitions as propaganda – a way of fomenting discord over wedge issues.

Of course, 99 percent of petitions have now moved online, and that has ramifications. Facebook "Likes", Twitter "Faves", and LinkedIn "Endorsements" are presented as community-builders. Aggregators like change.org, activism.com, moveon.org, and so on, provide a wealth of further options.

Crowdfunding sites are yet another flavour of participatory democracy, where we can vote with our dollars to support one cause or another.

What's a Buddhist to do?

There is a variety of petitions relating specifically to Buddhism, from support for the Rohingya in Myanmar, to protests against propaganda from the NKT, to saving a threatened Buddhist Studies university program, as well as platforms where Buddhist leaders have taken joint action on matters of national interest, such as immigration, sexual abuse, race relations, climate change, disarmament, and so on.

There is a another sort of petition, for which there is a longstanding history – for divine intervention. In a religious context, people might petition a deity through prayer, supplication, or offerings of various kinds.

The Buddhist approach is rather different. For starters, since there is no Creator God in Buddhism, and since Shakyamuni disavowed divine interventions, there is no Buddhist equivalent for religious petitions of that kind.

However, we often hear of Buddhists praying for the blessings of the Buddhas, Yidams, Gurus, and so on. Prayer wheels are spun, prayer flags are hung, incense is burned, offerings are made. Rather than simply dismissing these as vestiges of primitive beliefs about reality, or cultural idiosyncracies, these may be taken by Buddhists as practices to develop one's own mental continuum, rather than as something for which to expect external response. At least that is the contemporary Western Buddhist psychological perspective. The Pure Land notion of *tariki* is different.

As with many other Buddhist interpretations, the focus is on a turning about of the mind, rather than some external prime mover. We might say our modern focus on technology as the saviour is such a misplaced externalized focus, but quietism was not Shakyamuni's intent: "Not to commit evil, but to do all that is good, and to purify one's mind; that is the teaching of all the Buddhas." There's the doing part in the middle.

The difficulty becomes clear in the aphorism: the road to hell is paved with good intentions. For this reason, I believe that reasoned debate amongst diverse opinions is healthy, so that our intentions benefit from wide scrutiny and design thinking. There will always be powerful people and forces with agendas to promote. Speaking truth to that power will always be beneficial. Allowing a few to control the many, or for the many to limit their activism to petitions, are less than ideal consequences.

PETITIONS RESOURCES

- change.org
- activism.com
- moveon.org
- one.org
- www.petitions.net/buddhist_support_for_rohingya_people
- www.freetibet.org/petitions/3487

SLOGANS

80

Slogans suffer from the same pitfalls as petitions: they may wind up as superficial and ineffectual substitutes for real action. In some cases, they serve dark causes and inflame passions. Combined with images, slogans become memes (a term coined by **Richard Dawkins**): ideas and cultural information that are shared virally around the web, and their impact can be significant.

If people don't want to listen to you, what makes you think they want to hear from your sweater?

Fran Lebowitz

Memes are everywhere, not just on the web. Our branded clothing is just one example of how we affiliate ourselves with cultural groups through the way we present ourselves to the world. This reciprocal dynamic, of "joining the club" by displaying the signifiers and simultaneously proselytizing for it, has become a standard mode of self-identification in society. To put it another way (particularly for young people with heavy emotional investment in social media), memes have become the channel we tune in to, to define ourselves in relation to others. We are our own personal brands, looking for "likes" and "shares."

The unhealthy coupling of personal branding and compassion can be seen in the Icebucket Challenge, in which individuals agree to be filmed being doused with ice water as a symbolic accompaniment to a charitable donation, and then challenge another to repeat the process. The notion of helping is subsumed in the performance and chain-letter attitude of shaming if the challenged fails to take up the viral trend.

That is rather antithetical to the Buddhist notion of searching within for our true nature, or to the existential notion of creating our own meaning out of chaos, or simply caring about others in a humble way.

One of my favourite memes is a picture of Shakyamuni, with the line, "Pretty sure I never said that. – the Buddha" It's a tongue-in-cheek jab at all the other Buddhist memes out there that misquote Dharma to make a point that may or may not align with Buddhist teachings: fake Buddhist news, as it were. The psychology of twisting the words of others to fit our own purpose is beyond the scope of this book, but well worth considering.

Repeating slogans on your Facebook page, however erudite, uplifting, or engaging they may be, is simply pseudo-activism: #slacktivism. It is not a substitute for real life, nor really even much of a complement.

A certain degree of skepticism is necessary when we come in contact with slogans. Recognizing that they are always propaganda of some

ACTION

sort, we need to evaluate the source, the motive, and the implications. Consider the slogan "War on Drugs" and how that has played out. Or "Political power grows out of the barrel of a gun," Mao's famous dictum.

Investigative journalists (practitioners of an increasingly perilous profession) routinely explore the agenda behind the facade. This makes them dangerous to the powerful who prefer us to deal in passion for slogans rather than collaborative, informed understanding of what is really happening. Reality is so much messier, more complex, and boring.

Sadly, religious leaders are far from immune to this sort of cultish manipulation. In fact, quite the opposite. Adherence to religious dogma and ways of relating to authority have been masks for widespread, long-standing abuse by those with religious power. We want so much to believe that we are willing to doubt our own primal experience of the world to accommodate ourselves to fitting in. We put on the uniform and repeat the mantra slogans.

Here too, Shakyamuni was pretty clear about how his followers should not take anything on faith, but question everything to see if it made sense according to their own experience. Ultimately, he urged them to trust themselves.

I recognize the value of slogans; mantras have been a part of my personal practice for many years. But when I am with Westerners who are slavishly memorizing and reciting prayers, texts, and mantras in a foreign language they do not understand, because that language is supposed to be holy, it makes me sad. They are mistaking the pointing finger for the moon (which is, I know, a slogan).

The issue is not the slogan itself, but what we do with it. Do we deeply understand the meaning? Are we prepared to follow through on what it means? Can we see ourselves as larger than what the slogan says about us?

SLOGANS RESOURCES

- www.richarddawkins.net
- www.slogangenerator.org
- brandongaille.com/how-to-create-a-slogan-for-your-business/
- www.lionsroar.com/5-buddhist-slogans-office/
- theconversation.com/slacktivism-that-works-small-changes-matter-69271

BLOGS

■ Back in 2010, the University of British Columbia hosted a conference
81 called *Buddhism in Canada: Global Causes, Local Conditions.* I gave a presentation called CANADIAN BUDDHISTS ON THE WEB: *Push, Pull & Practice.*
At the time, my Sumeru blog had just won a Blogisattva award and blogs
were a big deal in the web world. That was
then, and this is now. As with everything else,
impermanence is the only constant.

> Times are bad. Children no
> longer obey their parents, and
> everyone is writing a book.
>
> *Marcus Tullius Cicero*

My interest in blogs began much earlier,
when I developed and taught one of Canada's
first courses focusing on the Internet, at Ryerson
University in the late 90's, entitled: *Publishing and the Internet.* I am one
of those dinosaurs who purchased one of the first personal computers in
the 1980's. I remember fax machines, the birth of the web, the advent of
email, HTML, and everything after.

Blogs took their original inspiration from *Star Trek*, a short-lived but
profoundly influential TV show in the 1960's, that commenced each episode with a voice-over from the "Captain's Log." They were personal web
pages featuring reportage, musings and opinions by individuals not associated with mainstream media. Like other cultural artifacts abounding
in the 500-channel cable universe, they featured something for everyone,
often with a lo-tech charm and a nerdy range of topics. They were subver-
sive, because they gave voice to a new class of commentator and a way for
others to follow them. A hot debate ensued: what is authoritative in the
realm of news media (an issue we still deal with, *viz* "#fakenews")?

Buddhist blogs walked the same uncharted path. Democratization
empowered fresh voices and that was good; but who was an authentic
teacher? Could lay Buddhists replace, or at least complement, ordained
monks and nuns as authoritative representatives of lineage? Were blogs
a door to, extension of, or substitute for, "actual" practice? What was the
relationship between a blog's value, the celebrity status (or lack thereof) of
its author, the sophistication of its digital *persona*, and the analytics of its
web traffic? How were we to relate to critical blogs that took a rebel stance
against the normative messages of Buddhist institutions (also an issue we
still deal with, *viz* "#metoo").

As the web evolved, so did blogs: they went mainstream. However,
that transformation was far from uniform within the Buddhist world.
Lineages with lots of western adherents (especially Zen, Vajrayana, and

secular Mindfulness) were very comfortable in cyberspace and savvy about their web presence. Other lineages (especially from Theravada countries) were much slower to embrace the possibilities of these new forms of participation in Sangha relationships. They were more comfortable with the traditional model of face-to-face practice.

Between 2011-2013, I undertook Canada's first national, sociological study of Buddhist organizations, with the assistance of the University of Toronto's Department of Religious Studies. Online presence was one of my significant topics of research. The study's key findings were published in *The Journal of Global Buddhism.*

As digital technology has evolved, so has our relationship to it. Blogs migrated to aggregators like Blogspot, moved to more robust content management systems like Wordpress, then narrowcasting services like RSS and podcasts, then social media platforms like Facebook and LinkedIn. The next wave of disruption came with virtual reality, as in Second Life. This was followed by Twitter, Snapchat, WhatsApp and other texting-type tools. These days, a Buddhist organization must embrace all forms of digital technology in its communications management plan.

Another important issue for Buddhists in this arena has to do with intellectual property. Is the Dharma free? Can we cut and paste from Dharma texts without attribution or remuneration? Is it okay to modify traditional texts and excerpts to make a point, or does this dilute the credibility of the teachings?

Crowdsourcing forums like Reddit and Dharma Wheel have become *de facto* hubs for discussion and seeds for cyberSanghas. Crowdfunding platforms like Kickstarter and GoFundMe allow us to follow our discussions with donations. Engaged Buddhist participation in other venues is also trending. I wonder what blockchain and AI will bring to the mix.

BLOGS RESOURCES

- cdn.shopify.com/s/files/1/2503/2728/files/Canadian_buddhists_on_the_web.pdf?9
- www.globalbuddhism.org/jgb/index.php/jgb/article/view/138/153
- www.webdesignerdepot.com/2011/03/a-brief-history-of-blogging/
- blogging.com/history/
- blogisattva.blogspot.com

FOOD

ALL BEINGS

82

Eating. What could be more vital in our wellbeing? Food consumes us, just as we consume food. It is important, first of all, to be mindful of the many facets of food's impact, and secondly, to choose wisely from among the buffet of perspectives, since not all will give us the same degree of physical or spiritual nourishment.

> Eat food, not too much, mostly plants.
>
> *Michael Pollan*

From the perspective of personal health, this quote from **Michael Pollan** crystallizes our best thinking at the moment, albeit only for those who possess the financial wherewithal to buy whatever they need. From a Buddhist perspective, it leaves me hungry for more. Don't get me wrong: it's advice I basically follow, but I would like to do better. I would like to see the big picture beyond my own personal wellbeing and eat for an equitable, sustainable future. Sadly, for most of the world, food insecurity is the norm.

Thinking about food from a design perspective, we can see our inter-being in the larger system of cultivation, harvest, manufacture, packaging, distribution, advertising, sale, medical implications, environmental implications, sustainability, and so on. Each of these has ramifications that deserve examination, as is alluded to in the *Oryoki* Zen Buddhist meal prayer: "First, seventy-two labors brought us this food; we should know how it comes to us."

In the following pages of this section, I hope to unpack some of these key themes of political, social, cultural, economic, environmental, and ethical issues surrounding food, from a Buddhist perspective.

The first Buddhist precept is to refrain from killing. That's a little different from the Judeao-Christian injunction against murder, in that it extends beyond other humans to include animals. In the best of all possible worlds, being vegan or vegetarian would be how to be. But Buddha did not preach veganism. In fact, when Buddhist monastics went on their alms rounds, they relied on the laity to provide them with food and were taught not to discriminate about what was offered. Buddha's goal here was more about freeing ourselves from obsessing about food and desire for more than is required for life.

In many Buddhist countries, a purely plant-based, healthful diet was simply not possible. Pragmatic accommodations were made.

However, now, with our global supply chain, we in North America each have more agency in terms of food. We are better able to see the long chain of cause and effect. Thus, our challenge extends beyond ourselves, to what is just and appropriate for every being involved in the food chain. This can be particularly difficult, since so much of our food comes to us through the efforts of multinational corporations whose agendas most often do not align with our aspirations. There is a political dimension to food that was never as dominant as it is now, because we understand that individual options are often constrained by institutional systems that put some at a disadvantage. For example, patent wars over intellectual property in the form of genetically modified organisms, fair trade agreements, or differential rates of obesity and other health disincentives based on socio-economic factors such as food deserts, are not issues that traditional Buddhist discourse would cover.

Environmental impacts from such practices as raising animals for food on an industrial scale, or the ubiquitous use of chemical additives such as pesticides or preservatives, have also become critical to modern discourse about food. These issues have synergistic impacts in other areas, such as sustainable fresh water and who gets it, chemicals in processed foods and how they affect health, fossil fuel consumption in our global supply chain, methane from organic waste in landfills, plastic ocean garbage, and so on.

Simply put, the four Bodhisattva Vows tell us that our choices must be for the betterment of others before ourselves. If that intention informs our food choices and our activism in the realm of food politics, we are on the right path. So I would say that in addition to Michael Pollan's excellent advice, we each need to be a food activist. There is too much at stake not to be. Even more than climate change, wild habitat destruction for agriculture is the number one cause for our alarming rate of extinctions on the planet. The shadows of palm oil and beef (for example) are long and dark. And do we really need 47 kinds of ice cream available at the supermarket?

ALL BEINGS RESOURCES

- michaelpollan.com
- www.foodpolitics.com
- fairtrade.ca
- www.greenpeace.org/usa/sustainable-agriculture/save-the-bees/
- npic.orst.edu (National Pesticide Information Center website)
- www.upaya.org/dox/oryoki-instructions.pdf

VICIOUS SAMSARA

83   In *The Jewel Ornament of Liberation*, **Gampopa** devotes an entire chapter to the vicious and intractable nature of samsara. In each of the six realms, beings suffer around food. The gods indulge in feasts while oblivious to the suffering of others. The asuras engage in constant plunder of the resources of others for themselves. Animals live in perpetual anxiety about finding their next meal, or being some predator's next meal. Hungry ghosts live in perpetual starvation. Hellions never even rise to the presence of mind to think of food, since their suffering is so immediate. Only humans have the space and clarity to make food choices that consider the implications for others (human and non-human).

Populations of vertebrate animals – such as mammals, birds, and fish – have declined by 58% between 1970 and 2012. And we're seeing the largest drop in freshwater species: on average, there's been a whopping 81% decline in that time period.
WWF Living Planet Report 2016

The problem is that our entire samsaric culture, all our secular institutions (and even most of our spiritual institutions), are set up to condition us into a particularly unhealthy relationship with food. Finding a better way is not easy.

Where food is concerned, the personal is definitely political. As Chan Master **Baizhang Huaihai** famously said: "A day of no work is a day of no eating."

What is the relationship between taste, the experience of eating, satisfaction, nutrition, and health? In the realm of the personal, what is our best approach? What is mindful eating, really? Given that North Americans typically eat one third of their meals outside the home, can we eat mindfully in restaurants? Is gratitude for that coffee at the drive-through enough? Is kombucha green tea really going to elevate our being, or is it just the latest fad? Can food be an addiction and a trap? Is food porn a real thing? Can we consume it if we didn't cook it or contribute to its creation? Is gratitude for the inter-being of food inescapable? Will we ever not need "temporary" food banks and soup kitchens?

In this Anthropocene, will there be enough food for the 11 billion people projected for the planet in the coming years? Who will eat and who will starve? How many domesticated animals will we kill? What environmental degradation will result from our industrial farming? How many wild animals and plants will become extinct because we have razed their habitats? Where will we put all the garbage? How can we make the entire system sustainable? What is our plan? Indeed, the questions are numberless and we vow to answer them all.

It's not as if we have no options here in North America. Organic, vegetarian food products are now widely available at competitive prices. Vege-burgers are available at most fast-food restaurants and are even the hottest IPOs for investors. South Indian vegetarian restaurants exist in most big cities. We can buy fair-trade products, and support social entrepreneurship through initiatives such as the Greyston Bakery, founded by the late **Roshi Bernie Glassman**.

We see the ravages of meat culture and processed edibles (I hesitate to call them food) everywhere around us, and yet we still keep Instagramming our meals. We see starvation as a weapon of war, as in Yemen, and yet do nothing beyond express some horror at a photo of a dying child. We may mindfully chew each samosa 32 times, volunteer at the food bank, participate in community gardens, recycle all our food waste, eat vegan, boycott Nestlé and Monsanto, buy acres of wilderness in the Amazon for habitat land trusts, and it will never be enough to end the suffering.

But…if we consider our world as a bodhimandala, *Bodh Gaia* (a portmanteau word), and understand ourselves as one small part of that living organism, our healthy choices help ensure the health of the whole. And, importantly, the health of the whole ensures our individual health. The ripples of our interbeing spread throughout the ten directions and the three times. The future of our planet is crowdsourced, by definition.

In Gampopa's time, karma was a rather mystical concept. Now, with our intimate understanding of supply chains, we see the workings of cause and effect in stark clarity. The ethical choices, the institutional inertia (if not outright hostility), the suffering of others, the future of the planet, our own personal shrug: nothing is hidden. May our efforts be worthy.

VICIOUS SAMSARA RESOURCES

- www.frozenark.org
- www.regjeringen.no/en/topics/food-fisheries-and-agriculture/svalbard-global-seed-vault/id462220/
- www.juul.com
- www.worldwildlife.org/experts/dekila-chungyalpa
- www.seachoice.org

FARM

■ 84 We have enough food for everybody, but they can't get it. They are like hungry ghosts. There is no shortage of problems involving farming these days. Some have to do with land use, some with the crops themselves, and some with social impacts on the other side of the fence. Here are just a few, specifically about farming (as opposed to the particular crops being grown).

> The real cause of hunger is the powerlessness of the poor to gain access to the resources they need to feed themselves.
>
> *Frances Moore Lappé*

Destruction of virgin forest to create croplands (for palm oil in Indonesia, for example) is reversing one of the planet's crucial carbon sinks, in addition to its impact in wildlife habitat destruction leading to a dramatic rise in extinctions.

Wasteful water use (such as for raising livestock), unsanitary water use (such as irrigating crops with potentially contaminated water sourced upstream from feedlots), and excessive water use (draining ancient aquifers and water tables), all put unsustainable stress on the ecology.

Monoculture has depleted heritage seed diversity, increasing the threat from blights and diseases, as well as distorting longstanding natural ecologies.

Concentration of control amongst large agri-businesses strips farmers of control and sustainable profits, while forcing them to bear the greatest risk. Marginal subsistence farmers are most vulnerable.

Genetic modification of organisms and patents over intellectual property create an unlevel playing field for small farmers, against whom multinational corporations launch crippling lawsuits or insupportable debt to nullify alternatives.

Since the 1950's, increasing dependence on synthetic fertilizers and pesticides limits agricultural options, threatens pollinators (e.g., bees) and other animals, creates toxic run-off, harms human health, and has proven to be an unsustainable system.

Healthy diets for subsistence farmers become disrupted as they switch from traditional crops to cash crops for sale and/or export, often with the need for much greater resource inputs.

Long-distance supply chains involve enormous amounts of carbon-based energy to bring food from farm to table. They also lend themselves to lax quality control, weak environmental oversight, and exploitative labour practices.

In all of this, governments often act with little awareness of potential unforeseen consequences, in thrall to the ideology and dollars of lobbyists.

On the other hand, there are some encouraging trends.

Consumers are increasingly conscious about their food choices. Organic, non-GMO, and Fair Trade products are now commonplace and often competitively priced. Slow food, local food, farm basket networks, and vegetarian options are gaining traction. The realities of good nutrition, the health risks of food additives and pesticide residues, and the ethical implications of food choices, are all transforming the food chain.

Historical Buddhism does not have much to offer on agricultural policy as it pertains to Right Livelihood, since monastics traditionally relied on alms for their sustenance. Romantic images of monks saving earthworms from the plow (as in the 1997 movie *Seven Years in Tibet*) are about as realistic as other fantasies about Buddhism (such as the 1937 movie *Lost Horizon*). Books on mindful eating, with their intensely personal focus, aren't much help either beyond the basics, since they rarely offer concrete advice on how to be an activist on the larger ethical issues.

Be that as it may, the guiding principle of Buddhist practice has always been to create the greatest happiness for the greatest number of beings (and that's all beings, not just humans), rather than short-term benefit for the individual at the expense of others. It does not take a rocket scientist to figure out that we are heading for a system crash. From **E.F. Schumacher** (*Small is Beautiful*), to **Frances Moore Lappé** (*Diet for a Small Planet*), to **John Robbins** (*Diet for a New America*), we can get the lay of the land. Systems thinking and design thinking can provide us with a framework for action. What remains is for us to find the will to act, and for some outspoken Buddhist leaders to take the initiative to make the discussion of agriculture a key component of our largely urban practice.

FARM RESOURCES

- www.smallplanet.org
- waldenlabs.com
- thehumaneleague.org
- chooseveg.com
- mercyforanimals.org

MEAT

▬
85
Right now worldwide, more than 150 billion animals are farmed for food each year – two-thirds in conditions that mean they can't move freely or live naturally. We kill 50 billion of them annually.

Beyond the ethical issue of killing animals, this industrial scale of raising them creates a panoply of very serious ecological problems.

In the time it takes you to read this sentence, approximately 4000 farm animals in the United States will be slaughtered.
animalclock.org

It takes 1800 gallons of fresh water to produce one pound of beef. That is equivalent to seven years of drinking water for the average human being – hardly the best way to use such a vital and limited resource.

Farm animal digestion (enteric fermentation) is responsible for 26% of US methane production. Landfill accounts for another 16%, much of it related to food garbage. More recent studies show that food system emissions could account for as much as quarter of all human emissions. That is 12% from agricultural production, another 9% from farming-induced deforestation, and a further 3% from things like refrigeration and freight.

If people just substituted beans for beef, but still ate chicken, pork and seafood, and if our energy and transportation infrastructure for the meat industry remained unchanged, that single transformative dietary act would have reduced US greenhouse gas emissions by about 50% of what would be needed for the country to have reached its 2020 targets.

However, we're moving in the opposite direction: the growing middle classes of developing countries are increasingly turning to meat-rich diets.

Doctors tell us repeatedly that red meat, processed meat, and meat preservatives are really, really bad for our health. Add to that the pesticides, heavy metals, and industrial chemicals that bioaccumulate as they move up the food chain: human breast milk included. Runoff from feedlots, pig manure ponds, and so on, has repeatedly contaminated vegetable farm irrigation with toxic bacteria such as *e. coli*. Animal feed made from animal byproducts, fed to cows (who are herbivores), resulted in Mad Cow disease in humans. Animal husbandry also gave us SARS and Bird Flu.

Buddhists should be concerned not just about killing and eating animals, but humane treatment of them. Caged animals spend much of their lives confined in unbelievably small cages. For example, a pig gestation cage (where mother pigs spend more than three-quarters of their lives) is 2' x 6.5'. That's not even enough room for them to turn around. The average chicken spends its entire life in a space 8"x10", smaller than a piece of paper from your laser printer.

Seafood is no better. Farmed fish live in similarly overcrowded conditions and are documented as being one of the most toxic foods around, because of the pesticides and antibiotics used to control disease and parasite infestations.

Wild-caught fish face other challenges. Indiscriminate overfishing has destroyed entire species populations. Wherever there is fishing, there is bycatch—the incidental capture of non-target species such as dolphins, marine turtles and seabirds. More than 40% of what gets caught is thrown away. Farm fish who escape wreak havoc on wild populations.

A vegetarian's foodprint is about two-thirds of the average American and almost half that of a meat lover. For a vegan it is even lower. The health benefits of a vegetarian diet are widely documented, from weight loss, to risk reduction for heart attack, stroke, and colon cancer.

Buddhism has never been explicitly anti-meat. Shakyamuni's instructions for the Sangha were to rely on food donations without discrimination. Under Right Livelihood, butchery was considered a bad choice, but the concept of consumers as activists, or even as active agents in a larger system, was hardly a doctrinal cornerstone. Even in Buddhist countries where vegetarianism was a viable option, the rationale rarely extended beyond avoiding killing. Ecology and climate change were non-issues.

Now, in the Anthropocene, we have so many compelling reasons to give up meat – reasons that are profoundly congruent with Buddhism. The Dharma teaches us that we are all part of interbeing. How can we legitimize killing when there is no self and other, no ontological difference between humans and animals? We are killing ourselves.

MEAT RESOURCES

- ourworldindata.org/meat-and-seafood-production-consumption
- www.beefresearch.ca/blog/cattle-feed-water-use/
- shrinkthatfootprint.com
- www.foodprint.io
- www.canadiancattlemen.ca/2017/10/27/k-d-langs-effect-on-the-beef-industry/

VEG

■ You may think that veg equals virtue. Sadly, the true story is much more
86 nuanced, as noted in "Why Salad Is So Overrated," **Tamar Haspel**'s article
from the *Washington Post*, Aug 23, 2015.

Salad vegetables are pitifully low in nutrition. A head of iceberg lettuce
has the same water content as a liter bottle

> Nothing will benefit human
> health and increase the
> chances for survival of life
> on Earth as much as the
> evolution to a vegetarian diet.
>
> *Albert Einstein*

of Evian (96% water, 4% bottle) and is only
marginally more nutritious. In that sense, lettuce is a simply a frightfully expensive vehicle
to transport refrigerated water from farm to
table. That is not the only problem. Lettuce has
a couple of unenviable top rankings in the food
world. For starters, it's the top source of food
waste (vegetable division), becoming more than 1 billion pounds of uneat-
en salad every year. And it's also the chief culprit for foodborne illnesses.
According to the Centers for Disease Control, green leafies accounted for
22% of all foodborne illnesses from 1998-2008.

Fruits, vegetables and condiments have been the basis for some of
humanity's worst crimes: Imperial spice wars of colonization; slavery on
sugar plantations; and establishment of Banana Republic dictatorships, to
name just a few. Chocolate and vanilla come at a bittersweet cost in child
labour, habitat destruction, and diversion of infrastructure resources.

Fruits and vegetables are a prime segment for genetic engineering.
About 70% of the processed foods in your supermarket include GE ingredients. This includes 88% of corn, 93% of soybeans, 90% of canola, and so
on. Most are modified to include resistance to diseases, pests or pesticides.
Others are modified to withstand long-distance transport, or to increase
expression of particular attributes (e.g., pink pineapple).

Sugar? Tobacco? Poppies? Cocaine? Hardly virtuous vegetables. Potato
chips? Hardly a nutritious staple. Konjack? Why do we need konjack?

Cut flowers? Growing them typically takes huge concentrations of
pesticides and 30x more water than agricultural crops. Refrigerating and
transporting them requires massive amounts of energy, since they are
mostly shipped by air. That also creates a lot of carbon dioxide pollution.
Kenya produces 33% of the world's cut flowers, while the Netherlands, the
world's largest flower-producing country, uses 6x more energy per flower
to heat and light its greenhouses. A single rose consumes enough energy
to drive your car 5 kilometers.

Ordering food online? If the Internet was a country, it would be the sixth largest energy consumer in the world.

There have been 7,500 varieties of apples recognized around the world. A hundred years ago, more than 700 of them were grown commercially in North America. Now we are down to fewer than 50. My local supermarket has about six types. Yet you can walk into a supermarket and see produce from around the world any day of the week. You don't see the hidden costs of those items because they are externalized.

Food waste is a huge issue. We throw away 40% of all the food we produce, and that includes the energy it takes to grow it, ship it, refrigerate it, and package it. If food waste were a country, it would be the world's third largest carbon polluter. In North America, that translates into more than 20 billion pounds of food each year.

Of all produce grown, as much a 30% of a harvest can be rejected, simply due to size, shape or color; they don't meet grocery store standards. We are under the tyranny of an aesthetic illusion that has nothing to do with nutrition. Eating "ugly" is fine, and in fact there are a number of advocacy organizations working on food justice by incorporating viable distribution networks for ugly vegetables. For example, Imperfect Produce will even deliver right to your door!

Most of America's fruits and vegetables are imported, even though one third of Americans are involved in growing food. You might consider reducing your dependence on the grid, by planting your own vegetable garden. It's fun and healthy, and your prize organic zucchini might just win top honours at the local harvest fair. As an added bonus, you might even have a bumper crop you can donate to a local foodbank. This could be the start of a beautiful friendship, because urban farming is a great way to build community. (There, I didn't mention Buddhism once.)

VEG RESOURCES

- www.foodcowboy.com
- www.rescuingleftovercuisine.org
- mealconnect.org
- www.misfitsproduce.ca
- outrider.org
- shabkar.org

FOOD INSECURITY

87 Walking into a modern supermarket, it is hard to imagine hunger. The aisles are filled with a staggering array of products: more than 45,000 on average. For any particular type of food, there are literally dozens of choices. Clearly, there is no shortage of food here, but for many people, it is an unattainable luxury.

> Imagine that you had just enough money to buy food for the week, with nothing left over to pay your utility bills or buy bus fare to get to work. Many hungry families face these tough choices every day.
>
> *feedingamerica.org*

One in six people in North America face hunger every day. For households with children, it's one in five. For disadvantaged communities, it's one in three! How could such a thing be "normal?"

Poverty is the main reason people go hungry. They can't afford to buy food. However, there is a larger, systemic issue: many impoverished communities are food deserts, where grocery stores, farmers' markets, and healthy food providers are noticeably absent. It's a health disaster, compounding the other problems.

In cities like Detroit after the collapse of 2008, citizens took matters into their own hands and began a variety of urban farming initiatives to counter the scarcity of fresh produce, but these types of community initiatives are the exception rather than the rule.

In olden times, Buddhist monasteries were supported by the farming communities around them. In Zen monasteries, daily physical work (*samu*) was part of practice, but it was not typically agricultural labour. Now the tables are turned. For modern-day Buddhist centres, I would suggest that samu could include community outreach food security initiatives. Those could be urban farming, volunteering at the local food bank, running a "pay-what-you-can" vegetarian meal program, a school lunch program, or many other things.

In **Bernie Glassman Roshi**'s Zen Peacemakers Sangha, homeless street retreats were a regular, if radical, example of how practitioners could directly experience the lived struggles of society's weakest citizens, and a powerful incentive for change.

In the larger global context, food insecurity is propelled by a confluence of factors, from global warming, to cash crop capitalism, to food access as a weapon of war. There are many think tanks and NGOs focused on food policy, tracking the problem and suggesting alternative solutions (although, admittedly, lots of them are politicized and instrumentalized as adjuncts of soft diplomacy initiatives, or economic development programs designed to alter current import-export ratios).

The typical argument around food insecurity says we need to grow more food for more people. It's presented as an open-ended challenge, rather than one of redistributing a finite number of resources more equitably. Ever since The Club of Rome published *Limits to Growth* in 1972, the focus has shifted in a variety of debates (such as energy and climate change), but food is a personal hot-button topic. For people at the top of the food privilege pyramid, the thought that they might actually have to do more with less (for reasons of equity, not health) is unpalatable (no pun intended).

For Buddhist practitioners, becoming involved in policy debate is a political decision at one remove from direct action, but it is an essential aspect of the social justice big picture.

Large Buddhist charities such as Buddhist Global Relief, Tzu Chi Compassion Buddhist Relief, the Buddhist Peace Fellowship, and Karuna have food programs as part of their mandate. Many temples and organizations who support orphanages and the like in Asia fund food programs. So there are many opportunities to deepen one's practice around food security within the context of Buddhist organizations.

However, consider the potential impact of bringing a Buddhist perspective to other broad-based organizations focused on progressive social policies! In many respects, your sweat equity is worth much more than your financial contributions.

This is a deeply-researched and hugely important issue, for which I discovered many more resources than I could possibly fit into the section below. If this is a topic of interest to you, you will find many great ideas online to help you actualize your inspiration.

FOOD SECURITY RESOURCES
- www.gifs.ca (Global Institute for Food Security)
- www.urbanfarming.org (Urban Farming USA)
- buddhistglobalrelief.me/category/food-insecurity/
- www.tzuchi.us/story/thought-for-food/
- www.agrowingculture.org/beyond-production-a-story-of-buddhist-farming/

EAT

88

Most popular Buddhist writing about eating focuses on mindfulness of the immediate act. In that regard, Buddhist/mindful eating is not so different from mainstream advice on healthy eating: listen to your body and stop when full; appreciate your food; chew slowly; be fully present.

> There is no love sincerer than the love of food.
>
> *George Bernard Shaw*

However, there is a much larger body of cultural baggage to consider. There are a lot of different reasons why we eat. Our food priorities include not only health, but also enjoyment, relationships, status, transference, and sublimation. Let's tease out a few themes.

The Buddhist origin story has Shakyamuni leaving a life of privilege, then starving himself with ascetic practices, and then realizing the error of his ways after eating a healthy meal offered to him by a passing maiden, before beginning the meditation that would take him to his ultimate goal: reaching Enlightenment. India had a well-accepted tradition of feeding yogins, so the notion of Shakyamuni accepting the meal was not a radical idea. However, Buddha's Middle Way was a departure from the extreme of asceticism as well as from the extreme of sybaritic indulgence.

Early Buddhist thinking about food focused on sustenance without attachment. Denying oneself was as much of a trap as over-indulging. That is still true today: obsessive attention to dieting and exercise is as unhealthy as over-eating and a sedentary lifestyle. Our unhealthy relationship with food includes celebrity diets, celebrity chefs, food fads, and a variety of other food porn variations in the booming industry of food-TV and cookbooks. It could also include fetishization of mindful eating, Zen-style *oriyoki*, tea ceremonies, *tsok* offerings, Buddhist cookbooks, and other Buddhist food culture. These may be essential for some, beneficial for many, but hardly a full practice for most. What's anybody other than a *tenzo* to do? We don't want to throw the udon out with the pasta water.

The new wrinkle is how food, exercise and health have been digitized for a quantified life. We want to know how many calories, what type of calories, how many steps, our body mass index, blood pressure, heart rate, carb-to-fiber ratio, and so on. And we want to post them all to social media along with our food selfies! Soon our insurance plans may be demanding the data from us for compliance purposes.

Eating with others is a natural and healthy thing. However, restaurants are complicated. As customers, we are in a privileged position. The workers may not be well-treated. Fast-food restaurants mostly offer unhealthy food. The atmosphere is not conducive to reflective eating. We often eat out because we are in a rush, tired, or distracted. Sometimes we eat out simply because we can; it's not cheap. So how can we eat mindfully when we can't eat optimally?

Restaurant critics, from the elite to the crowdsourced Yelp reviewer, often focus on food as a status symbol. "Look how cutting edge, how rich, how health-oriented, and how sophisticated, I am." Insert your own image of a wine snob here. As far as status symbols go, what you eat has got to be one of the most ephemeral. Here today; turd tomorrow.

Eating as an act of transference? You are what you eat, the saying goes. Mass marketers of edible products know all too well how to ping our neural response centres with food additives and excito-toxins that can short-circuit our rational relationship to what we eat. We'll eat poison gladly if it tastes good, costs little, and works really slowly. As you can imagine, there are so many emotion issues tied to eating, it's hard to know where to begin.

Eating is often a proxy for body image in general. Every day, we are bombarded with body-shaming messages meant to distract us from more meaningful issues, and to disempower us. One has only to look at the covers of women's magazines in the drug store to see the process in action. Barbie rules, right down to the thigh gap! What choice to we have but to eat our suffering? The result: dysmorphia.

Sharon Suh (*Occupy This Body: A Buddhist Memoir*) sees mindful eating as a way of reclaiming our relationships to our bodies. In a world where food is a weapon, a prize, or a drug, simply listening to our hunger and thirst, and responding without the overlay, can be a revolutionary act of liberation.

EAT RESOURCES

- mygoodplanet.com/
- mygoodplanet.com/veganism-time-high/
- www.meatfreemondays.com/ (Paul McCartney)
- thecenterformindfuleating.org/
- www.meatless.nl/
- gebis.org/community/

DRINK

■ 89 Water is a powerful metaphor, and it appears often in Buddhism. We bathe the baby Buddha, put water offerings on the shrine, see the moon of truth reflected in the water of delusion, see the universality and clarity of water as a stand-in for Tathagatagarbha, speak of how the lotus grows from muddy water, refer to it as one of the five psycho-cosmic elements of a Vajrayana *chorten*, pay homage to Naga water serpents, and so on.

> They both listened silently to the water, which to them was not just water, but the voice of life, the voice of Being, the voice of perpetual Becoming.
> *Hermann Hesse*
> Siddhartha

The builders of Angkor Wat had an exquisitely sophisticated understanding of hydrological engineering, but that is not what we think of when we think of that ancient city. Somehow, in our modern era, we have forgotten about the actual reality of water.

Freshwater makes up a very small fraction of all water on the planet. While nearly 70% of the world is covered by water, only 2.5% of it is fresh. The rest is saline and ocean-based. Even then, just 1% of our freshwater is easily accessible, with much of it trapped in glaciers and snowfields. In essence, only 0.007% of the planet's water is available to feed and quench the thirst of its 7.7 billion people.

Ecologists talk about the water cycle: where water is, where it goes, and how it gets there. There is the same amount of freshwater on earth as there always has been, but the population has exploded, leaving the world's water resources in crisis.

We are tapping into fossil water underground faster than the thousands of years it will take to replenish. Fracking for fossil fuel extraction is contaminating our aquifers. Industry is polluting our rivers and lakes. Municipal water treatment plants can't keep up with the deluge of excreted medications in our drinking water. We irrigate our vegetable farms with water contaminated from adjacent feedlots. Multinational corporations buy up water rights at the expense of local populations, and then sell that water at a price and in forms that benefit only their shareholders. The world's largest reservoirs of freshwater, the polar ice caps and glaciers, are vanishing. Right now, 92% of the world's flowing freshwater is behind dams, and in many cases, those rivers never reach the sea. Inland seas (like the Aral Sea) and great lakes (like Lake Chad) are shrinking and drying up. All of this ecosystem havoc has so disrupted the water cycle that pernicious drought has reached pandemic proportions.

Water is indispensible to life. As such, it is a right, and explicitly recognized as such by the United Nations. Nevertheless, as a resource in short supply, freshwater has become a source of international tensions (as with the Mekong River) and withholding it has become a weapon of war (as in Yemen).

On the flip side, commodified water is packaged in power drinks, soda pop, vitamin water, and a plethora of plastic bottles. We'd rather ship bottles of fancy water halfway around the world than clean up the water in our own proverbial backyards. Just ask native Canadians who've lived with boil-water advisories for years, because the government won't invest in clean water for them (investing instead in contentious oil pipelines to get the world's dirtiest oil from Alberta to the coast).

According to inventor **Dean Kamen**, half of the world's infectious diseases could be eradicated if everybody had access to clean drinking water. He's been working on a simple, inexpensive distillation device (the Slingshot) to do it. His technology is sound, but so far the idea hasn't taken off. Meanwhile, another of his inventions, the mix-your-own-soda-flavour machine at your local movieplex, has been a big hit.

Lifestraw is another clean-water technology (using filtration) that has popped up to respond to the market opportunity of contaminated water. In both cases, clean water is a market opportunity instead of a right. That's not a very Buddhist approach, in my humble opinion, but if that's what it takes to solve the problem, and if harm reduction beats puritanical extremism, I'm good with it.

The sad fact is that I cannot find any resources about water management policy and implementation from a Buddhist perspective, except for passing reference as part of generalized environmental orientations. I am thirsty for more.

DRINK RESOURCES

- www.slingshotdoc.com
- www.lifestraw.com
- 12.000.scripts.mit.edu/mission2017/dams-and-reservoirs/
- www.ecology.com/water/
- www.internationalrivers.org
- www.ottawariverkeeper.ca

PACKAGE

Buddha's prime directive was: "see reality for what it is; don't be fooled into thinking your labels and projections have inherent substantiality." That is diametrically opposed to the advertising dictum: "Sell the sizzle, not the steak." Nowhere is the latter approach more evident than in food packaging. You know what I mean: you bought a bag of something and discover it's half empty (sold by weight, not by volume). The picture on the box looks soooo good (not shown actual size). The sealed plastic clamshell and cardboard frame are enormous, compared to the product (for theft control). We are seduced by elaborate printing, foil stamping, lenticular and holographic onsets, die-cutting, embossing, promotional offers, iconic container shapes and exotic materials. Are we buying the item or the package? Often, it's the design we are consuming.

81 Incredibly Evil Packaging Designs That Will Seriously Infuriate You
Šarūnė Bar, BoredPanda

Most packaging is single-use and then discarded. Only one-third of recyclable packaging (glass, metal, cardboard) is recycled. Many types of packaging are only semi-recyclable (plastic). Some packaging is designed for the landfill (tetras, foils, amalgams). Even with recycling, most re-use is downcycling. We actually pay a premium for recycled, post-consumer recycled, and biodegradable packaging!

Packages are like a big, dangling carrot. The goal is to convey as little information as possible about the ingredients, while maximizing the emotional allure and promote frequent purchases. Producers have fought pitched legal battles for years to limit nutritional information, allow questionable health claims, disguise or omit ingredients, use misleading "sell by" dates, promote over-packaged individually-portioned and take-out product lines, and market to children. Industry consolidation has resulting in a handful of giant corporations who control all of this, giving us the illusion of choice instead of real, sustainable options. Ironically, the only plain packaging we see is for sex toys, cigarettes, and cannabis.

We live in a world of media franchise brand tie-ins (think Disney or Star Wars). Contests, puzzles, coupons and other offers make packaging itself the product (here in Canada, we have Tim Horton's Roll Up The Rim To Win coffee cups, or McDonald's McMonopoly french fries pouches). Market segmentation by gender, age, region, ethnicity and other demographic markers is the norm (think of a basic item like a toothbrush then visit that aisle in the store).

Packages are designed to fit into store planograms, and packagers pay enormous premiums for specific shelf placement, end-caps, stand-alone displays, and such. The constraints of supply chain management mean secondary packaging must also be considered; not just the plastic bag you might need to get your purchase home, but the pallet-wrapped, container-friendly, barcoded boxes or crates, and all the infrastructure involved in shipping and inventory control too.

But enough ranting from me about the evils of packaging. Let's get back to the Way of the Bodhisattva.

Fifty years ago, *How to Wrap Five Eggs: Traditional Japanese Packaging*, by **Hideyuki Oka**, was a bestselling book. It focused on the aspect of Japanese design known as *tsutsumu* – the art of wrapping objects and gifts. With reusable materials and minimalist design sophistication, the showcased packages showed us another way to be. (Think of **Marie Kondo**'s Tidying Up method, for some sense of the aesthetic.) Tsutsumu is complementary to the minimalist Zen approach to possessions in the MariKon Method, and analogous to the broader, secular applications of mindful simplicity derived from *satipatthana*.

Doing away with excess packaging seems to me to go hand-in-glove with Buddhist sensibilities. Cardboard is better than plastic; simplicity is better than ornament; reusable containers are better than single-use. The other day I bought some blueberries. They came in a cardboard box instead of a plastic clamshell. I was practically beside myself with joy, because I hadn't seen blueberries without plastic in years, since I was a kid when they came in wood veneer tubs.

Basically, packaging is, for the most part, garbage in every sense of the word; think carefully and do your research before you buy. Whenever possible, look for the product with the least packaging.

PACKAGE RESOURCES
* www.zerowasteweek.co.uk
* ec.europa.eu/eurostat/statistics-explained/index.php/Packaging_waste_statistics
* toxicsinpackaging.org/faqs/
* challenges.openideo.com/challenge/circular-design/ideas/assignments/mission-reimagine-the-package-design-for-zero-waste1

HEALTH

BIRTH

91 Birth is suffering. That's how the Buddha's list of sufferings in the Four Noble Truths begins, but for the Bodhisattva in 2020, reproduction ethics and politics demand deeper scrutiny. Birth has become the battleground for so many other agendas.

If we are to heal the planet, we must begin by healing birth.

Agnes Sallet Von Tannenberg

Buddhist scriptures say we all share pristine Buddha Nature, but Buddhist leaders mostly seem to treat women as second-class citizens, denying them full agency in their own paths to enlightenment, in denial about that systemic discrimination, and content to ignore the suffering women experience because of it. In this, they are merely mirroring the patriarchal societies where they find their expression. However, modern feminists are having none of it, and more power to them! **Rita Gross**, author of *Buddhism After Patriarchy* has lots of good advice in that regard.

The current battle over reproduction, with a *Handmaid's Tale* on one side and women's experience on the other, shows no signs of easing up.

It's a myth that birth is a private matter between two people in a socially-approved union. Society has always been proscriptive in that regard. Now, modern interventions have separated reproduction from sex with technologies like birth control, artificial insemination, *in vitro* fertilization, genetic screening and manipulation, embryonic stem cell research, and so on. Society has not caught up to reality.

We could consider that "birth" really is a process with seven parts: preconception; conception; gestation; birth; after the birth; bonding; and infancy. In each phase, the wellbeing of mother and child depend on a web of factors that we hope start with the best of intentions, followed by all the support required for a healthy outcome. There are some books about enlightened pregnancy, mindful childbirth, Buddhism for mothers, and the like. It's good to have a birth plan, because without it, one is at the mercy of standardized procedures designed for the benefit of the healthcare industry as much as, if not more than, the parents themselves.

Bodhisattvas today need an activist perspective. For example, how do you feel about denial of access to contraception? Rollbacks of sexual education courses? Sexualized violence? Cancellation of funding for midwives? Mothers in labour turned away from hospitals because they don't have insurance coverage? Lack of quality daycare? The fact is that birth does not occur in some isolated vacuum; it is part of a continuum.

HEALTH

Many of today's socially progressive initiatives focus on empowering women and girls, and there are a variety of Buddhist organizations, such as Karuna.org, which sponsor programs like that, but if you search for contemporary Buddhist literature on any of the broader issues, you will be deeply disappointed by the lack of any substantive discourse about the more technologically-challenging aspects of modern birth.

We are in unfamiliar territory. Is fertility a right? Is infertility a disease? What are the privacy issues around sperm and egg donors or recipients? Can you sell sperm, eggs, or embryos? What are the legal rights and responsibilities of a surrogate? When does an embryo become a fetus? When does a fetus become a person? If prenatal gender testing can lead to infanticide, should we not allow that testing? What is the fate of unneeded research embryos? What are the acceptable limits to embryo manipulation?

On the other hand, one aspect of birth that has received a fair bit of attention in Buddhist writing is death, and grief around stillbirth or abortion. Jizo, the Japanese personality of Ksitigarbha, is well-known as the patron Bodhisattva of unborn children. Another example of Buddhist views on birth: we are told that all beings have been our mothers, and so we should treat them with the same respect and love we show our mothers. Instead of getting caught up in sentimental visualizations, I suggest that treating the actual half of humans who give birth in ways that will empower and support them would be a better interpretation of that advice.

Rebirth is a concept integral to Buddhism. We hear that our lives are the result of our past karma, that we should see problems as opportunities, and that some reincarnated beings (i.e., *tulkus*) are *a priori* better than others. With no scientific evidence, I remain unconvinced. I would much prefer to see more enlightened approaches to birth in <u>this</u> lifetime.

BIRTH RESOURCES

- tricycle.org/magazine/rita-gross-female-birth/
- www.facebook.com/enlightenedpregnancy
- killingthebuddha.com/mag/confession/birth-is-suffering/
- www.ncbi.nlm.nih.gov/books/NBK235272/
- www.nytimes.com/2017/01/06/well/family/the-japanese-art-of-grieving-a-miscarriage.html

OLD AGE

■ Here in the developed world, we are facing a silver tsunami of aging baby
92 boomers. Don't worry, millennials, we'll be gone soon. In fact, in the developing world, we are already a much smaller segment of the population than people under 25. So you'll get a chance to run the place in no time at all. Hey, meanwhile, sorry about the mess.

I thought growing old would take longer.

That is cold comfort for our cohort, as we come face to face with our own impermanence, but there are many myths on offer to help us during this phase of our lives: active retirement when we get to enjoy the fruits of our labours; a time of reflection, a celebration, and "going forth" into mystical opening; elderhood where we get to mentor the young; the opportunity to give back; and so on. In the shadows are other alternative futures: loss of faculties; loss of independence; age-ism; loneliness; regret; anticipatory grief; and disillusionment. The greatest of these disillusionments is perhaps that the "upbeat" myths we've been served are just marketing fluff, or half-truths at best.

In reality, old age is personal, visceral, and utterly front-and-centre in our daily experience. There is no narrative we can construct to sugar-coat it. As my mother used to say: old age is not for the faint of heart, but it's better than the alternative. We have more yesterdays than tomorrows, and even a mid-life crisis has passed its Best-Before date.

I'll be more specific. Very few people have the luxury of active retirement with no financial worries. The hale and hearty grandparents you see cavorting in television pharma ads bear no resemblance to real people struggling with chronic illness, dementia, social isolation, and so on. And even those who win the old age health-and-wealth lottery cannot escape the dukkha of old age.

Of course, we all suffer from anticipatory grief and must learn to accept the things we cannot change. As **Elizabeth Kübler-Ross** noted, it's a process. It's easier said than done to let go of the holy grail of "the good death," knowing we may exit in a coma, drugged up, or in palliative care. Focusing on rebirth in Amitabha's Pure Land, or practicing *Phowa*, are wonderful practices, but no substitute for what we did for years before our final moments. **Stephen Jenkinson**, author of *Die Wise*, offers some interesting thoughts on a new vision for Elder Culture, with a touch of shamanism and a hint of **Robert Bly**'s *Iron John*. He's turned his thoughts on elderhood and death into a cottage industry. But....

Most of us will wind up diminished by age, and in need of care. The "hero's quest" style of Buddhist practice, which may have worked for us in our youth when we were trying to make our mark on the world, simply no longer makes sense. The yin and yang of practice in old age involves receiving support with grace and gratitude, as well as offering ourselves in active service (such as chaplaincy).

But there is more here than coming to terms in our personal practice, according to Buddhist social theory, as well as from the perspective of design thinking. Old people are the most frequent users of institutionalized healthcare and have the most complex needs. The staff who care for them are often overworked, underpaid, and conflicted by moral distress – leading to burn-out, and increased rates of turnover. Could Buddhist practice provide the grounding in compassion and self-care that healthcare workers need to lessen their work-life stress? Shouldn't our Buddhist practice encompass improvement of our healthcare system as a way of alleviating suffering? And isn't death (not just avoidance of it) central to healthcare?

Most North American Dharma Centres have been established as places of teaching and meditative practice. They do not follow the Abrahamic traditions offering a wide range of social services to congregants, and they are struggling to make the transition. This probably one of the major drivers behind the rise in Buddhist chaplaincy training programs, and it's about time we supported pastoral work and chaplains better.

Buddhist teachings have much to offer for making sense of the loss of identity that comes with old age, but we have much to learn from others about the breadth of compassion we could be manifesting. After all, if Buddhist teaching is all about interdependence, then surely our communal future is as much the valid locus of our practice as the search within. There are many more resources on this topic available, in addition to these.

OLD AGE RESOURCES

- www.lionsroar.com/forum-when-im-sixty-four
- orphanwisdom.com
- www.nursingtimes.net/roles/nurse-educators/nursing-with-dignity-part-2-buddhism/205660.article
- www.buddhanet.net/tib_heal.htm

SICKNESS

93

Our modern view of medicine has evolved a long way from the animistic ideas from Buddha's day. Not only do we have a greater understanding of the viral, bacterial and genetic causes of disease, but our vision of illness now includes mental health, disabilities, addiction, chronic conditions, and the many lifestyle and social factors leading to poor health outcomes.

Physician, heal thyself.
An ancient proverb

Modern medicine is not content to consider illness as ripening karma, or a motivator to heighten and enrich our practice of non-attachment. Now we fight back – not just with allopathic treatment, but increasingly with naturopathic and homeopathic modalities, Traditional Chinese Medicine, Tibetan medicine and other holistic approaches. We've taken the Hippocratic Oath far beyond "Do no harm." In fact, to some degree, we've even shifted the entire medical paradigm from one of illness to one of health (or lack thereof).

Buddha was sometimes called the Great Doctor, and Dharma called the Medicine, but he was never an evangelist for faith healing. His advice on treating the sick was practical and rational. However, while his approach was what we might today consider proto-scientific, it was hardly compatible with many of the views of mainstream Western medicine.

We have seen tremendous medical advances in our lifetime, in diagnosis, treatment, technology, techniques, pharmacopia, holistic integrative medicine, use of Big Data in medical geography, and so on. Vaccination and antibiotics have transformed lives around the world. We've even recognized the value of promoting prevention, such as lifestyle changes and public health initiatives, rather than focusing on cures.

Of course, there are still many medical mysteries to solve. The rise of superbugs with broad-spectrum antibiotic resistance may soon end our epoch of easy infection fixes. Globalization and climate change may launch pandemics for which we are unprepared. As excellent and sophisticated as our healthcare system is, it is always on the verge of collapsing under the weight of its own complexity. We should not be complacent.

Medical advances have done wonders and miracles in reducing suffering, and we are working hard on the challenges, but modern healthcare is not without its ethical dilemmas. These include debates over environmental causes of disease, stem cell and animal research, the profit-driven agendas of drug companies, cosmetic surgery, ideological barriers to reproductive procedures, stigma around STIs, medically assisted end-of-life, inequitable access to healthcare, effective responses to gun violence or air pollution and the like, and many other topics.

We may have taken doctors down from their white-coat pedestals and empowered ourselves in our own health journeys, but we still need experts, and in terms of Right Livelihood, medicine is certainly one of the more noble options. One healthcare design thinker I greatly admire is **Peter Jones**, author of *Design for Care: Innovating Healthcare Experience*.

Perhaps the most dramatic dissonance between Western medicine and a Buddhist approach has to do with knowing how to stop fighting. Doctors who prioritize process over patient constantly push for extreme treatments with the goal of extending life for as long as possible, regardless of the quality of that life. Ironically, the medical advances that help us all live longer result in our spending our final days in slow decline in horrific long-term care facilities: 50% of our lifetime medical expenditure comes in the last 10% of our lives. Palliative and hospice care are still the exception rather than the norm, but even before we get there we must run the gauntlet. **Toni Bernard**'s Buddhist approach is even more rare.

What, specifically, can Buddhist teachers and community leaders offer in the realm of healthcare? Well, for starters, mindfulness-based interventions (as pioneered by **Jack Kornfield** and **Jon Kabat-Zinn**) have had a huge impact and these seem only poised for greater uptake.

Buddhist social theory is also congruent with increased focus on public health initiatives, and universal access to healthcare and economical pharmacare. These are critical system upgrades needed to ensure the widest alleviation of suffering caused by ill-health. There is also a strong social justice component to this, since poverty and barriers to access put entire populations at greater risk. Buddhists need to join forces with healthcare activists to make these changes.

SICKNESS RESOURCES
- www.envisioning.io/legacy/health
- rosenfeldmedia.com/books/design-for-care/
- upaya.org/uploads/pdfs/NicolleThesisFORWEB.pdf
- www.tonibernhard.com
- www.buddhistdoor.net/features/buddhistdoor-view-rethinking-retirement

DEATH

■
94

There is no doubt that humans have a fearful fascination with death. Our culture ruminates obsessively over violent deaths (murder mysteries, freak accidents, serial killers, etc.) and the pathos of loss (medical dramas, bereavement rituals, the tropes of obituaries, and so on.).

Gracious dying is a huge, macabre and expensive joke on the American public.

Jessica Mitford
The American Way of Death

We speak of loved ones "passing." The phrase used to be "passing away" but we can't seem to bring ourselves to say that. We create elaborate afterlife scenarios rather than face the possibility of a universe without us in it, whether the scenery involves heaven, hell, rebirth, or some other plane of existence.

My goal here is not to delve deeply into our sick relationship with death. Instead, I simply want to explore how Buddhist thought, combined with design thinking, might lead to more meaningful and sustainable death practices.

Theravada Buddhist discussions of "a good death" focus on acceptance, awareness, and a clean karmic slate. The first precept (non-killing) and care not to interfere with the workings of karma are the pivots around which the debate swirls. However, the locus of death is still firmly identified as the individual in transition. The death-centric practices of the Vajrayana (such as *Chod*, *Phowa*, *bardo* prayers, and recognition of *tulkus*) may prepare us for death, but the narrative focus is again on the individual.

From a Mahayana or Zen perspective, there is no self and no individual who is dying. The transition is a pulse in the cosmos that we misconstrue as termination. This view best expresses my limited understanding.

The modern scientific paradigm looks at death in a different way, as an organic process rather than as a morality tale or mythic narrative. **Sherwin Nuland**'s book, *How We Die*, should be required reading for anyone attempting to pontificate on the nature of death, and I would venture to say he does a better job of describing the process than any Buddhist text I've read or any initiation that has been conferred on me.

So let's run with the no-self scenario, since it seems to fit most closely with our modern scientific understanding. We'll relieve ourselves of agonizing over Schrodinger's Cat as a surrogate for our own dilemma. Less than 10% of us are likely to be conscious at the time of our demise, and the likelihood of elation is vastly less than that! **Stephen Jenkinson**'s *Die Wise* goal and **Katy Butler**'s *The Art of Dying Well* are mostly out of reach, even though the Good Death business is booming. If we can set aside our concern for the individual and think about death as a design problem, what would we say?

What if we saw the biosphere as a loved one, or even as our own super-self? Would we strive more diligently to protect it from death? Our attachment to our individuality is the very reason for our short-sighted behaviour, careening from death denial to delusions peddled by the death industry. All in all, we suffer from a lack of grief literacy.

Even though we now know that our corporeal existence is a symbiotic relationship with more bacteria within us than we have human cells, and that we need those bacteria in order for us to live, we still find it difficult to see our own microbiome as part of the larger system of Gaia. Indeed, we even have difficulty seeing any parallels between the deaths we fear for ourselves and the deaths we so blithely inflict on the animals we eat.

Much of our media portrayal of death ignores the social conditions that lead to the fateful outcome. To play on a frequent Buddhist image, we focus on saving the drowning person without ever questioning why there are so many people in the river. Solving public health and infrastructure problems, providing clean water, removing barriers to healthcare caused by greed and corruption, or improving our disposal of the dead may not be as glamorous as a handsome young detective catching a killer, or as heroic as a psychologically-complex doctor striving to save a child, but the long-term effects are much more profound. Ponder this.

What is the most environmentally-friendly way to dispose of the dead? Certainly not embalming, coffins, cremation or dispersal of ashes into waterways. Simply allowing a cloth-wrapped corpse to be buried and to decompose naturally is the least energy-intensive and least toxic solution. Why is it so difficult for people to access this option?

DEATH RESOURCES

- www.buddhistchaplains.org
- www.talkdeath.com
- www.thebuddhistsociety.org/page/buddhist-funerals
- www.urbandharma.org/udharma5/viewdeath.html
- www.accesstoinsight.org/lib/authors/walshe/wheel261.html
- www.upaya.org/being-with-dying/

BIOTECH

▬

95

Could we clone the Buddha? Maybe not, but it would certainly be a big deal if we could sequence the **Dalai Lama**'s DNA, and then use CRISPR to insert his genes into *tulku* embryos! Or, could we use machine learning to create an AI algorithm of **Thich Nhat Hanh** and keep a virtual version of him alive after he dies (like *Max Headroom*)?

The potential for synthetic biology and biotechnology is vast; we all have an opportunity to create the future together.

Ryan Bethencourt

Or, why not just develop an Enlightenment Pill, and give it to everybody?

Seriously, I think that when people think of biotechnology their thoughts immediately go to over-the-top scenarios of utopias like *Avatar* or dystopias like *The Matrix*. The reality is somewhat more, well, realistic.

We've learned a lot about biology in the past 2500+ years. From antibiotics to vaccination, prosthetics to transplants, diagnostic tools to hospital management software, or a myriad of other developments, we've improved the lives of people dramatically (and, it could be argued, many animals as well). Nobody wants to go back to the olden days of exorcisms, bloodletting, or reading sheep bones for portents. In that regard, Buddhist teachings would have little fault to find with modern medicine.

There are, obviously, other aspects of biotechnology in modern medicine about which Buddhists can and should be more ethically ambivalent. These are my focus here. We'll start from the fundamental premise of Buddhism: reduce suffering.

Just as endosymbiotic organisms evolved higher orders of structure to provide systemic benefits to all their constituents, we might say that a well-organized society offers more benefit to its citizens. Healthcare is one of those benefits. Improvements in healthcare, of any kind, are beneficial, so long as they are universal. Why universal? Because access to healthcare based on wealth or affiliation includes the inherent dualism of those who are excluded from benefit, thus increasing their suffering. In political terms, this means healthcare cannot be optimal when it is based on the profit-motive. And, in terms of our globalized existence, solving health problems wherever they appear on the planet is in our own enlightened self-interest.

Of course, it is unrealistic to expect that every technological advance is going to be affordable on a wide scale. Healthcare needs to be sustainable. Demand for services must be weighed against the revenues available. Research and development need funding. Universal, affordable access to higher education is a corequisite and enhancer for universal healthcare. Equity is not the same as equality. (In case you haven't figured it out by this section of the book, I am a socialist.)

As the planet's population continues to peak, we in the North are experiencing a lopsided bulge of baby boomers and this puts a lot of strain on our healthcare system. However, people under 25 make up 43% of the world's population, and 60% of the population of developing countries. One could certainly make a case for focusing limited healthcare dollars on the world of the future, while maintaining a certain level of dignity for those elderly patients here who will experience 50% of their lifetime healthcare needs in the last 10% of their lives. Boomers, none of us is going to live forever! Let's not get carried away with expecting heroic measures. Accept death.

Similarly, solutions to healthcare problems that are overly ideological or reliant on technological fixes are suboptimal. For example, condemnation of addicts is merely a way of externalizing the social determinants leading to addiction, and the attendant costs. Fervent embrace of guns perpetuates the curse of gun violence. Self-driving cars will never be ubiquitous enough to end motor vehicle mayhem. Better blood sugar testing devices are no substitute for reducing obesity before diabetes sets in.

In many cases, appropriate simple technology is much more powerful than advanced technology. For example, consider social entrepreneurs like **Dr. Govindappa Venkataswamy** (whose low-cost corneal implants have helped millions of Indians suffering from cataracts) or Vestergaard (whose LifeStraw portable water purification and PermaNet insect vector control have helped millions of people around the world).

A Buddhist equivalent to **Rick Mercer'**s "Spread the Net Challenge" could be a very viable, yet low-tech, biotech Bodhisattva act!

BIOTECH RESOURCES
- online.sfsu.edu/rone/GEessays/Buddhism%20and%20Biotechnology.htm
- www.pfb.info.pl/files/kwartalnik/1_2005/Wachowicz.pdf
- books.google.ca/books/about/CLONING_the_BUDDHA_The_Moral_Impact_of_B.html?id=T7eblRJnpUQC&redir_esc=y
- archive.org/details/cloningbuddhamor00heinrich

LIFE SUPPORT

96

Let's talk about dying, medicine's dirty little secret. For 99% of us, it's going to be a slow, physically, financially, and emotionally draining process, with the added kicker of diminished cognitive ability. That certainly doesn't sound like something we'd like to last even longer than it has to, does it? Given the inevitability of death, the quality of life in our transition is clearly more valuable than the quantity of minutes by which we can postpone it. At least, that's the Buddhist view; we can't outrun our karma. Non-harming and compassion must be carefully weighed when deciding on heroic measures such as life support, Do Not Resuscitate (DNR) orders, or medically-assisted death.

"Do Not Resuscitate" (DNR) laws are one of the successes of the bioethics movement, which replaced the traditional model of physician-dominated paternalism with an emphasis on patients' rights.

Barron H. Lerner

Often, death becomes a conflictual situation where patients, loved ones, and the medical establishment are at odds about how to proceed. For example, there is still plenty of debate about when we actually die, and patients in persistent vegetative states or being considered for organ donation are often involved in lawsuits about the validity of life support. Similarly, recent acceptance for medically-assisted death has opened the way for a radical re-think of how we die.

Traditional Buddhist discussions of this topic usually centre on the dying person's previously-stated wishes, whether that person was able to form active consent, and whether the intervention complicates one's karmic consequences.

The resource section for this topic includes several Buddhist responses to the question of whether or not withdrawal of life support is appropriate. For example, from the perspective of non-harming, withdrawal of artificial feeding and hydration (ANAH) would be considered to be contrary to the first precept: non-killing. From the perspective of compassion, ANAH may be considered an unwanted intervention that is preventing a person from their natural karmic transition through death. These discussions show the blurred lines between withdrawal of life support and active euthanasia.

Palliative care is a recognized branch of medical practice, and there are thousands of hospices in North America. There are many, many caring professionals dedicated to diminishing the mental, emotional, and spiritual turmoil of death. Chaplains are often on the front lines here, and we've seen an increase in training programs for Buddhist chaplains as North American Buddhism goes more mainstream. The problems arise when these institutions (such as the San Francisco Zen Hospice, which closed recently due to lack of funding) do not receive the type of governmental support they deserve.

There are always going to be dramatic stories of miracle cures, amazing advances in organ transplant technology, and sensational lawsuits swirling around the topic of life support. It's important to remember that these are outliers. As long as they remain the focus of our attention, end-of-life care for the masses will be starved for oxygen.

For example, the University of Toronto recently launched a graduate Buddhist chaplaincy program as a development of their Buddhist Psychology and Mental Health program. For all its merits, it is offered as a full-time program, which means students cannot continue their day jobs while attending, and the University freely admits that there are few paying jobs for chaplains upon graduation from the program. To my way of thinking, there is an unfair expectation that Buddhist chaplains will volunteer their services while earning a living elsewhere: a guaranteed recipe for burn-out, and a condition that will hobble the program's success.

Why aren't more Buddhist teachers actively writing and speaking about real-life end-of-life in professional magazines and the popular media? *Buddhist Care for the Dying and the Bereaved*, edited by **Jonathan Watts** and **Yoshiharu Tomatsu** (2012) is one of a very short list of practical contemporary Buddhist books on the subject.

Merely restating time-worn tropes about the need to be aware at the moment of death, resolving karmic debts, emergence of the Clear Light in the bardo, or other transcendentalist teachings are not going to cut it. Let's pull the plug on outmoded responses to end-of-life care.

LIFE SUPPORT RESOURCES

- www.buddhistchaplains.org
- www.buddhismcanada.com
- www.jpsmjournal.com/article/S0885-3924(12)00262-X/fulltext
- www.tandfonline.com/doi/full/10.1080/15524256.2013.794060
- www.ncbi.nlm.nih.gov/pmc/articles/PMC3307077
- en.wikipedia.org/wiki/Buddhism_and_euthanasia

ABORTION

97

There are few ethical problems that draw more fire than the issue of abortion. Not much is said about abortion in traditional Buddhist texts, since it was not something possible at the time. However, we can look to the first Buddhist precept, not to kill, for guidance. According to the teachings of Buddha, five conditions must be present to constitute an act of killing: 1) the thing killed must be a living being; 2) you, the killer, must know or be aware that it is a living being; 3) you must have the intention to kill it; 4) there must be an effort to kill; and 5) the being must be killed as the result.

> No woman wants to have an abortion.
>
> *Kate Michelman*

All those conditions are met in abortion, so from the Buddhist perspective, abortion is a bad thing. Nevertheless, modern arguments for and against do not stop there.

Those on the pro-choice side say that in situations where a woman has decided to have an abortion, she should have the opportunity to do it in a safe and effective way, without extra complications (physical, emotional, or financial). Pro-life advocates say the rights of the fetus take precedence over the rights of the mother since life is inviolate, the fetus is defenceless, and other options are available.

To compound the issue, access to safe abortion has become a battleground for patriarchy versus feminists. Reproductive rights have become a surrogate for other gender politics where patriarchy is resisting women's equality and rights of agency, or penalizing women for being on the mommy track. In many cases, lack of access to abortion is yet another hurdle for oppressed classes. Then there's the whole problem of selective abortion of female fetuses in many developing nations. In other words, the problem is less about abortion *per se*, and more about deeper societal problems.

I would never counsel anyone to have an abortion as opposed to contraception or adoption, but I recognize that women will continue to demand that right and I support their ability to do so in a safe way. If the overall goal is harm reduction and the act is going to occur, why destroy two lives rather than one? In cases where the birth may impose great hardship on a family, or the child will be severely disabled, or where the child was conceived through sexual violence, a more nuanced approach is obviously necessary.

Furthermore, pro-life can't be just a knee-jerk anti-abortion reflex. Life doesn't end at birth. How can one be pro-life while defunding early child development programs, separating immigrant children from their families, disproportionately imprisoning young people from the oppressed classes, failing to ban the guns responsible for school shootings, or supporting other initiatives designed to hobble some children once they are born? (And don't get me started on our dysfunctional foster care system.)

In Japan, Jizo (Ksitigarbha, Skt.) has become the patron Bodhisattva of aborted, miscarried and stillborn children. His statues can be seen in many cemeteries and he serves as a focus for rituals and emotional catharsis for the parent(s) of those children. Perhaps Japanese Buddhists' efforts to reconcile abortion and Buddhist doctrine provides a model for flexibility and compassion in a complicated and emotionally-charged decision where there is no "right" answer.

I would like to see more Buddhist contributions to the debates about abortion to move past short-term right/wrong dualism and augment them with long-term practical ways to counsel the grieving parent(s).

But even more so, I would like to see Buddhist contributions to the debates about abortion to focus explicitly on the social factors that make it disproportionately problematic for certain segments of society. If the reasons why women find themselves having to consider abortion were removed, that would take a lot of steam out of sexual politics. In other words, even if Buddhists consider abortion to be a bad thing, we can certainly work for sexual education, contraceptions, better parental leave, and a host of other options that will reduce the number of women walking the abortion path. I'm pro-choice, but abortion is not the only choice.

Reductionist frameworks limiting access to those options, and then prioritizing the fetus over the mother, are products of absolutist ideology that will inevitably result in anguish. They come out of a war on women, not a respect for life.

ABORTION RESOURCES
- www.plannedparenthood.org/learn/abortion
- www.morgentaler.ca/faq.html
- www.learnreligions.com/buddhist-perspectives-on-abortion-449712
- www.urbandharma.org/udharma/abortion.html
- rcrc.org/buddhist/
- tricycle.org/magazine/anti-abortionpro-choice

DRUGS

■ 98 When talking about drugs, we need to recognize that different classes of drugs require different approaches. For example: medicines; narcotics; hallucinogens; freely available intoxicants like alcohol and tobacco; illegal intoxicants like cocaine or ecstasy; excitotoxins in food, such as artificial ingredients, sugar, salt, caffeine or trans-fats; and industrial chemicals pervading our environment. There is no one-size-fits-all Buddhist societal approach neatly encapsulated in the fifth precept against taking intoxicants.

Not necessarily stoned, but beautiful.

Jimi Hendrix

Chögyam Trungpa is the poster-child for alcoholic Buddhist teachers, but he is certainly not the only addict in the bunch. Putting aside the sexual scandals engulfing his Shambhala legacy, he and his Dharma heirs have never really been able to convince the larger Buddhist world that drinking or otherwise self-medicating is a valid Buddhist practice. Perhaps the problem here is that addicted teachers are also addicted to teaching! To me, the solution seems relatively straightforward: if you have an addiction problem, get help. Take a sabbatical from teaching. I'd say Vinaya applies here to lay teachers as much as it does to ordained monks and nuns: no intoxicants, period.

The uneasy relationship between psychedelics and meditation is another focus. We're in a bit of a revival, and ayahuasca is the trending hallucinogen at the moment. We're a long way from the heady days of **Timothy Leary**. Yes, psychotropic drugs such as SSRIs are very helpful in stabilizing patients suffering from brain chemical imbalances, and new research indicates LSD might be helpful in dealing with depression, but these are not being touted as spiritual wormholes to a higher reality; their goal is simple sanity. If you choose to indulge, call it what it is, but don't try to equate it with higher realms and Dharma practice.

Painkillers with sedative effects are another hot topic, particularly when used at end-of-life. The Buddhist default is that they impair awareness that is critical at death, but nobody wants a loved one to suffer.

Balancing the intellectual property rights of pharmaceutical companies with access to safe medicine for all is an ongoing struggle. Unethical drug-peddling (viz. Perdue Pharma and Oxycontin), price-gouging (viz. **Martin Shkreli**, *aka* "Pharma Bro"), and the high cost of Insulin or EpiPens are merely tips of the iceberg. You've no doubt been subjected to endless drug commercials where the side effects list goes on longer than the sales pitch, or offer a needless medical solution to a non-medical "problem" (Rogaine, anyone?). I'm a Buddhist, and I support a national pharmacare plan with a single-payer structure.

Addiction counselors usually focus on addiction and how to deal with it. **Vimalasara**, co-founder of Eight Step Recovery Using The Buddha's Teaching to Overcome Addiction is a good example here of a Buddhist response. But let's move beyond the obvious.

The "War on Drugs" has been revealed to be a cover for imprisoning huge numbers of black and hispanic Americans in modern-day slavery. Production and distribution of illegal drugs funds many failed state and terrorist organizations. Do Buddhists support decriminalization?

Our addiction to sugar and salt is killing us; not only can you buy them everywhere, but it's virtually impossible to avoid them even if you want to. Pesticides, steroids, antibiotics, and hundreds of "approved" artificial ingredients are an essential component of our food chain, but eliminating them is way less sexy than gluten-free, keto, paleo, or countless other diets. I'd like to see Buddhist support for vegetarian diets be expanded to embrace healthy, drug-free and chemical-free foods in general.

And what about all those drugs we put on our skin? Whether or not beauty products are physically harmful to us (and many are), do we really need to invest hundreds of billions of dollars each year in the cosmetics industry? **Kodo Nishimura** notwithstanding, make-up has never been much of a topic for Buddhist teachers (who are predominantly men). Where is the Venn diagram overlap of Buddhism, beauty culture, and the empowerment of girls and women?

We're flooded with chemicals, carcinogens, hormone-disruptors, and thousands of others for which we have no clear understanding of the synergistic effects. Where are our Buddhist eco-warrior role models?

DRUGS RESOURCES

- en.wikipedia.org/wiki/List_of_largest_pharmaceutical_settlements
- www.newyorker.com/magazine/2017/10/30/the-family-that-built-an-empire-of-pain
- www.drugpolicy.org/issues/brief-history-drug-war
- www.plantteachers.com/allan-badiner/
- tricycle.org/trikedaily/psychedelics-buddhist-revival/

MENTAL HEALTH

99

Buddhists often talk about mental health, and, indeed, the sales pitch for modern Western Buddhism often focuses on how meditation can confer psychological benefits in the here and now. From Mindfulness to **Marie Kondo**, we have been redefining the pursuit of happiness with significant input from Buddhist teachers and apologists.

90% of all families are dysfunctional. The other 10% are in denial.
Fridge magnet

In a clinical sense, our recognition of the validity and pervasive nature of mental distress, and society's willingness to find real solutions, are wonderful advances. Pharmacology has been at the forefront of these developments. But for the general population, for whom mental health issues may not reach the point where acute intervention is needed, much remains unresolved. As long as we're "functional," society has little regard for our needs.

Some will seek better mental states by developing healthier coping mechanisms, eliminating maladaptive responses, or choosing better friends. Corporations will jump on the bandwagon to raise their public profile (as highlighted by the recent backlash over the "free publicity" aspect of Bell Canada's "Let's Talk" campaign). For those who live with privilege, this is how the world works. For the oppressed, a more radical approach presents itself because they are acutely aware of the societal determinants contributing to mental health challenges.

As **Jiddu Krishnamurti** said, "It's no measure of health to be well adjusted to a profoundly sick society." Other thinkers, such as **Gabor Mate** have explored this theme as well. I'm also a fan of **John Bradshaw**'s systemic approach to family dynamics, moving the locus of distress from the individual to the roles we assume to play our parts in the psychodrama of our lives. The public sphere and the world of work are just different modalities for our dysfunctional family relationships.

Fortunately, acceptance of diversity has eased the strictures causing suffering for many people. When you realize you aren't the cause of your distress, or that you are not living an inauthentic life, your view of normative society undergoes a radical transformation; society's dysfunction and coercion become starkly visible. A new journey to health opens up, and Buddhism often becomes the vehicle for that journey.

Buddhist teachers and chaplains have done a spectacular job in bringing mental health-promotion techniques to both the public and the medical profession. Kudos to them, but as you probably know this far into the book, I'm interested in poking at the problems with a stick. Improving mental health without challenging the status quo is like Bompu Zen: great as far as it goes, but it doesn't go very far.

Traditional Buddhist explanations of karma locate it within the individual, and it is tempting to mis-interpret this in a reductionist way, saying whatever happens to you is your own fault. However, that is really a neo-liberal conceit of social Darwinism, masquerading as Dharma. Buddhist teachers who fall into the trap of failing to explain the co-dependent and synergistic societal dynamics of karma are presenting a rather narrow explanation of fourfold dependent arising.

Can we go further? Let's move beyond the "Mindfulness" model to embed Buddhist perspectives that incorporate social justice activism into mainstream psychological thought, rather than simply being a sub-genre that resonates mostly with the privileged.

So what would mental health initiatives look like if we combined Buddhist teachings, design thinking, and social activism? Widespread adoption of Buddhist businesses with hiring policies like those of the late **Bernie Glassman Roshi**'s Greyston Bakery? Disenchanting ourselves from narratives of salvation by gurus and empowering our Sanghas? Decommissioning of Buddhist teachers who are abusers? Or a dramatic increase in chaplaincy work by Buddhist activists? Greater participation by Buddhists in mainstream mental health publications and colloquia? These are all excellent initiatives.

At the very least, when we Buddhists talk about mental health, let's be sure to include the dialectic of our place in society, on the receiving end of external stressors, but also as (possibly complicit) participants in the creation of mental stress for others. Better would be to talk about active application of the Five Precepts as the antidote to the latter.

MENTAL HEALTH RESOURCES

- www.mentalhealthamerica.net/co-dependency
- drgabormate.com
- www.who.int/mental_health/publications/gulbenkian_paper_social_determinants_of_mental_health/en/
- www.theatlantic.com/health/archive/2019/03/buddhism-meditation-anxiety-therapy/584308/

PLANET

BODHIMANDALA

100

The term Bodhimandala traditionally refers to the place where a Buddha attains Enlightenment. Although it is much less commonly used than the term mandala, (67 thousand Google results vs 207 million), it has some important meanings for our discussion here.

That men do not learn very much from the lessons of history is the most important of all the lessons that history has to teach.

Aldous Huxley

Broadly speaking, the outer meaning of a Bodhimandala is a sacred place to Buddhists. Bodh Gaya, Swayambhu, Kailash, Wutai, Shwedagon, Borobudur, and the Potala are examples. Any Sangharama or temple can be a Bodhimandala. The inner meaning is revealed by the way architecture or practice in these places recreates Buddhist cosmology. The secret meaning is revealed when we carry the Bodhimandala perspective into our everyday lives.

Peter Herschock, author of "Built Space as Bodhimandala: The Architectural Meaning of a Practised Buddhism," parts 1 and 2, in *Architectural Theory Review* (1999) explores the inner meaning, and expands his exploration into the secret meaning with his book, *Valuing Diversity: Buddhist Reflection on Realizing a More Equitable Global Future* (2014).

In the *Great Compassion Repentance Ritual*, we recite: "The worshipped and the worshipper are empty and still in nature. The response and the Way are intertwined, inconceivably. This Bodhimandala of mine is like a wish-fulfilling pearl; the Buddhas appear before me, and I appear before the Buddhas. Bowing down, I return my life in worship."

I have always found this particular passage profoundly moving, and it is part of the bedrock for my environmental activism. Consider: if it is part of every Bodhisattva's Vow to create a Pure Land, when does that start? Here and now, obviously. This very *saha* world is our Bodhimandala.

(If you are interested, **Vimalakirti** gives **Glorious Light Bodhisattva** a more detailed description of the constituents of a Bodhimandala in the *Vimalakirti Nirdesa Sutra*.)

Back in 2007, the Buddhist Channel launched an international program to fund ten Buddhist social action groups. The program website, www.bodhimandala.net, now defunct, ran for several years and can still be found on the Internet Archive Wayback Machine. Following the links there quickly reveals a plethora of amazing organizations with many inspiring ideas for action, largely in the arena of social justice.

Since that time, environmental issues have moved from the margins to the central focus of global attention. Rather than ameliorating conditions for those in need, there has been a value shift toward the more fundamental issue of survival. Buddhists have been behind the curve in rallying to the cause, and I have yet to see more than a few Buddhist organizations that have progressed from endorsement to active campaigns.

Buddhism places emphasis on intention, but implicit in that is the need to clarify our underlying values. Herschock makes a distinction between problems, for which there are logical solutions, and predicaments, which come from clashes of values and solutions for which require fundamental embrace of diversity in our relationships.

I'd venture to say that Buddhists are as aware as anybody else of the predicaments we face. Buddhism's understanding of interdependence could be a great place to begin that reorientation. However, to do so, Buddhists must fully embrace our little blue planet as the Bodhimandala, with what His Holiness **the Dalai Lama** refers to as Universal Responsibility.

Bryan Norton, a well-known ecologist, coming at it from a secular perspective, concurs that the solutions to our predicaments will not come from fixed, utopian objectives, but achieved through experimentation, incremental learning, and adaptive management. In other words, the way forward is through a new focus on process rather than perpetuating what has proven to be a paradigm that is no longer workable.

The prospect of a more volatile future is a likely consequence as more people are pushed to their limits. The dilemma, as I see it, is that people and organizations who have a selfish and/or short-sighted interest in maintaining the status quo are not going to invest in the kind of change that will involve sacrificing some of their privilege for the greater good.

This section of the book explores these themes in greater detail.

BODHIMANDALA RESOURCES

- ecobuddhism.org
- davidloy.org
- www.oneearthsangha.org
- compassionateearth.wordpress.com
- arcworld.org
- greenfaith.org

EARTH

101

If you have seen any of **Edward Burtynsky**'s giant aerial photographs of human activity, you have some visceral sense of the extent to which the Anthropocene is an undeniably appropriate name for our age.

As I write this, Canadian mining giant, Barrick Gold, is in the process of trying to buy its rival Newmont, to become the largest gold miner on the planet. The devastating effects of Barrick operations in locations as far-flung as Chile, Zambia, and Papua New Guinea are shocking, but gold is hardly the only driver in this global plunder. Critical components of our digital infrastructure come from conflict minerals such as Tantalum, Tin, Tungsten, and Gallium (*aka* T3G). The world is facing serious shortages of these and other important elements (such as Ag, As, He, Sn, and Y) in the near future, a trajectory that is sure to lead to further volatility.

> We are as gods and might as well get good at it.
> *Stewart Brand, 1968*
> We are as gods and *have* to get good at it.
> *Stewart Brand, 2009*

We produce about 20,000 plastic bottles every second. We dump the equivalent of a garbage truck full of plastic into the ocean every minute; that's 1,440 truckloads a day, every day. Recent investigations have even found plastic debris in the bottom of the Mariana Trench, the deepest recess of the ocean! Recycling programs are insufficient to deal with the problem, by many orders of magnitude.

I'd hate for this book to be a jeremiad, but....

Back in 2014, *Minding Nature* journal published an article called: "Should Environmentalists Study Asian Philosophy?" A more crucial question might be: "Why aren't more Buddhists studying Environmentalism (let alone playing an activist role)?" To wit, there are no Buddhists on the Parliament of World Religions' Interfaith Climate Action Task Force, and Buddhist voices are barely represented in the Alliance of Religions and Conservation.

As a high school teacher promoting sustainability curriculum, I've made extensive use of resources from **Annie Leonard**, founder of the Story of Stuff Project. Your Dharma centre could run a powerful workshop series based on their many superb videos.

If you are looking for a sustainability organization reaching out to an adult audience, have a look at the Post Growth Institute. In fact, the international degrowth movement is quite large, and well-worth exploring, even if off the radar of mainstream media. I can't imagine a better fit with degrowth than Buddhism's voluntary simplicity, but a Google search for "Buddhism and degrowth" reveals virtually nothing beyond the usual suspects (like **E.F. Schumacher**, who died in 1977).

Earth, Water, Fire, and Air are the four elements symbolized in Buddhist stupas (as **Lama Anagarika Govinda** described in his 1976 book, *Psycho-Cosmic Symbolism of the Buddhist Stupa*), as well as in many indigenous spiritual traditions. It should not be foreign to us to respect and care for them, and yet somehow we have lost our groundedness in the Earth, our indebtedness. Thought leaders like **Tom and Kitty Stoner** (*Nature-Sacred*), **Richard Louv** (*Nature Deficit Disorder*), and **Naomi Klein** (*This Changes Everything*) have shown a path but there is a lot of resistance.

Nichidatsu Fujii, founder of the Nipponzan-Myohoji Buddhist Order, has inspired Buddhists to construct more than 80 Peace Pagodas around the world. **Dilgo Khyentse Rinpoche** and **Dzongsar Jamyang Khyentse Rinpoche**, founders of the Peace Vase Project, have inspired Buddhists to plant more than 3,300 Peace Vases around the world. **Goi Sensei**, founder of the May Peace Prevail on Earth movement, has inspired the installation of more than 250,000 Peace Poles around the world.

Where is the Buddhist leader who will capture the public imagination to focus on environmental issues with the same dynamism?

I recently read *Ecology, Ethics and Interdependence: The Dalai Lama in Conversation with Leading Thinkers on Climate Change*, edited by **John Dunne** and **Daniel Goleman** (published in 2018). A host of Buddhist luminaries took part in the discussions, and I was excited by the prospect of reading it, but the book left me feeling discouraged at the tentativeness and vagueness of their comments. If this is the best that Buddhism has to offer, we are in a bad way, folks. That type of disappointment is why I have written this book and provided all these specific resources.

EARTH RESOURCES

- www.storyofstuff.com
- resources4rethinking.ca/en/
- plasticbaggrab.com
- parliamentofreligions.org/program/climate-action
- www.teachthefuture.org
- naturesacred.org

WATER

102 There are many references to water in Buddhism. It's a metaphor for mind, clarity and purity. The moon of truth is reflected in it. Naga serpent Dharma protectors live in it. It's fluid, but able to wear down the tallest mountain. We bathe the baby Buddha in it. We offer water bowls on shrines daily. Many Buddhist centres feature it in their names. Before and after Enlightenment, we are encouraged to carry it, along with chopping wood. But to what degree do we recognize the actual, physical importance of water? How many Buddhists could explain even the basics of the hydrological cycle?

All the water that will ever be is, right now.
National Geographic

Less than 2% of the world's water is potable, and that's shrinking. Lack of access to clean water is responsible for about 50% of disease around the world. And as almost every schoolkid knows, we are 98% water.

Josephine Mandamin, a grandmother water walker in the Anishnaabe Nation in Ontario, Canada, has walked more than 20,000 kilometers to promote water awareness. Her 13-year-old niece, **Autumn Peltier**, an internationally-recognized environmentalist from the Wikwemikong First Nation, has addressed the Canadian government and the United Nations on water issues. In the United States, aboriginal water keepers from the Sioux Tribe galvanized the world at Standing Rock with their efforts to protect their freshwater resources from an oil pipeline. In Western Canada, aboriginal communities are at the forefront of the fight to stop the Transmountain Pipeline. Brazil's indigenous communities are similarly at the forefront of trying to protect the Amazon River watershed from logging, mining and other forms of attack from the country's right-wing government.

It is commendable that indigenous leaders have become our saviours in the fight to preserve and protect our freshwater resources, and that they have inspired many allies. More power to them.

In 2013, Soto Zen teacher **Shodo Spring** led a four-month "Compassionate Earth Walk" along the route of the Keystone XL Pipeline. In 2017, Buddhist nun **Jun Yasuda** (from the Grafton Peace Pagoda) led a 90-mile "Water Walk for Life" in protest of the Pilgrim Pipeline.

These are outstanding contributions, but I am looking for something more sustained and broad-based than consciousness-raising walks.

The Himalayas have sometimes been called the Third Pole. Glaciers there feed some of the world's most populated watersheds, the Mekong, Yangtse, Salween, and Irrawaddy to name a few. All the countries in the region are reporting water problems. Given that these rivers all flow through Buddhist countries, it stands to reason that Buddhists there would be active in regional water politics. For example, His Holiness **the Karmapa** founded the Khoryug Movement to promote environmental initiatives, but other than an annual conference, it does not reveal much on its website. Mlup Baitong (a Cambodian NGO), the "ecology monks" of Thailand (dating back to **Phrakhru Pitak Nanthakun**'s groundbreaking initiatives in 1975), the Bhutan Trust for Environmental Conservation, and The Small Earth Nepal have all been active in environmental issues, but with integrated agendas that do not focus specifically on water security.

A search of the Asia-Pacific Water Forum website and publications for the keyword "Buddhist" reveals zero results. Nothing from The Water Project's website either. Ditto for Friends of Nature, China's oldest registered NGO. Ditto for the UN Global Analysis and Assessment of Sanitation and Drinking Water. In other words, while there have been Buddhist initiatives, they remain in silos, unintegrated with secular initiatives.

Pollution of our oceans has become another focus of environmental concern. Whether it's micro- or macro-plastic waste, agricultural run-off, oil spills, or radioactive isotopes from Fukushima, there is no denying that the world's oceans are under assault from humans. For those of us who do not live in maritime communities, it can be difficult to understand the intimate, essential relationship we have with the ocean, but that does not mean the relationship does not exist.

There are many other water issues but space does not permit me to explore them in any detail here. Suffice it to say, any realistic water management strategy must address every phase of the hydrological cycle to achieve maximum value. There is no shortage of places where Buddhist voices would be welcomed.

WATER RESOURCES

- www.shidhulai.org
- www.waterpolitics.com
- www.policyalternatives.ca/publications/monitor/water-politics
- www.water-alternatives.org/
- www.khoryug.com
- mlup-baitong.org

FIRE

103

There are many references to fire in Buddhism. It's a metaphor for consciousness, purification, and burning away desire. Wrathful Bodhisattvas and Dharma Protectors are wreathed in it. The Burning House is a key parable from the *Lotus Sutra*. Fire is a symbolic component in stupas. We offer butter lamps on shrines daily. We conduct fire pujas. Chinese Buddhist monks and nuns use it to permanently scarify their heads at ordination. **Thich Nhat Hanh**'s teacher, **Thich Quang Duc**, serenely burned himself to death in it to protest the war in Vietnam. More than 150 Tibetans have self-immolated in similar fashion to protest the Chinese occupation of their country (a number so alarming that His Holiness **the Dalai Lama** had to make a public plea for them to stop). Fire is where all that wood we chopped at the Zendo winds up. But to what degree do we recognize the actual, environmental impacts of fire? How does today's Bodhisattva respond to fire?

> Only YOU can prevent forest fires!
>
> *Smokey the Bear*

Massive wildfires, the likes of which we've never seen in our lifetime, are now commonplace. Newscasters speak nightly of "unprecedented" climate events, but there is nothing unusual or unknown about them now.

The causes are complex, but the underlying answer is global warming. Of course, wildfires make for riveting news video. Unfortunately, our everyday use of fire to heat or cool our homes, cook our food, power our cars, and so on, rarely provides anything so dramatic. To mix my metaphors, it's the 90% of the iceberg we never see. It has a name, carbon-based energy, and scientists are virtually unanimous in their recognition that the oil and gas industry fuelling it is the primary cause of the global warming that is causing all those wildfires. But there's a cognitive disconnect.

The science of alternative energy sources is not complex. Solar, wind, geothermal, hydroelectric, and tidal energy are abundant, non-polluting, and entirely renewable. It is only the world's addiction to fossil fuel and nuclear energy (and the money they generate) that keeps us hooked. And as long as governments and big business are unwilling to invest in the infrastructure needed to transform, we're going to stay hooked. More on that in the section on Energy.

Many religious organizations are speaking out for conservation and alternative energy sources. Some are now divesting from their fossil fuel assets. Some Buddhist centres are investing in renewable energy as well.

Another facet of the fire picture involves clearcutting and burning jungle to make way for plantations. This is a big problem in places like Indonesia, where palm oil is a global cash crop, and Brazil, where the government has pretty much given land grabbers *carte blanche* to slash and burn the rainforest for ranching. We are losing more than 150 acres of rainforest every minute of every day, and most of it goes up in smoke.

Deforestation, aside from being a primary vector of species extinction through habitat loss, generates a positive feedback loop that has devastating effects on the environment. When the forest loses its trees, it loses its ability to generate enough rain through transpiration to sustain itself. Bye bye forest. Hello wildfires. Bye bye carbon sink. Hello carbon emitter.

I am sure that you know all about the problem with fossil fuels, so there is no need here for a lengthy explanation about how burning oil, gas, coal and wood all contribute to global warming, or about how temperature rise triggers a lot of other knock-on effects that accelerate the process. Suffice it to say, if your Dharma Centre has not undertaken a serious environmental retrofit to reduce your carbon footprint in every possible way, that's not cool.

The Forum on Religion and Ecology at Yale has a selection of climate change statements from spokespeople from World Religions. Follow the link below to read the nine Buddhist statements (2003-2016). The site also contains an extensive bibliography of publications relating to Buddhism and Ecology, compiled by **Duncan Ryuken Williams**.

The journal, *Religion*, has an interesting article from 2019 entitled: "Environmental Revolution in Contemporary Buddhism: The Interbeing of Individual and Collective Consciousness in Ecology."

In other words, if you dig around a bit, you will find some articles to spark your interest and light a fire under your initiatives.

FIRE RESOURCES

- tricycle.org/magazine/awakening-age-climate-change/
- tricycle.org/trikedaily/growing-buddhist-movement-responding-ecological-crisis/
- oneearthsangha.org/statements/the-time-to-act-is-now/
- fore.yale.edu

AIR

104

Pristine mind is like the clear sky, always present whether obscured by clouds or not. The illusions and delusions of samsara are like a city of gandharvas, with no true nature.

My first awareness of environmental issues came with stories recounting the air pollution in Victorian England. It was only years later, in the latter half of the

The health effects of air pollution imperil human lives. This fact is well-documented.

Eddie Bernice Johnson

1970's, while working for Pollution Probe, that I started reading of other types of pollution, like acid rain, heavy metals in landfill or industrial effluent, toxic byproducts of garbage incineration, and a Pandora's Box of other nightmares. And it seems not much has changed between the Love Canal disaster of 1978 and the Flint, Michigan water scandal of 2014. In a sense, you could say air pollution was the canary in the coal mine, but nobody cared when it died.

When I think of the world's environmental problems, I think air pollution is perhaps the most insidious. It is the engine for global warming, and that in turn is the cause for so many other problems. However, the impact is so incremental, so distributed, that we just don't notice until we float over a tipping point and enter an exponentially greater danger zone.

Anything you can do to enhance the planet's atmospheric oxygen supply is good. Reducing atmospheric carbon dioxide and methane is good. Reducing sulfur and nitrous oxide emissions is good because they combine with water in the atmosphere to create acid rain.

Repairing the ozone hole caused by CFC refrigerants has been one of the environmental movement's success stories. But there are other gases in the atmosphere too. For example, did you know the world is facing a helium shortage. And there's the whole problem of particulates.

For most of us, driving is our most obvious contribution to air pollution. The problem is just so much bigger than any one of us can realistically change; so much of it seems out of our control. Going electric, keeping an older car, finding employment closer to home, riding your bike, or simply taking public transit are viable alternatives, but not always realistic. Until our economy moves away from fossil fuel and builds the infrastructure required to fully enable alternative energy sources, we're screwed. Have a look at the documentary, *Who Killed the Electric Car* and its sequel, *Revenge of the Electric Car*, to get some sense of the scope of the problem. Just be prepared to be demoralized.

There is no mystery to air pollution. We understand the ozone hole, the greenhouse effect of atmospheric carbon dioxide and methane, how forest fires in Alberta can darken skies in Ontario, and the health impacts of many airborne industrial chemicals. What seems to be lacking, however, is the political will to prevent these problems from occurring; instead, we play a never-ending game of catch-up.

I cannot recall any specific reference in traditional Buddhist literature to air pollution, nor any exhortation there to modify our lifestyles in the interest of clean air. Consequently, if we want to find a Buddhist guide, we're going to have to extrapolate (as we have for many other modern problems). For example, I've stopped burning incense at home, but that's the only specifically Buddhist air quality offering I've modified.

Well, then, what's an environmentally-conscious Bodhisattva to do, beyond small personal changes? Three excellent air quality initiatives might be to plant trees, rewild your temple lawn, and do whatever you can to reduce your centre's carbon footprint. If you have a retreat centre, you might also consider deeding the property to a wild land trust instead of selling it, if you no longer have need of it.

Does your Dharma centre have and display a comprehensive environmental policy document? If so, you are in the minority! Have you actively sought connection with the EcoDharma centre, One Earth Sangha, or another Buddhist organization that puts environmental activism at the centre of their practice? They have so much to offer!

And of course, there are a variety of interfaith organizations dedicated to fighting climate change.

The Canadian Association of Engaged Buddhists, for example, is a member of the Canadian Climate Action Network, along with more than 100 other organizations. Imagine the synergy!

AIR RESOURCES

- www.interfaithenvironment.org
- www.interfaithsustain.com
- www.interfaithpowerandlight.org
- climateactionnetwork.ca
- www.buddhistdoor.net/news/air-pollution-levels-threaten-birthplace-of-the-buddha

BIOSPHERE

▬▬
105

In the *Avatamsaka Sutra*, **Shakyamuni Buddha** uses the metaphor of Indra's Net to present a fractal image of the cosmos, in which infinite worlds nest one within the other, reflecting one another perfectly across the ten directions and the three times. The Huayan Patriarch, **Fazang**, interprets this as a teaching on emptiness and dependent origination, just manifestations of the vitality of the Tathagatagarbha.

The totality of life, known as the biosphere to scientists and creation to theologians, is a membrane of organisms wrapped around Earth so thin it cannot be seen edgewise from a space shuttle, yet so internally complex that most species composing it remain undiscovered. The membrane is seamless. From Everest's peak to the floor of the Mariana Trench, creatures of one kind or another inhabit virtually every square inch of the planetary surface.

Edward O. Wilson

In the modern retelling of the Gaia myth, **James Lovelock** and **Lynn Margulis** call our attention to the biosphere as one living organism, in which the Earth's life forms are themselves responsible for regulating the conditions that make life on the planet possible. We are all just manifestations of the vitality of the biosphere.

That perspective is congruent with Huayan Buddhist thinking in some important ways. By situating us within the larger system, and recognizing we are a manifestation of it rather than apart, interbeing becomes the wellspring for us to create the causes and conditions necessary to sustain life. From a design thinking perspective, this focus on General Systems Theory brings structure and texture to the discussion.

However, our world is unlike the fractal universe of Indra's Net in one key way: we live in an incredibly thin membrane about 12 miles thick, from the peak of Mount Everest to the pit of the Mariana Trench. For all intents and purposes, our biosphere is essentially two-dimensional. The causes and conditions we must regulate to exist are specific and unforgiving.

To consider ourselves the crown of creation is delusional; our world is ruled by bacteria, fungi, green plants, and other animals – we need them more than they need us (not to mention the fact that each of us has more symbiotic bacteria in us than "human" cells).

Insofar as evolution has endowed us with awareness, intelligence, and agency, we humans are on the karmic hot seat. At the very least, the future of humanity is our climate-change responsibility. The planet could arguably get on without us, and might even be better off for it. But in a self-correcting system, we will very likely be the aberration that gets eliminated to achieve equilibrium. Furthermore, once we write ourselves out of the story, it's unlikely we'll be back. After all, it took the planet almost three billion years to evolve us.

However, that's the best-case scenario (at least from the human perspective; the cosmos does not care). It's not hard to see that we are taking down most of the planet with us through our degradation of the biosphere. We are well into the planet's sixth great extinction event and what it's going to look like on the other side isn't pretty. Our paradigm of unregulated progress has proven to be cancer.

It's important to remember Gaia is not an externalized deity to be worshipped. Gaia is our transformed vision of a sanctified nature. All those animals we are pushing into extinction, all those rainforests we are razing to make palm oil plantations and ranches, all those oceans we are filling with plastic, that's US. In other words, we're talking here about suicide.

Three hundred Buddhist teachers signed the Global Buddhist Climate Change Collective statement to world leaders in 2015, but the GBCC website lists nothing more recent. I wonder what each of those teachers is doing now. A Google search for "Buddhism and the biosphere" reveals many articles about, but few articles by, Buddhists. News stories about releasing lobsters off the coast of Nova Scotia are a classic example. A specialized search within h-Buddhism, the academic Buddhist Studies portal, reveals zero hits for "biosphere," and slim pickings for anything environmental.

What Buddhist teachers are currently championing this eco-manifestation of the Bodhisattva Vow? Not many. **David Loy** has been doing all the heavy lifting; he has single-handedly kept environmental activism at the centre of Buddhist practice for many years. He gets held up as the Buddhist poster-child for EcoDharma, but making him a celebrity simply illustrates our slacktivism. Show us your "True. Nature."

BIOSPHERE RESOURCES

- www.ecodharma.com/articles-influences-audio/systems-theory
- ecodharmacentre.wordpress.com
- www.buddhistdoor.net/features/halting-the-economics-of-extinction-how-a-spiritual-resurgence-in-china-could-save-the-biosphere
- www.the-scientist.com/reading-frames/book-excerpt-from-buddhist-biology-38019

ENERGY

■ In a landmark case, Juliana v United States, a group of 21 young people are
106 suing the government to stop subsidies, permits, and support for the fossil
fuel industry. Their complaint, commenced in 2015, asserts that, through
the government's affirmative actions that cause climate change, it has vio-
lated the youngest generation's constitutional
rights to life, liberty, and property, as well as
failed to protect essential public trust resources.
Their evidence comes from more than 50 years
of government documents acknowledging the
direct cause-and-effect relationship between
fossil fuels and global warming.

> Exercising my "reasoned
> judgment," I have no doubt
> that the right to a climate
> system capable of sustaining
> human life is fundamental to a
> free and ordered society.
>
> *U.S. District Judge Ann Aiken*

In spite of repeated federal government
attempts to quash the suit, it is proceeding. If
the young plaintiffs win, it will signal a dramatic reversal from the "busi-
ness-as-usual while we rearrange the deck chairs" approach we've seen
so far. After all, the United States is now the world's largest producer of
oil and gas. There are more than one million active oil and gas facilities
in the United States. Because of lack of proper reporting requirements,
nobody has a clear idea of how many of them employ fracking or other
unconventional drilling or stimulation techniques.

The San Francisco Zen Center is one of a variety of faith organizations
(and the only Buddhist organization) who have supplied *amicus* briefs
supporting the plaintiffs.

The case is remarkable in two ways: it directly targets the fossil fuel
industry, and it illustrates how young people are tired of listening to our
generation dither about how to fix the problems we have created. In fact,
I have seen an increasing number of news articles about youth climate
strikers and activists like **Greta Thunberg**. Shame on us for leaving it to
children to solve the world's problems.

In 2018, the Canadian government paid the jaw-dropping sum of
$4.5 billion CDN to buy a pipeline that does not even exist yet on paper,
has not cleared environmental assessments, and lacks endorsement by all
the indigenous communities along its proposed path, to pump Alberta's
bitumen (from the dirtiest oil sands in the world) to the British Columbia
coast. Our government says we must convert to alternative forms of
energy, but that we need to "transition" to that. Well, by investing in a
pipeline, the government is committing to continue pumping that oil for

40 more years. And what of a similar investment in renewables (other than hydroelectric, which is already mostly built out)? The government's own promotional pieces put it at way, way less, by several orders of magnitude. As I mentioned in the previous section on "Air," I see oil as the distilled karma at the root of our global environmental problems. It is simultaneously the source of our carbon dioxide crisis, our plastic crisis, and our global resource conflict crisis.

This is not to imply that the oil industry is the sole villain here. Every type of energy production and transmission exacts environmental costs. I have been opposed to nuclear power for decades, for a variety of reasons, but I have also read some very compelling arguments for the value of this technology. What I don't understand is why the industry hasn't moved to cheaper, safer Thorium and salt-cooled systems.

If you have experienced a black-out or a brown-out recently, you probably heard or read news stories explaining how our electrical grid is many decades old and insufficient for the increased urban density that our cities and factories demand. Who should pay to maintain the grid? Is going off the grid realistic? Can we build Net Zero infrastructure?

We have been so seduced by megaprojects that we have lost any awareness of appropriate, localized solutions. There are more than 84,000 dams in the United States. Precious few use more environmentally-friendly run-of-the-river technology. But let's get close to home (and off the grid). Has your retreat centre ever considered a pico hydro generator? Does your urban centre have a wind turbine? Do either of them have a Tesla Powerwall? A geothermal heating system?

Don't be like the Buddhist centre who has been actively fighting a multi-year legal battle to stop wind-farms near their 530-acre retreat centre (just one of four they own in the area).

ENERGY RESOURCES

- www.ourchildrenstrust.org/juliana-v-us
- www.earthguardians.org
- www.international.gc.ca/investors-investisseurs/assets/pdfs/download/vp-renewable_energy.pdf
- www.cbc.ca/news/canada/toronto/80m-temple-project-in-rural-ontario-threatened-by-wind-turbines-buddhists-say-1.3652314

CAPACITY

107 "Enough." That is a concept close to the hearts of Buddhists, but unappealing to most people. For those who feel the world's current environmental crisis is essentially one of spiritual orientation, it is the crux of the matter. As long as we thirst for "more," we suffer the consequences.

It does not require more than a simple act of insight to realise that infinite growth of material consumption in a finite world is an impossibility.

E.F. Schumacher
Small Is Beautiful

Only the short-sighted still see "ownership" of the world's resources as a zero-sum game with only one winner. We know that we would need six planets to supply the demands of our current growth model, and we clearly do not have that. "Stewardship" is the new watchword.

Some say that Buddhism might be operating with a similar set of blinders. As **Glenn Wallis** points out in his recent, provocative book, *A Critique of Western Buddhism: Ruins of the Buddhist Real*, when Buddhism purports to have answers for every problem and fails to be open to other ways of thinking, it creates the very causes and conditions for its own irrelevance. The need to project Buddhism as "sufficient" creates edifices designed primarily to protect that sufficiency. Like that child in the schoolyard who doesn't play well with others, modern Buddhism has sidelined itself from the most important, "real" transformation the planet now faces: survival. There has to be a willingness, not just to join environmental groups so the Buddhist voice can be heard, not just for Buddhists to listen to what other faith groups and secular groups are saying, not just to join with them in projects, but to actually and humbly learn from them.

If there is such a thing called Engaged Buddhism, then what does Disengaged Buddhism look like? What is the price of disengagement?

Like **Christopher Queen** in his 1995 book, *Engaged Buddhism in the West*, I'm proposing a new, Fourth Yana. He coined the term Navayana; I've westernized it as Novayana. **Stephanie Kaza**, now retired, is another lion of Engaged Buddhism with an environmental focus, from the 1990's. Outside of academia, how familiar are their names, and where are the vast numbers of ecosattvas who were to have taken up the mantle of their work? We Buddhists are in need of some heavy-duty capacity-building!

Where's the disconnect in praising these vanguards, but failing to bring their cause into the mainstream? We've marginalized them by celebrating their "outlier" status. Their work has yielded a withered branch with bitter fruit. Am I mad? Yeah, you bet.

Remember that old adage when questioning the value of someone's tangential argument, "What does all that have to do with the price of tea in China?" Well, with General Systems Theory, we now know that it has everything to do with it. On Spaceship Earth (to use the phrase coined by **Buckminster Fuller**), we are all in this together. There is no us-versus-them, no here-versus-there, and no Plan B. The solutions to our predicaments must be resolved by all of us together. What I'm proposing is that now and in future, Enlightenment will be crowdsourced, however difficult that might sound.

Shakyamuni Buddha certainly didn't talk about crowdsourcing, but he did make the Sangha one of the Three Jewels. It has been arguably the weakest of the three in Buddhism's journey to America. One cause may be our culture of individualism. Another may be our unhealthy emphasis on gurus and roshis. In the Novayana, gurus are passé (or at least putting them on pedestals is; I still respect and feel profound gratitude towards my teachers). Pratyekabuddhahood is equally off the table. We need to be more like rhizomatic aspen trees. (Look it up; the image is apt.)

The only serious response to our finite capacity is degrowth. There is no point in talking about grandiose projects like geo-engineering our way back from the nine planetary boundaries we are traversing. In fact, we've already gone too far. It's not a one-off event; it's a myriad of ugly new vectors radiating out into the future. The climate refugees are already in motion; watch *Human Flow*, by **Ai Weiwei**. Mitsubishi has pushed the bluefin tuna to near extinction by catching and deep-freezing as many as they can, cornering the market for when they're all gone. Fukushima and Chernobyl are gifts that keep on giving.

Rewild the planet and terraform Sukhavati? The reality is more like Blackleg Ticks, Zika, and Wild Parsnip.

LIMITS RESOURCES

- www.uvm.edu/~skaza/publications/assets/saveallbeings.pdf
- en.wikipedia.org/wiki/Stephanie_Kaza Mindfully Green (2008) Dharma Rain (2000)
- www.uvm.edu/~skaza/?Page=publications/default.html#articles
- www.sunypress.edu/p-2307-engaged-buddhism.aspx
- www.thezensite.com/ZenEssays/CriticalZen/Engaged_Buddhism.htm

THE COMMONS

■
108

When people talk about "The Commons," the usual image that comes to mind is a town square or college campus dining zone – a shared space for interaction. An older definition is land or resources belonging to, or affecting, the whole of a community. More recently, the term has come to include virtual and cultural resources. These resources are held collectively in the public sphere, not privately. World heritage religions also fall into this category.

"In a competitive world of limited resources, total freedom of individual action is intolerable."

Garrett Hardin

In 1833, British economist **William Forster Lloyd** introduced the concept of "the Tragedy of the Commons," in which individual users acting for their own self-interest behave contrary to the common good of all users. In 1968, ecologist **Garrett Hardin** updated the concept with contemporary implications. His argument exposes the fallacy of rational actors that is at the heart of neoliberal, free market capitalism.

Governance of the Commons has become a central theme in modern politics and economics, from healthcare, law, finance, and security, to infrastructure (energy, transportation, water, communications, and so on). Whether or not we label this as socialism, maintenance of public institutions is a fundamental responsibility of government and the prime measure of the success of a society. What makes America great is not the power of its economic engine, but the application of the universalist values of its Constitution in providing services to all its citizens.

As the Information Age has morphed through the Age of Personal Computing, the Networking Age, and the Age of Convergence, our concepts of ownership have morphed with the times. **Jeremy Rifkin** crystallized this change in his book published in 2000, *The Age of Access*. He talks about our disruptive shift from ownership of property (including data) to a sharing economy where access to services in networks is central. This is certainly visible in the domain of information (from streaming video to subscription software to social media), but it also applies in more physical domains as diverse as transportation (ride hailing apps), real estate (timeshares), or medical care (HMOs). It is a trend that purports to support the public good, but does not.

A rebuttal of sorts, *Reinventing the Wheel: A Buddhist Response to the Information Age* (1999), by **Peter Herschock**, joined other alternative voices in exploring the dark side of the digital revolution.

Rifkin speaks of this new economic paradigm as a collaborative commons, but one can clearly see how this so-called post-capitalist utopia has been co-opted by retrograde oligarchies in the twenty years since his book was published. We have the gig economy, with all its inequities: either you have servants or you are one.

On the flip side, we've seen the development and deployment of many initiatives that foster the public good, such as alternative forms of copyright (Creative Commons), open-source software (Firefox), disintermediated peer-to-peer networks (Wikipedia), tool libraries, microfinance, and the like, as well as organizations which promote companies who uphold that ethic (such as B Corporation).

Amidst all of this, there is growing understanding of the value of our Global Commons and Global Public Goods. However, we are still faced with the predicament of clashing value systems.

In 2014, in his book, *Valuing Diversity: Buddhist Reflection on Realizing a More Equitable Global Future*, **Peter Hershock** casts a Buddhist light on all this, positing GCs and GPGs as the way to cut through the Gordian Knot.

In the best of all possible worlds, Engaged Buddhists will actively pursue their chosen agendas such as social justice or environmentalism, and take leadership roles. Every voice is to be valued, and every contribution to the Commons is needed. In this world, however, Manjusri's sword may be required. Or, like Milarepa, we must sit with our hands to our ears, silent, and listening intently to the lessons our world is teaching us moment to moment. This is not the time for dismissing voices that do not come from "accredited teachers." Each of us must become the practitioner of no rank.

Shakyamuni twirled the lotus flower and you smiled. Now he's handed it to you. Don't panic.

THE COMMONS RESOURCES

- blogs.dickinson.edu/buddhistethics/files/2016/12/Hershock_Clippard_16-1.pdf
- www.foet.org (Jeremy Rifkin)
- www.eastwestcenter.org/about-ewc/directory/peter.hershock

REFLECTION

REFLECTION

Writing this book has been a more-than-two-year journey. There have been many changes in the world during that time; new leaders have emerged and disappointed us, the political process has sunk even further into ineffectual partisanship, and priorities have changed. Foremost among those changes has been the growing consensus that we, the planet, are on the brink of death, brought on by our own human activity, with the corollary that we seem entirely incapable of altering our course, much as we would wish and hope for the opposite.

Although I have known of the challenges for many years, I did not anticipate the emotional component that these recent changes would bring, and I am still struggling with the feelings they have awakened in me – feelings of grief and helplessness, yes, but also an acute awareness of my own contributions to the mess in which we find ourselves. When I was a teen-ager full of the enthusiasm of the 1960's, I certainly did not imagine I would be witnessing the very real possibility of global annihilation within my lifetime. The threat of nuclear war never held the certainty of climate change, mass extinctions, pollution, and other planetary boundaries we are traversing, as quickly as we can, it would seem. And I was oblivious to the cumulative effect of my small, personal choices, combined with those of multitudes of others – effects that are inescapable now.

This is clearly a turning point in world history. The diagnosis is critical, the situation is urgent. Continuing with the same old same old is not just kicking the can down the road; it is suicide.

Perhaps my cynicism is the logical conclusion of the counterculture ethos of my youth. De-schooled by activists, evangels, and songwriters, I became disillusioned with society's willful blindness to the problems in its midst. I took up Buddhist practice as a way to create an alternate narrative with more substance. What I did not know was that in my old age, disenchantment would lead to such a generalized misanthropy. In retrospect, my mother or some other acute critic would say, "You became enchanted by Buddhism because you did not see the opportunity for enchantment within the religious tradition in which you were raised or the one you saw all around you, and enchantment seemed like something you felt was a necessary component of a life well-lived." Point taken.

Everywhere I look, samsara seduces us into busy-ness, a preoccupation with things (*prapança* – mental proliferation), that is shallow and meaningless at best, or vicious and self-destructive. Is this revulsion enough of a basis for renunciation? I do not know, but I do know that the way forward must include acceptance of this sense of not belonging, and the accompanying anticipatory grief.

In the same way, I feel a sense of great shame for what we have done. When I walk into the grocery supermarket to buy food, I look at us all and wonder how it came to this state of obscene over-consumption. And yet....

What has also surprised me is the commitment I feel. This Bodhisattva Vow is a driving force. Whether I succeed or fail does not matter; what matters is that I act. The Vow invites me into deeper practice while I am still left with unanswered questions, doubts, and decisions. What does that practice look like: is it more personal, more interior, or more engaged, more activist? Where's the balance?

For the past two years, writing this book has been the answer to those questions. But now it is done. I'm not interested in turning it into a mission, or a business, stumping across America to promote it (although I'm happy to talk if people are interested and seek me out). In fact, now I'm focused on writing an altogether different book – one I have been pondering and researching for almost 30 years – the story of the Panchen Lamas, told as the imagined diary of their linked lives. So I guess the pendulum is swinging more toward private practice.

My old friend **Suwanda Sugunasiri** left home and ordained last year after his wife died. He is now **Bhante Mihita**. That's an inspiring act. I don't think I could do it, but I understand the intention to purify, refine, and reduce to essentials. In my case, going forward looks like more mystical communion with the wellspring of the mandala, refreshing the vitality of the initiations I received so long ago. It's not just personal preparation for a good death, but a radiant aspiration for how to be in the face of our unprecedented, shared fate.

❁

A number of friends have served as early readers of the preliminary drafts of this books, and I offer my thanks to them for their willingness to offer constructive advice. One of the recurring comments was that it would be valuable to include a list of specific things individual readers could do, a distillation of the solution, as opposed to going on and on about the problems. In each case, the writer gave examples drawn from their own experience and area of specialization. In other words, they responded to my conversation-starters with engagement and a search for solutions. That's exactly the level of involvement I hope to generate in every reader. But as for answers, I have not so much to offer.

❀

Over these past two years, my thoughts evolved on how this book should be sequenced. It's not a linear progression, but there is the aspiration on my part to make it flow intelligently and enjoyably in some over-arching way, perhaps like a melody line, if not reaching some climactic conclusion. This reflection, if you will, is a coda rather than the dénouement of a crime novel. In that sense, there is no "right" order for things and a bit of improv has been thrown in there. If you skipped around in a contrapuntal way, that's okay.

For those of you who are fans of **John Cage**, and perchance have read his book, *Silence*, yes, this book is a typographic homage to him. That book was iconic for me in my 19th year. And for those of you who are fans of **Richard Saul Wurman**, and perchance have read his book, *Information Anxiety*, yes, the design of this book is also a typographic homage to him. I discovered him in later years, but his approach to dealing with complex information resonated for me; I have used it many times with clients and in curriculum-creation for high school students.

❀

I hope you will return to this book from time to time, approaching the bookshelf with a skip in your step to read a couple of pages, even at random. If it quenches your thirst for meaningful discourse, stokes the fire of an impassioned speech, or inspires you to some achievement for the common good, I'll be happy. With any luck, it won't wind up on a bonfire at 451° Fahrenheit, get you in trouble for possessing a copy, or simply lie mutely buried in some landfill or blowing sediment until Wall-e or the aliens arrive. Write me a letter from the future to tell me how it's all turning out.

NOTES

www.ingramcontent.com/pod-product-compliance
Lightning Source LLC
Chambersburg PA
CBHW031245090426
42742CB00007B/314